It has been a great source of satisfactio‌‌‌‌‌‌‌‌‌‌‌‌‌‌‌‌ ‌‌‌‌‌‌‌‌‌‌‌‌‌‌‌‌ ie
movement taking place across Scotland t‌‌‌‌‌‌‌‌‌‌‌‌‌‌‌‌ ‌‌‌‌‌‌‌‌‌‌‌‌‌‌‌‌ al
population level. It has become possible ‌‌‌‌‌‌‌‌‌‌‌‌‌‌‌‌ ‌‌‌‌‌‌‌‌‌‌‌‌‌‌‌‌ in
and healing from childhood and adult tr‌‌‌‌‌‌‌‌‌‌‌‌‌‌‌‌ ‌‌‌‌‌‌‌‌‌‌‌‌‌‌‌‌ y
require, so that all can benefit from a he‌‌‌‌‌‌‌‌‌‌‌‌‌‌‌‌ ‌‌‌‌‌‌‌‌‌‌‌‌‌‌‌‌ re
is now a cross party working group in S‌‌‌‌‌‌‌‌‌‌‌‌‌‌‌‌ ‌‌‌‌‌‌‌‌‌‌‌‌‌‌‌‌ of
childhood trauma, which is quite somet......., ..., ..., . .,.....nt on the almost unbearable presence of child abuse in our world, takes bravery and courage for all involved.

Clea Thompson, Principal Clinical Child Psychologist, Child Psychology Service, Fife.

...Unless we support families and assist with the parenting skills then the cycle would never be broken. How do you know how to support your child emotionally if you have never been shown this from your parents? How do you help to be a buffer for your child at times of adversity when you are dealing with your own issues and have no one to contain you?

Lynn Sweeney, Community Safety Advocate, Scottish Fire and Rescue Service.

The beauty of the Solihull Approach, we quickly discovered, was that it does not conflict with any other approaches. It values the practitioner's experience and knowledge, and simply offers a framework to their way of working. Since our first delivery of the Foundation Training we have not received a single negative evaluation of the training. We have delivered the training in Shropshire to approximately 600 multi-agency professionals to date.

Karen Ladd, Parenting Strategy Coordinator, Shropshire Council.

It's all about recognising emotions in yourself and your child and understanding how they impact upon behaviours rather than the old fashioned praising of good behaviours and ignoring of bad. It acknowledges that perceived bad behaviours need attention too as the cause may be stress/unhappiness/anxiety and those things shouldn't be ignored but supported.

Jen Hopkins, parent.

The Solihull Approach has been particularly powerful and practically useful. The 'bottom-up' approach in the development of the model, where practice informs theory and theory, in turn, informs practice means that the Agnes Unit staff, mostly new to the field of perinatal and infant mental health, have been able to quite naturally grasp the integrated psychodynamic and behavioural theoretical concepts in the model and start using them in their practice. Their day-to-day clinical work with the parents and infants admitted to Agnes Unit then brings the theories to life, which in turn promotes reflective clinical practice.

Vivian Lee, Perinatal and Infant Psychiatrist and Georgina Timmins, Registered Mental Health Nurse and Family Therapist, Victoria, Australia.

It isn't possible to compartmentalise how the Solihull Approach is used within my role. I feel that it is intrinsic to my role and to myself as a compassionate human being. The Solihull Approach is so embedded in my work that it works unconsciously.

Amy Sadler, Infant Feeding Specialist, Solihull.

The Solihull Approach has changed both my personal and professional life. I am a better mum and much better practitioner. I consider it a privilege to be involved in delivering training for practitioners and also the UYC programme for parents. Delivery in the prison setting has been particularly rewarding and fascinating. I have enjoyed building relationships with the dads and getting to know them as dads and not prisoners. They have taught me lots about adverse childhood experiences and I am both amazed and grateful for their openness, honesty and trust in us. However, the proudest achievement has been the impact that the group has had on their children. The knowledge that the groups have enhanced the interactions and relationships that the dads have with their children and knowing that this will make a difference to their children's future, is the greatest reward of all.

Cheryl Valentine, Solihull Coordinator, North Lanarkshire Council.

Hopefully not sounding too evangelical, but the Solihull Approach training opened a window to a whole new world for me and way of viewing that world. I have been involved in work with young people for over 30 years and it changed the way that I engage not just with young people but colleagues and family.

Alistair Macintosh, Youth Engagement Officer, Scottish Fire and Rescue Service.

There is a growing body of neuroscience research concerning the brain development of the unborn and new born child and, it can be argued, 'we are the first generation to have this knowledge at our fingertips, we ignore it at our peril'. The Solihull Approach introduces this neurological information to social workers, for some for the first time, and sets it beside familiar theory. It is, therefore, an approach at once familiar and brand new which has received very positive training evaluations from a profession that can be weary and wary.

Sheina Rigg, Learning and Development Coordinator (Children's Community Services), Belfast Health and Social Care Trust.

The Solihull Approach *in Practice*

Edited by
Hazel Douglas

© Solihull Approach 2018
University Hospitals Birmingham NHS Foundation Trust,
Bishop Wilson Clinic, Chelmsley Wood, Solihull, B37 7TR.

First published 2018

ISBN 978-1-908960-42-9

All rights reserved. No part of this publication may be reproduced, stored in a retrieval system or transmitted in any form or by any means electronic, mechanical, photocopying, recording or otherwise, without the prior permission of the publishers.

Printed and bound in Great Britain by Quorum Print Services Ltd.

Copies of this book are available from:
Solihull Approach Team, University Hospitals Birmingham NHS Foundation Trust
solihull.approach@heartofengland.nhs.uk
www.solihullapproachparenting.com
0121 296 4448

Facebook Page: Solihull Approach
Twitter: @SolihullAproach

Printed on paper manufactured from responsibly sourced material.

Cover and text design by Rebecca Johnson and Hannah Hassan.

Published by Solihull Approach Publishing.

9564841
Printed on Carbon Captured paper

This book is dedicated to all the practitioners, parents, commissioners and managers who have contributed to the development of the Solihull Approach. You know who you are. Thank you!

Contents

1	Introduction *Hazel Douglas*	17
2	The Solihull Approach model *Hazel Douglas*	19
3	How the Solihull Approach started *Hazel Douglas*	25
4	A note on theory into practice *Hazel Douglas*	34
5	Managing a large roll out of the Solihull Approach: Shropshire *Karen Ladd*	36
6	From small beginnings: the Solihull Approach in Northern Ireland *Averil Bassett*	45
7	The Solihull Approach in the antenatal and postnatal period *Mary Rheeston*	51
8	IT'S A GIRL! (A mother's experience of the Solihull Approach antenatal group) *Terezie Leach*	59
9	NO WAY! (A father's experience of the Solihull Approach antenatal group) *Jackie Leach*	61
10	Using the Solihull Approach in a therapeutic parent and infant unit in rural Australia *Vivian Lee and Georgina Timmins*	63

11	The Solihull Approach and Peer Breastfeeding Supporter training	77
	Mary Rheeston, Elaine Kindred-Spalding and Amy Sadler	
12	The Solihull Approach Postnatal group 'Understanding your baby'	86
	Mary Rheeston	
13	The Solihull Approach: a children's centres perspective	94
	Louise Moreton	
14	The Solihull Approach and schools	104
	Rebecca Johnson	
15	Solihull Approach Workshops for parents	110
	Karen Ladd	
16	Ravenswood Primary School: a school's experience of teaching children the Solihull Approach	113
	Jacklyn Purdon	
17	Delivering Solihull Approach training in primary and secondary schools in North Lanarkshire Council	119
	Cheryl Valentine	
18	Implementing the Solihull Approach in the Scottish Fire and Rescue Service	130
	Cheryl Valentine	
19	Social workers and the Solihull Approach	142
	Sheina Rigg	
20	Delivering the 'Understanding your child' parent programme in a prison setting	157
	Denise Kelly, Sean McCracken, Catarina Smith and Cheryl Valentine	
21	Solihull Approach for adults: Keeping Trauma in Mind	178
	Clea Thompson and Andrew Summers	
22	The evidence	185
	Rebecca Johnson	

Contributors

Averil Bassett
Senior Education Manager, Clinical Education Centre for Nursing, Midwifery and Allied Health Professionals, Northern Ireland

Hazel Douglas
Clinical Psychologist and Child Psychotherapist, Director of the Solihull Approach

Rebecca Johnson
Clinical Psychologist, Solihull Approach Development Manager

Denise Kelly
Development Worker, Getting Better Together, Shotts, North Lanarkshire

Elaine Kindred-Spalding
Infant Feeding Coordinator, Solihull

Karen Ladd
Parenting Strategy Coordinator, Shropshire Council

Jackie Leach
Father

Terezie Leach
Mother

Vivian Lee
Perinatal and Infant, Child and Adolescent Psychiatrist, Australia

Sean McCracken
Residential Officer, HMP Shotts

Louise Moreton
Senior Health Lead (Children's Centres), Birmingham

Jacklyn Purdon
Acting Principal Teacher, Ravenswood Primary School, North Lanarkshire

Mary Rheeston
Health Visitor, Manager of the Solihull Approach

Sheina Rigg
Learning and Development Coordinator (Children's Community Services), Belfast Health and Social Care Trust

Amy Sadler
Infant Feeding Specialist, Solihull

Catarina Smith
Prison Officer, HMP Shotts

Andrew Summers
Consultant Clinical Psychologist, Adult Psychology Service, Fife

Clea Thompson
Principal Clinical Child Psychologist, Child Psychology Service, Fife

Georgina (George) Timmins
Registered Mental Health Nurse and Family Therapist, Australia

Cheryl Valentine
Solihull Coordinator, North Lanarkshire Council

Other contributors

Thank you to those who have shared their experience of the Solihull Approach in practice in this book.

Mary Cruickshank, Head Teacher, North Lanarkshire

David Dalziel, First Line Manager, National Integration Centre, HMP Shotts

Sam Giles, Specialist Health Visitor, Maternal Mental Health Lead, Solihull

Jen Hopkins, Mother

David Jackson, Crew Manager, Scottish Fire and Rescue Service

Avril Jones, BFI Community Coordinator, Aneurin Bevan University Health Board, Caerleon

Alistair Macintosh, Youth Engagement Officer, Scottish Fire and Rescue Service

Gordon McGuire, Station Manager, Scottish Fire and Rescue Service

Siobhan Slavin, Change Manager, Early Intervention Transformation Programme, Belfast

Lynn Sweeney, Community Safety Advocate, Scottish Fire and Rescue Service

Thank you to all the parents and practitioners who have contributed quotes to this book.

Biographies of chapter authors

Averil Bassett

Following ten years of health visiting practice in Northern Ireland, I joined the nursing and midwifery education staff in 2002. My teaching relates to health visiting and public health. Subjects of special interest include: infant mental health; perinatal mental health; domestic violence; attachment; and brain development.

Since 2010 I have led on the provision of Solihull Approach programmes by the Clinical Education Centre, commissioned by the Department of Health and the Public Health Agency across health and social care, voluntary and community settings. This has developed through partnerships with the Director of Solihull Approach programmes, stakeholders across children's services and membership of regional groups contributing to the workforce development of the Infant Mental Health Framework, Northern Ireland.

The other passions in my life are family, my husband, three children and grandchild. I love walking, tennis, cycling and all things outdoors. Holidays with a good book, good food and good wine, but only after I have put my trainers to good use, preferably on a beach where I can enjoy magnificent views!

Hazel Douglas

Hazel began her career as a clinical psychologist working with adults, but soon developed an interest in early intervention and prevention. This led to her training as a child psychotherapist, working in children's mental health. She led the project to develop the Solihull Approach, aiming to embed key messages from research about emotional health and wellbeing into training for practitioners and into courses for parents. She advocates looking at this from a public health perspective, across populations.

Rebecca Johnson

Dr Rebecca Johnson is a Consultant Clinical Psychologist with 20 years of clinical experience in the NHS, predominantly in the field of Child and Adolescent Mental Health, with a special interest in infant mental health and parenting. Her most recent clinical work was in perinatal mental health in Warwickshire. She has been a Solihull Approach trainer and contributor since 2001, has worked in Solihull since 2003, and is the Solihull Approach Development Manager. She is also the mother of two school aged children.

Denise Kelly

I am a Development Worker for Getting Better Together in Shotts, a rural community in North Lanarkshire. The main focus of my role is developing services to support children and families visiting their loved one at HMP Shotts. I am passionate about my work and care deeply about making differences to their lives and long term outcomes. I live with my two children who are 15 and 12 years old, they keep me on my toes every day and I treasure my relationships with them. On a Sunday, I am to be found engaging with my inner child while playing on my mountain bike, travelling at speed down the side of a mountain! The Solihull Approach has enhanced my relationships with my children and has transformed my practice and understanding of the problems some of the children and families I work with endure.

Elaine Kindred-Spalding

I am a Registered Midwife, Infant Feeding Coordinator and Tongue Tie Practitioner working in Solihull 0 to 19 Community Services, within the Infant Feeding Team. I love my job and have worked within this same team for 10 years. I feel very privileged to work with such passionate and dedicated people and to be in a position to support women and their families at such an important time in their lives. I have two children, Tom, aged 27 and Sophie, who is 25 and following their births I was motivated to work towards changing my 20 year career as a medical secretary to that of a midwife, as I saw what a difference a good midwife could make and I wanted to be that person. It was a long journey from there; six years of taking three 'A' Levels, one after the other whilst looking after my children and working part-time, before I was in a position to apply to start my midwifery degree at the grand old age of 37! Following that I worked as a midwife on the wards of my local hospital and also delivered antenatal parentcraft classes, at which point I was introduced to the Solihull Approach team. Since then I have been involved in aspects of the Solihull Approach work, contributing to writing, and delivering various courses. Solihull Approach underpins all the work that we do and how we communicate with mothers, families and colleagues and what a wonderful difference this makes to all of us!

Karen Ladd

Karen Ladd, Parenting Strategy Coordinator, Shropshire Council, has worked as Shropshire Council's lead for parenting support since 2012. Prior to this Karen was trained and worked as a nurse, both home and abroad and spent several years in education. Parenting delivery has drawn on her knowledge from all of her previous roles, not least her role as a parent and a grandma.

Terezie and Jackie Leach

Terezie and Jackie Leach are the mother and father of their new baby girl. They attended the Solihull Approach Antenatal Group 'Understanding pregnancy, labour, birth and your baby.'

Vivian Lee

Dr Vivian Lee is a Perinatal and Infant, Child and Adolescent Psychiatrist. She has been working at the Latrobe Regional Hospital in Traralgon ever since she became a fully qualified psychiatrist over five years ago. She has loved it so much that she has remained with the service ever since, despite still not making the move to escape to the country. She feels very fortunate to be offered the opportunity to help set up a parent and infant unit so early in her career. Perhaps this will be her only major career achievement; she doesn't see herself leaving Agnes Unit! Vivian works two days a week with the infants, parents and families at the Agnes Unit and two days a week in her own child and adolescent private practice in the south eastern suburbs of Melbourne, where she focuses on offering longer term psychodynamic psychotherapy.

Sean McCracken

I am 46 and am married to Nicola with three children: Sam (6); Sophie (4); and Finn (1). I have worked for the Scottish Prison Service for the last 22 years at HMP Shotts, during which time I've worked Detached Duty at HMP Edinburgh, HMP Perth, HMP Zeist, HMP Peterhead and HMP Aberdeen. I now work in the National Integration Centre as a Residential Officer at Shotts. I have really enjoyed working with Cheryl Valentine, Melissa Keys, Cat Smith and even Denise Kelly since the Solihull Project first started in early 2016. Long may it continue.

Louise Moreton

Louise Moreton's background is in early years and adult learning with a career which began 24 years ago and includes being an NVQ assessor and tutor. She has a postgraduate qualification in early years. She was involved with setting up Sure Start services and developing children's centres in Warwickshire for seven years before taking a position in 2008 with a voluntary sector organisation commissioned to provide a number of children's centres in Birmingham. For the past five years her focus has been on antenatal and perinatal provision, including developing breastfeeding support services.

Jacklyn Purdon

I qualified with a Bachelor of Education (Honours) Degree from Strathclyde University, which prepared me for primary teaching in Scotland. I have been a class teacher in North Lanarkshire Council for over ten years, recently undertaking the role of Acting Principal Teacher in Ravenswood Primary School. I am thoroughly committed to the teaching profession and have appreciated the opportunity to share our experience with a wider audience.

Mary Rheeston

Mary Rheeston is the Solihull Approach Manager and has been involved with the project since it began in 1996. She is involved in Solihull Approach developments, resources and training. She has a strong commitment and belief in supporting emotional health and wellbeing for everyone, from the antenatal period through to adulthood. She began her professional career as a nurse and paediatric nurse and then trained as a health visitor in Solihull where she became involved with the Solihull Approach.

Sheina Rigg

Sheina Rigg has been a social worker since 1990, trained at Edinburgh University. Originally from Ayrshire in Scotland she has lived, volunteered, worked and brought up her family in Belfast. She became a Solihull Approach trainer in 2014 and immediately saw the value of the approach for social workers. The theory underpinning the Solihull

Approach is familiar to social work but the model gave staff a common language to communicate with their health visiting and Sure Start colleagues. The Public Health Agency Northern Ireland (2016) Infant Mental Health Framework gave further impetus to extend the course provision within social work. Sheina continues to find the Solihull Approach a well-considered addition to social workers' skills and knowledge. In her role she delivers training to the social work force but also to colleagues in nursing, psychology and other allied professions . She is committed to the vibrant community and voluntary sector in Belfast and coordinates a project with a community development ethos regarding best practice in safeguarding children. She loves dancing (lindy hop/ east coast swing) and cycling and is committed to the integrated education movement in Northern Ireland as a former parent and as a governor for Lagan Integrated College, Belfast. Her chapter came from her dissertation as the final part of a Masters in Applied Social Sciences, Strategy and Leadership course at Queens University Belfast in 2018.

Amy Sadler

My career started in 2007 where I worked as a midwife in my local hospital for eight years providing antenatal, intrapartum and postnatal care for women and their families. After the births of my own children I further valued the importance of timely and expert breastfeeding support. My personal experiences of feeding my children and receiving support from an Infant Feeding Midwife is what inspired me to pursue my current role as an Infant Feeding Specialist for Solihull Infant Feeding Team and to subsequently train as a Tongue Tie Practitioner and Lactation Consultant.

As part of my role, I currently lead on the Solihull Approach peer breastfeeding support course which enables mothers to train to support other mothers on their feeding journey. This is an incredibly important part of my role, as peer support is vital to the continuation of breastfeeding.

Helping others is my purpose in life and I aim to help women reach their feeding goals whilst treating them with compassionate care. I absolutely adore my job, I get so much satisfaction from helping families, because I know how much it is appreciated and valued.

Catarina Smith

I am a Prison Officer. I have worked in HMP Shotts for 12 years. I started in the Operations group, but now I work in Residential. The area I work is Allenton Level 4 which is called the NIC (National Induction Centre).

This was the area in HMP Shotts where the Solihull Approach Programme was first delivered. The programme has allowed participants to engage with their children in a more positive manner. It was due to this success and talking to the participants that I became interested in taking part. Out of prison I go to the gym, cycling at the weekend and spending time with my family.

Andrew Summers

Andy Summers is a Consultant Clinical Psychologist working in adult mental health within Fife's Health and Social Care Partnership. He has lead responsibility within Adult Psychology for developing services for people who have experienced complex trauma.

Clea Thompson

Clea Thompson is a Clinical Psychologist, working in a primary care psychology service with children and families. For over ten years she has had a lead responsibility for developing the Solihull Approach in Fife and more recently has had a role with National Education Scotland developing trauma informed services in Scotland. Clea provides consultancy and training to multi-agency partners and the family nurse partnership focusing on early intervention and prevention of developmental trauma. She is a member of the Scottish Trauma Advisory Group and is the Child Psychology representative for the Division of Clinical Psychology, Scotland.

Georgina (George) Timmins

Georgina (George) Timmins is a Registered Mental Health Nurse and a Family Therapist, who has worked at Latrobe Regional Hospital for over 19 years, enjoying many roles, including clinical practice with children, young people and families with the Child and Adolescent Mental Health Service. George currently divides her time between two roles, coordinator of the Families where a Parent has a Mental Illness Program and as a clinical nurse educator. It is in her capacity as a clinical nurse educator that George joined with Vivian to deliver the Solihull Approach 2 Day Foundation training, initially to their new colleagues at the Agnes Unit. George particularly embraced this therapeutic model of care due to its ability to support and empower families to be with, understand and communicate with one another in a very 'person centred', 'developmentally appropriate' and 'recovery focused' manner and to provide both a rigorous and flexible framework to support and empower clinicians in their therapeutic and reflective practice, whether working individually, dyadically or systemically.

Cheryl Valentine

I have been married to my husband for 26 years and we have two grown up children who are aged 22 years and 24 years. I have been working in the early year's sector for 33 years and have a particular interest in promoting and supporting emotional wellbeing in not only children, but also parents/carers and our staff. My recent work experience is the post of Head of Centre in a Family Learning Centre in Coatbridge, Scotland where I worked for 16 years. We used the Solihull Approach in our centre and saw the impact it had on our children, their families and on how we worked together as a team. Since 2014, I have been on secondment from my head of centre post to the role of Solihull Approach Training Programme Coordinator. This opportunity was presented to me as a result of the work we were doing using the Solihull Approach in our centre. I have learned lots in the past four years and have had the privilege of working with a wide range of service practitioners e.g. health, social work, education and third sector, in addition to police, fire and prison services. More recently I have been employed through the Scottish Attainment Challenge to deliver the Solihull Approach training to our schools in North Lanarkshire. I am passionate about the Solihull Approach as I have seen first-hand the impact it can have on individuals…in short, it changes lives… it works!

1 Introduction

Hazel Douglas

The idea for this book grew out of the 'Learning Together' Solihull Approach conferences. These are an opportunity for practitioners to share with others how they have applied the Solihull Approach model in their area. It is always amazing to see the enthusiasm and hear about innovation and dogged determination from people who want to make a difference.

At the time of writing, times are difficult in the UK for children and families. The political choice of austerity since 2010 has led to massive cuts in services, especially to those supporting parents and children. In its first ten years, the Solihull Approach developed during times when services to families were expanding, including the advent of Sure Start and then Children's Centres. It has then continued to develop during a further decade when services were decimated. During the difficult times, the original design of a cascade training programme, utilising effective resources, has supported areas who continued to focus on the wellbeing of children.

There is now overwhelming evidence for the cost effectiveness of support in the early years of a child's life making a difference across the life trajectory. More ACEs research, following on from the first paper published last century in 1998[1], continues to show how Adverse Childhood Experiences impacts on both mental and physical health from childhood to old age. The UN publication in 2013[2] encouraged countries to take a strategic view of supporting early child development. So, at some point, the world will turn and there will be more countries and more services in this country focussing resources on supporting children and their families.

The Solihull Approach aims to contribute to the emotional health and wellbeing of children and families, through supporting practitioners and parents in their communities. This book brings together the experience of practitioners from different areas of the UK and internationally from Australia. It also covers a wide range of applications of the Solihull Approach model, from antenatal and postnatal support, to a perinatal unit, children's centres, schools, prisons and firefighters.

There is a growing body of research on the Solihull Approach model, both quantitative and qualitative and including an RCT (Randomised Controlled Trial), on the effectiveness and high acceptability for both practitioners and parents. There is a brief overview of the published research studies (at the time of writing), but as this grows every year, the most up to date list is on our website for practitioners (www.solihullapproachparenting.com). We do encourage everyone to have a go at research!

The Solihull Approach model is increasingly being used across the age range from preconception to the emergency services working with adults. We think that it can

18   Introduction

probably be used whenever one human being works with another human being. The only limitation has been our imagination! Luckily, though, the Solihull Approach is much wider than the core Solihull Approach team and people who have taken the Solihull Approach on board have seen applications for it and then worked with us to extend its reach.

We are delighted that at least some of those innovators are represented in this book.

References

1. Felitti, V.J., Anda, R.F., Nordenberg, D., Williamson, D.F., Spitz, A., Edwards, V., Koss, M.P. and Marks, J.S. (1998). Relationship of Childhood Abuse and Household Dysfunction to Many of the Leading Causes of Death in Adults -The Adverse Childhood Experiences (ACE) Study. *American Journal of Preventive Medicine*, 14(4), 245-258.

2. Britto, P.R., Engle, P.L. and Super, C.M. (2013). *Handbook of Early Childhood Development Research and its Impact on Global Policy*. New York: Oxford University Press.

2 The Solihull Approach model

Hazel Douglas

Introduction

The theoretical model for the Solihull Approach emerged from practice. It is not a theoretical model crafted elsewhere and then applied to practice. This is, perhaps, a pedantic observation, but it may explain why the Solihull Approach model has resonated with practitioners from the beginning.

The model facilitates an understanding of emotional health and wellbeing, as well as mental health. It can be applied to working with families, with individuals, with groups, with a community or with a large population from a public health perspective. It can be applied across the age range of a child from preconception to adolescence and across the life trajectory. It has been used in different cultures, in different countries. It speaks to what it means to be a human being; understanding what supports us in our development and what hinders us. It reminds us of the importance of relationships.

There are more details about the model in the First Five Years Resource Pack[1] and the School Years Resource Pack[2]. If you are particularly interested in theory, a more in depth look at the concepts of containment and reciprocity is also available[3].

The model

The UK has historically had a strong grounding in learning theory and behaviour theory. So it is no surprise that in the late 1990's the explicit concept being used by health visitors was behaviour theory, with specific knowledge of factors such as reinforcers. Listening to health visitors talk about their cases, their frustration was palpable. A mother would describe a sleep problem with their child, the health visitor would give good advice grounded in behaviour theory. Nothing would change. The good thing about behaviour programmes is that, if they are carried out, they generally work. The bad thing is that, for them to work, they have to be carried out! It became obvious, through discussion, that parents were often not in an emotional state to think clearly, in order to apply a new technique or change their behaviour.

The concept of containment from psychoanalytic theory, although not an easy bedfellow with behaviour theory (there has been much animosity between the two camps over the 20th Century in particular), looked like it explained this and gave a way forward. Containment was first described in the 1950s by Bion[4], a psychoanalyst. It describes how we, as human beings, learn to process our emotions in concert with another and how we continue to do this throughout our lives. Starting at the beginning of life, a baby may be full of an emotion. After all, what sense does a baby make of the intensity of feeling frustrated or angry or frightened? Adults help with this. By recognising something of the emotion the baby is experiencing, trying to understand it (mirror neurones may be involved here) and then reflecting it back to the baby in a manageable form, the baby learns that emotions can be borne and processed or managed.

If the adult does not help, then what happens? If the adult ignores the experience of the baby, the baby is left to manage these states by themselves. And this has lifelong consequences, because of the early development of the architecture of the brain. If the adult is themselves overwhelmed by the emotion, then what does the baby experience? That emotions cannot be understood or processed? Again, this has lifelong consequences.

This sounds simple, but it is fundamental to our experience of the world. It will subsequently affect how we relate to others: friends; colleagues; and partners. It is likely to affect how we relate to the world and even to the big questions of our day. Voter analysts have a large category of voters they describe as using high emotion and low information.

The striking point of containment is not just about developing the capacity to experience and process emotions, it is that containment restores the capacity to think. This relates to the research on the anxiety/arousal and performance curve. We need some arousal or lift in our available energy in order to perform. An actor going on stage usually wants to feel slightly anxious, in order to perform. This also applies to athletes. And indeed, to all of us! You will upregulate yourself or downregulate yourself according to the task you want to do.

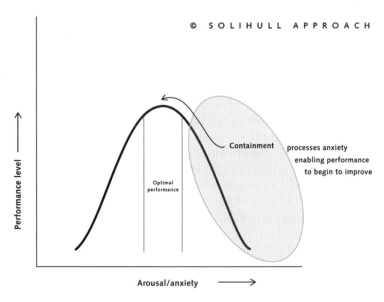

On the anxiety/arousal and performance curve, performance increases as anxiety increases, but there will be a point, which is different for all of us, where performance will decrease as anxiety increases, on an inverted U shape. Past this point, a person about to do a speech in public, for example, may 'dry up' (a symptom of anxiety as the sympathetic nervous system takes away the energy from the salivary glands and digestive system and directs it to the muscles, thinking that a flight or fight is about to happen) and feel unable to think clearly.

So, to come back to the health visitor and the parent, the health visitor firstly needs to contain the parent, to restore the capacity to think in the parent. The parent can also then determine their own course of action. There are many descriptions of real interactions between parents and practitioners in the Solihull Approach Resource Packs illustrating this.

The Solihull Approach model now had two components: containment and behaviour management. However, again, in discussion with health visitors about their experiences, it quickly became apparent that there was something missing, that containment and behaviour management on their own were not sufficient to illuminate the interaction between a practitioner and a parent. There needed to be another concept about the rhythm of interaction and attunement.

The next component was reciprocity, from the world of child development research. This was described by Dr Berry Brazelton[5], a paediatrician and researcher. At a time when most researchers saw babies as passive beings, Brazelton's research showed them to be socially active from birth. Analysis of the interactions between mothers and their babies, showed that there was a rhythm to the interaction, the 'Dance of Reciprocity', with specific steps. Subsequent research showed that parents and babies live in a millisecond world[6] , adjusting to each other subconsciously with incredible sophistication.

At the time (late 1990s to early 2000s) integrating this concept into the model meant that there was a way of understanding when things went wrong with feeding and toileting in particular. It allowed a description of spoon feeding, for example, as an activity between two participants, where it was important to be attuned to the child. It is easy to see how moving to solid foods might be difficult if the parent was trying to move the spoon without reference to the rhythm and cues of the baby. It is also an opportunity lost for reciprocal interaction around an everyday activity.

Understanding reciprocity showed how these interactions happened around everyday activities and emphasised how important the interactions between a parent and child are for the development of the child.

As well as illuminating an aspect of the relationship between the mother and child, reciprocity does the same for the relationship between the practitioner and parent. Containment explains how a practitioner can listen and help a parent to process sometimes overwhelming emotions, restoring the capacity to think in that parent. Reciprocity provides a concept to use in thinking about the rhythm of interaction between the practitioner and parent. The interaction will not be experienced as helpful if the two are out of tune with each other.

Reciprocity was used by Tronick[7] to think about upregulation and downregulation of activity within an interaction, sometimes the mother helping the baby to become calmer (downregulate) or more active (upregulate). Eventually we learn to do this for ourselves. Children have to regulate themselves all the time at school, to be able to sit still at a table, or upregulate to participate in an activity. And this is the same for everyone. At work sometimes you will need to relax and calm down, during a meeting for example, or sometimes you will need to walk about or make a drink in order to elevate your energy level to finish your task.

These three concepts were found to be sufficient to provide a foundation for thinking about human relationships and development. They provide the scaffold to understand previous learning and training and to integrate future learning and training.

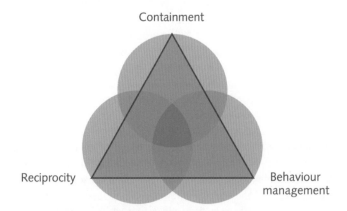

Many practitioners found the model helpful not only in understanding their interactions with clients, but also their interactions with colleagues at work. This included supervisory relationships where containment was sometimes required in order to work through the anxiety of the practitioner and restore the capacity to think about a way forward. Reciprocity was helpful in thinking about the attunement and the pace of interaction between the supervisor and practitioner. And behaviour management was helpful for a consideration of boundaries or other issues.

Because we are human beings in relationship to other human beings, whether we are at home or work, practitioners on the 2 Day Foundation Training often comment on how they begin to think about their own families. We have had many comments over the years about how helpful the model has been at home as well as work.

The model illuminates what people have experienced or seen hundreds and thousands of times over their lives. The model just gives the vocabulary to put it into words. Many practitioners have found this helpful when trying to explain an issue to a colleague or in writing reports. Similarly, which is reported elsewhere in this book, practitioners have appreciated having a shared language to describe their experience to colleagues in their own agency and with practitioners in other agencies.

Some people on the 2 Day Foundation training describe experiencing a 'lightbulb moment', as the concepts help them to make sense of their experience. Wittgenstein[8], the philosopher, considered the importance of language; that naming something allowed it to be talked about or thought about and conversely 'what we cannot speak about we must pass over in silence' (Wittgenstein).

There are several consequences of using the model. Practitioners often find that the parent is enabled to find their own solution that suits them and their particular circumstances. Or, put in another way, the parent works out and applies their own customised behaviour management. Practitioners find that that behaviour management comes at the end of a process of using containment and reciprocity. Sometimes they use containment and reciprocity and may not need to contemplate behaviour management.

Instead of having to use a toolkit, where items in the toolkit are generalised for everybody to use, understanding the situation allows for either a toolkit not to be used, because the parent has found their own solution, or for items in the toolkit to be customised for the individual.

Another consequence of using the model is that practitioners often experience a rise in job satisfaction[9]. One reason might be that if they are using a toolkit from somewhere, they are now not using it by rote, making their job more interesting. There may be an increase in solved difficulties. And, because we are social beings, concentrating more on relationships may be intrinsically more satisfying.

The Solihull Approach has been going for 20 years now. Over that time the importance of behaviour management has diminished, whilst the importance of a consideration of relationships has grown. For instance, before the Solihull Approach, sleep difficulties were often dealt with using a behavioural approach. Using the Solihull Approach meant that time was given in the assessment phase to understanding the story behind the sleep difficulty. Sometimes containment of the parent was needed, sometimes containment of the child. Sometimes an understanding of reciprocity and an attuned relationship was important. And sometimes this then led to a customised behaviour management programme. Or not. As understanding grew, so did the importance of containment and reciprocity and relationships in considering the difficulty of a child sleeping. This is not to throw the baby out with the bath water. Behaviour management is still helpful in many circumstances, but not in isolation. It is used as part of a process.

Another indication that the culture is changing is that, when the Solihull Approach parenting group was developed in 2006, we called it 'Understanding your child's behaviour', because then it seemed a step too far to call it 'Understanding your child'. Now, in 2018, some areas running the group have already dropped 'behaviour' from the name and advertise the group as 'Understanding your child'.

Conclusion

The Solihull Approach model consists of three concepts, each with their own rich background: containment; reciprocity; and behaviour management. The integration of these concepts within one model facilitates understanding of the relationship and how to apply this understanding when intervening in family or personal difficulties, thinking about trauma and the impact of Adverse Childhood Experiences[10] or when promoting wellbeing within a community.

References

1. Douglas. H. (Ed) (2017). *The First Five Years: Solihull Approach Resource Pack.* Cambridge: Jill Rogers Associates.

2. Douglas. H. (Ed) (2017). *The School Years: Solihull Approach Resource Pack.* Cambridge: Jill Rogers Associates.

3. Douglas, H. (2007). *Containment and Reciprocity.* East Sussex: Routledge.

4. Bion, W. (1959). Attacks on linking. In W.R. Bion (1990) *Second Thoughts.* London: Karnac.

5. Brazelton, T., Koslowski, B. and Main, M. (1974). The origins of reciprocity: the early mother-infant interaction. In M. Lewis and L. Rosenblum (Eds) *The Effect of the Infant on its Caregiver.* London: Wiley.

6. Beebe, B. and Lachmann, F. (2002). *Infant research and adult treatment.* Hillsdale, NJ: Analytic Press.

7. Tronick, E. Z. (1989). Emotions and emotional communication in infants. *American Psychologist*, 44, 112-126.

8. Wittgenstein, L. (1921/2001). *Tractatus Logico-Philosophicus.* London: Routledge Classics. Proposition 7, 89.

9. Douglas, H. and Ginty, M. (2001). The Solihull Approach: changes in health visiting practice. *Community Practitioner*, 74(6), 222-224.

10. Felitti, V.J., Anda, R.F., Nordenberg, D., Williamson, D.F., Spitz, A.M., Edwards, V., Koss, M.P. and Marks, J.S. (1998). Relationship of child abuse and household dysfunction to many of the leading causes of death in adults. The Adverse Childhood Experiences (ACE) Study. *Am J Prev Med.*, 14(4), 245-258.

3   How the Solihull Approach started

Hazel Douglas

There are a few versions around about how the Solihull Approach started. This, however, is the definitive one as I was there!

In 1996 a health visitor came back from a seminar about sleep. She went to her manager with the idea of opening a sleep clinic. Her manager contacted me (I am trained as both a clinical psychologist and child psychotherapist) in the Child and Adolescent Mental Health Service about meeting together with the health visitor and the health visitor lead. After hearing that all health visitors had a good proportion of parents of children and babies with sleep difficulties on their case load, it seemed to me that a first step would be to work with the health visitors to see what they needed, otherwise a sleep clinic would quickly develop a waiting list. A sleep clinic could be developed later if necessary.

Several health visitors came along to a subsequent meeting to explore the idea. It became apparent that several health visitors had been to various conferences on sleep and had brought back resources on what to do and resources for parents, but these were scattered haphazardly through various clinics; nobody really knew where. There were some leaflets available from other organisations that could be purchased from a small budget, so this added another complication in a busy clinic.

It was decided that everyone would look around at what was available and bring them back to the next meeting. The plan was that we would review the resources and decide which ones would be best to use and then put in place a system for making them easily available to all the health visitors. I thought that would be it. There was no point in reinventing the wheel and there were bound to be great resources out there that we could use with minimal work.

I was wrong. Most leaflets were very behavioural. As a trained behaviourist I knew that behavioural programmes worked, but only if they were put into practice. Listening to the health visitors talk about the families they were working with, many parents seemed too overwhelmed to change what they were doing. Some behaviour programmes were written as though one size fits all and others were harsh, both for the parents and the child. Other leaflets were too expensive to be available on a broad basis. Also, as a psychotherapist, I had access to other ideas, such as those of Dilys Daws[1], which could be integrated with the behavioural concepts to produce a benefit from both worlds.

We decided to form a project group and write our own leaflets alongside a commentary. This took months. At the end, we had a folder with leaflets and an explanation of how to work with families with babies with sleep difficulties that included behaviour management and containment. This was presented to the health visitors who were delighted with the results of our labours and I confidently expected that would be the end of it.

I was wrong. The health visitors pointed out that most of their caseload fell into four categories: sleeping, feeding, toileting and behaviour management difficulties. Now they had the resources for sleep difficulties, please could they have the same for the other three. This was an unexpected turn of events, but the health visitors signed up for three project groups to repeat the method of looking for suitable resources. I thought there would definitely be at least one of the categories that we would not need to develop resources for.

I was wrong. Again. The project groups took the view that we needed to develop our own resources, especially as a model of working was emerging that also included the concept of reciprocity. Listening to the discussions in the project group around feeding, it seemed to me that containment and behaviour management as concepts were not enough to describe the experience of the parent, baby and health visitor. I introduced the concept of reciprocity, the idea of there being a rhythm to an interaction, where the baby was an active partner. This helped in understanding the interaction around feeding. Having established reciprocity as part of this new model around feeding, it was easy to then integrate it into an understanding of toileting.

It took months to develop these resources to cover all three areas. Each section included an explanation for health visitors on how to use the resources together with photocopiable leaflets for parents.

We now had four folders. The next idea was to bring all the resources together. We decided on a loose leaf folder to make it easy to take out and photocopy leaflets. By this time it was beginning to look like a resource pack.

This all took about three years to develop the materials for the local team. This might have been the end of the development, but another area, Bristol, heard through the grapevine about our efforts and asked us to train their health visitors. We didn't have a training. Mary Rheeston (Health Visitor) and myself put together a half day training. It began with the development of a baby's brain to put into context why the role of the health visitor was so important for prevention and early intervention and why the four areas of sleeping, feeding, toileting and behaviour management were linked to infant mental health. The feedback was excellent.

We decided to work with someone who knew what they were doing about educational resource production and found Jill Rogers of Jill Rogers Associates. She project managed turning our loose leaf folder into a formal Resource Pack, at the same time designing it as a distance learning resource for those who wanted a more in depth look at the model after the training.

The first professionally produced First Five Years Resource Pack

It took a lot of effort to develop, as it included many case studies drawn from practice to show how the model worked, as well as an explanation of the theory. The first publication was in 2001, retaining the loose leaf format so that practitioners could still photocopy leaflets. It was called The First Five Years and featured our new logo.

The original Solihull Approach logo

Word of mouth began to lead to requests for training and the training developed into a two day format with two weeks inbetween to allow for some processing of the theory and application of the model to practice. Jill Rogers worked with us to turn our notes for the training into a detailed Training Manual that could be used by others to cascade the training within their own organisation. This was a deliberate strategy to make the training affordable and accessible for large numbers of practitioners. However, this then requires a consideration of governance, so that cascade trainings are of a similar quality to the original training. Four systems were designed: a training for practitioners to cascade; a detailed manual on how to deliver the 2 Day Foundation Training; an inbuilt evaluation for every training for feedback to the trainers and for the Solihull Approach office; and telephone support. One of the 'early adopters' was Derbyshire where Rebecca Johnson, Clinical Psychologist, became a cascade trainer.

Then the school nurses said 'what about us?' as the First Five Years did stop at five years. Three years later we had the School Years Resource Pack in 2004, followed by a Resource Pack in 2008 for those working in fostering and adoption and then in 2010 a Resource Pack for the antenatal team.

Ideas for covers for the next Resource Pack

From right to left: Jill Rogers, Lynda Ross, Helen Lake, Mary Rheeston.

As you can imagine, the number of Solihull Approach Resource Packs and manuals was growing on the shelf.

The name emerged probably for the following reasons: it was a team effort involving a large number of people in Solihull, so it was called after the place it originated in. It is an approach and not a programme. It is not telling practitioners or parents what to do. It introduces people to key messages from research and also to concepts which help to illuminate how we develop and live in the world, with an emphasis on relationships.

From the time where we knew we had a separate entity called the Solihull Approach, we began a parallel programme of research, as we had clinical psychology trainees who needed research proposals for their doctorate. We were receiving good feedback for the efficacy of applying this new model, but we needed something more robust to demonstrate that the model had an effect.

As we developed, so did the logo. In 2012 we decided on this logo, as it had more of a presence online.

Then in 2014 we 'refreshed' the logo again.

Parents

In the meantime, in the early 2000s, the Child and Adolescent Mental Health Service were asked to look at parenting programmes with a view to recommending one. The same method was used, of examining current programmes. Some were rather too behavioural. Mellow Parenting had a similar ethos to the Solihull Approach, but was a targeted programme. We decided to use Mellow Parenting for parents in substantial difficulty, but reluctantly decided to develop our own programme for use universally. We also wanted it to be relevant for parents across all stages of a child's development, as many programmes focussed on a specific age range.

There began to be a realisation that the Solihull Approach was all about relationships, that relationships underpinned development, attachment and emotional wellbeing across the life trajectory. We wanted to call our new parenting programme 'Understanding your child', but because many of the parenting groups on offer were about behaviour, we felt we had to be pragmatic and called it 'Understanding your child's behaviour'. The facilitator's manual was ready in 2006. Of course, then we had to develop a training programme for facilitators which required another manual, in order to create a cascadable training.

After the parenting programme came the antenatal parenting group 'Understanding pregnancy, labour, birth and your baby' (2012) and the postnatal group 'Understanding your baby' in 2015.

In 2011 we were part of a Government Programme called CANparent, which aimed to offer a menu of free parenting classes in three different areas of the country. There were many learning points from this experience[2], for example 'The analysis suggests that future government parenting support initiatives would be advised to reflect on the weaknesses of the quasi-market delivery model'. For me, the major point was the unwelcome realisation of just how stigmatising people felt it was to attend a parenting group. I think this is mainly because of many years of referral systems for parenting groups for targeted families. This has led us to champion the cause of universal groups to take away the stigma and to call them 'courses for parents', not 'parenting groups', which insinuates that the group is targeting your parenting because there is something wrong with it. The idea of curious parents just wanting to learn more is not yet a common idea in our culture. The other positive result for us from the CANparent programme was that it jolted us into developing an online course for parents based on the face to face course. This can be offered universally across a population to contribute to removing the stigma from the face to face group.

The three face to face groups for parents: antenatal; postnatal; and 'Understanding your child's behaviour', have been recreated as online courses for parents. This means that the same content is available to partners who cannot attend the face to face courses. It also provides choice for parents who cannot, or don't want to, attend a face to face group, but who still want to learn more about babies and children. There is not usually a place for grandparents in groups, as places are at a premium, but many, especially those involved in childcare for their grandchild, want to see what's new from the time when they were parenting a child. The online courses provide that opportunity.

The online courses are beginning to be translated into other languages, providing further access for parents.

Large roll outs

As you can see, the Solihull Approach was developed from practice on the ground, within the NHS in the public sector. From Public Health comes the idea of raising the average; that gains can be made, not just by making large changes within individuals, but by making small changes across a large number of people. This applies to mental health. On the one hand is the need for highly trained practitioners in mental health. But they will always only be able to see the tip of the iceberg in terms of need. On the other hand, most practitioners who come into contact with children and families in their work can support emotional health. Indeed, so can communities. The Solihull Approach, if it could reach large numbers of practitioners, has the potential to raise awareness and to inform skills. In order to do this, the training model had to support the ability to reach large numbers effectively and at low cost. This is where the cascade system came in, with detailed manuals and trainings for practitioners on how to deliver a training.

Commissioners and managers began to see the potential of rolling out the Solihull Approach across their area, because the ability to cascade meant that roll outs could be delivered across thousands of staff at a relatively low cost. Kent was the first major roll out, planned by Dr Alex Hassett.

These strategic roll outs involve planning for moving theory into practice. They also involve planning for sustainability. Roll outs usually include four to six follow up work discussion sessions, Solihull Approach Advanced training days and a local conference (see later Chapter for more details).

It became clear that for these large roll outs practitioner enthusiasm was not enough. It was essential for the Solihull Approach to be part of a planned strategy with commissioner and manager involvement. When there was a designated person leading the project then amazing things happened. You can read about some of them in this book.

> Just wanted to say we are using SA in Wales a lot! As an overview, we deliver SA 2 day basic training to all our health visiting staff; generic, 'flying start' and 'families first'. Also our school nurses are now being trained in-house too. Caerphilly Borough have piloted a responsive feeding team of community nursery nurses and established a care pathway from SA antenatal course, through to 2 years (usually first 1000 days work). There is a postnatal support contact at 72 hours and the feedback from the families is great!
>
> Avril Jones, Baby Friendly Initiative Community Co-ordinator,
> Aneurin Bevan University Health Board

Further developments

Nowadays we have a plan with a list of resources arising from horizon scanning or requests. Sometimes one of these rises to the top of the 'To do' pile because of a request to the office; 'Have you got...?'. Developing a peer breastfeeding supporter training is one example. Another is the development of free addendums that customise the 'Understanding your child's behaviour' group for parents of children on the autism spectrum, or parents of children with physical and/or learning disabilities and for adoptive parents.

Other developments have taken place where an area had a particular need and then customised the resources for that group in conversation with us. You can read about working with firefighters in a later chapter.

Updating the Resource Packs

With moving theory into practice in mind, in 2017 when we updated the Resource Packs, we thought about how to make the Packs more appealing to encourage people to read and reread the case studies and the application of the model. We had also had several requests for a digital format. The design of the Resource Packs had been chosen to facilitate distribution of the leaflets to parents by photocopying. However, technology has moved on and often it is easier to download to print rather than photocopy. At the same time, some people prefer to read books on a screen rather than on paper.

We took the decision to turn the Resource Packs into a book format, to encourage people to read it as they would a book. At the same time, we also offered it in a digital format, so that there was a choice in how to read the resource. Digital books also contribute to a move to paperless offices in some boroughs. As we are now training outside the UK, some people prefer a digital version rather than the international shipping system.

Language

Language changes and develops over the years. In the early 2000s, the language was around the impact of stress. Nearly two decades later the language is more about trauma.

In another two decades it will have changed again, but the message is the same: stress/ trauma/adverse childhood experiences have an impact on us in childhood both mentally and physically and this can continue across our lives. And the strategic actions remain just as difficult. For instance:

- Governments investing in the antenatal period and the early years and supporting parents
- Developing a culture where the trauma is taken seriously of people who self-medicate with drugs or alcohol or who are in prison. (The Netherlands have so few prisoners they sell space in prison to other countries[3])
- Developing a culture where those on the 'far right' have their trauma taken seriously. (One study[4] showed that 45 percent of those interviewed reported being the victim of childhood physical abuse while 21 percent reported being the victim of childhood sexual abuse; 46 percent of those interviewed reported being neglected as a child).

Conclusion

I find the story interesting for several reasons. The Solihull Approach did not arise from a plan. It grew organically, developing in response to need. In the beginning it was a small local initiative. There was no sense of it growing and no plan for it to do so. It was crafted by and in response to the people who were going to use it, which I think is one reason for its success. It was fit for purpose and had from the beginning a high degree of acceptability woven into it, because it was created with the people who wanted to use it.

Initially the Solihull Approach did not grow through strategies developed many levels above practitioners. It grew through practitioners' recognition that the model was helpful and then through word of mouth recommendations. Neither did it develop because an organisation created an intervention and then designed a marketing strategy to sell it to other organisations.

After a few years, as it became clear that the Solihull Approach was an entity and of interest to others, it required the structure of a creative organisation: a focus on incremental innovation; research and development; horizon scanning; communication; skills development; cost control; and the rest.

It has been a rollercoaster of a journey. Sometimes it is difficult, especially when we are developing something new and have to learn a lot from our mistakes! The emails, tweets and phone calls from people who use the Solihull Approach and find it beneficial and often transformational are both humbling and encouraging.

We are engaged in culture change. Increasing emotional health from conception onwards will have profound consequences for the way we treat each other and the world.

References

1. Daws, D. (1993). *Through the night: Helping parents and sleepless infants.* London: Free Association Books.

2. Cullen, S. M., Cullen, M. A., and Lindsay, G. (2017). The CANparent trial—the delivery of universal parenting education in England. *British Educational Research Journal*, 43(4), 759-780.

3. *The Dutch prison crisis: A shortage of prisoners.* https://www.bbc.co.uk/news/magazine-37904263 accessed 12.10.18.

4. Simi, P., Bubolz, B., McNeel, H., Sporer, K. and Windisch, S. (2015). Trauma as a Precursor to Violent Extremism: How Non-Ideological Factors Can Influence Joining an Extremist Group. *START Newsletter*.

4 A note on theory into practice

Hazel Douglas

Moving theory into practice is always a challenge. training can be a waste of time and money if there is no thought as to how it applies outside the training room.

As the number of areas taking on the Solihull Approach training increased, it became important to make sure that the training made a difference. Practitioners evidently enjoyed the training and reported that it was very useful, but if the learning stays in the training room then what good is it? Ways of supporting theory into practice is a constant consideration in the Solihull Approach team. Often the actions are not complicated, but they require planning to operationalise them (there is a list of actions on the Solihull Approach website[1]).

At the most basic, the Foundation training has a two week gap between day 1 and day 2. This is to give time to process the concepts and to come back to day 2 to revisit them, as well as, in line with social learning theory, to support 'homework' and to see the concepts in action in real life. Occasionally, as it is operationally easier, we receive requests for the training days to be consecutive or for there to be one long training day. One area did carry out a programme of delivery over one day. However, their own evaluations showed that the delegates did not gain much from the training and they had to put on extra sessions to compensate. We have thousands and thousands of post training evaluations from around the UK and elsewhere, so we can compare one area's results with an expected average.

Kent, in its large roll out, included work discussion sessions after the 2 day Foundation training and generally areas now build in mandatory attendance at four to six work discussion sessions to their plan for roll outs. Northern Ireland developed a toolkit to support the provision of these sessions, as did North Lanarkshire, and they have generously made these available for download on the Solihull Approach website.

Some areas hold an annual Trainer's day for their Solihull Approach cascade trainers. Cascade training in itself usually moves practitioners into a greater understanding of the model, both because of the further training and because they really have to understand the model in order to explain it to others.

Some put on a conference so that practitioners can showcase their work using the Solihull Approach. Arranging an event can be helpful to support practitioners to move theory into practice.

Many areas follow up the 2 day Foundation training with training to run the Solihull Approach groups for parents. Again, this training, together with the experience of running a group based on the model, usually moves practitioners onto a higher level of understanding.

The Solihull Approach Advanced training days have been designed to introduce or deepen knowledge, using the Solihull Approach model as architecture to incorporate new knowledge more easily. They are one day courses which can be used in a theory into practice plan. They are run after the 2 day Foundation training and can accommodate up to 40 people in one training, depending on the confidence of the trainers. An area can organise a rolling programme of the Advanced trainings. They act as a quick refresh for understanding the model and then introduce new information on the topic, followed by a recent relevant area of research and time for reflection to integrate this new knowledge with the Solihull Approach model. Brain development in the 2 day Foundation training concentrates on the early years, to set the scene for why risk factors and resilience factors have an impact on us. The Advanced training covers brain development from the antenatal period through to adolescence. It also provides a brief introduction to the relatively new area of research into mirror neurones and then integrates the information in the seminar with the Solihull Approach model. These trainings can also be helpful to contribute to practitioners' CPD (Continual Professional Development).

The Advanced trainings are:

- Brain development (from antenatal to adolescence, which includes mirror neurones)
- Attachment (which includes epigenetics)
- Understanding trauma (includes Adverse Childhood Experiences: ACEs)
- Refresher training.

When added to the 2 day Foundation training, they can lead to the award of Solihull Approach Advanced Trained Practitioner status by the Solihull Approach Head Office.

For any training, the challenge is to move the knowledge out of the training room and into practice. The concepts in the Solihull Approach model are about how we are in the world with each other. Understanding the concepts in the training is augmented by seeing how this understanding is used in practice in the work discussion sessions. The Advanced training days show how containment and reciprocity underpin the quality of an attachment and are central to an understanding of reaction to and recovery from trauma. They explain why Adverse Childhood Experiences have such an impact. They show how to support emotional health.

When planning your Solihull Approach training, whether it is for 10 colleagues or 3,000 practitioners, the most value will be wrung out of your investment if you put in place a plan for moving theory into practice.

References

1. www.solihullapproachparenting.com/making-it-happen/

5 Managing a large roll out of the Solihull Approach: Shropshire

Karen Ladd

Shropshire is a large rural county of 319,736 hectares, or 1,235 square miles. We have a population of 311,400 and the population density in Shropshire is 0.96 people per hectare compared to 4.09 across England[1]. 95.4% of residents describe themselves as white British. Over a half of residents live in rural areas as defined by the 2011 rural urban classification scheme.

There are an estimated 59,386 children, under the age of 18 and this will decrease to 58,915 by 2031[2]. Although two thirds of the families that our Children's Services currently support live in the larger market towns, a third of families who need our support live in much smaller and rural areas, many with poor transport links. Shropshire has the reputation of being a beautiful county, but for many of our services its rurality is our biggest challenge.

The 2011 riots in London and across the country, lead to an investigation carried out by local authorities into their support offer for parents. The riots occurred between 6 and 11 August 2011. The protests began in Tottenham, London, following the death of Mark Duggan, a local man, shot dead by police on 4th August. Thousands of people rioted in cities and towns across England. By 10 August, more than 3,000 arrests had been made across England, with more than 1,000 people issued with criminal charges for various offences related to the riots. In a public speech on 15 August, the then Prime Minister, David Cameron, blamed a 'broken society' in 'moral collapse'. The Ministry of Justice report that followed, noted that rioters brought before the courts were disproportionately male (89%) and young (53% were aged 20 or under, with the number of 'juveniles' ranging from 26% in London to 39% in Merseyside). The spotlight of responsibility was very much focused on parents and the deterioration of standards within family life.

The significant spending cuts of the coalition government in the United Kingdom at this time, including planned cuts to police budgets and scrapping of the Education Maintenance Allowance, and trebling of university tuition fees, combined with high youth unemployment, meant that there were additional pressures on services to work in a cost effective way. David Cameron set out plans to invest £448 million over the course of the Parliament to turn around the lives of around 120,000 'troubled families' in England. The Troubled Families programme consists of a range of targeted interventions for families with multiple problems, including crime, anti-social behaviour, truancy, unemployment, mental health problems and domestic abuse. The introduction of the Troubled Families programme encouraged Shropshire Council to investigate what offer of support it already had in place for families across all levels of need.

In Shropshire in 2012, there was evidence of four different parenting approaches being worked with by different agencies, and although these approaches were all evidence based, agencies were rarely recognising the integrity of these programmes of delivery. Shropshire had chosen to 'localise' the delivery of our parenting offer; groups had been shortened, workshops had been adjusted to meet perceived need, and professionals were reporting that parents would not attend anything for longer than 4 weeks. We knew that being a predominantly rural county, transport links were a problem, but we had no evidence to back up our professionals' comments, other than low numbers and lack of engagement from families. It would appear that parenting approaches come with strong professional alliances, most likely because people involved in the delivery of these approaches are parents themselves and have benefited from their knowledge first hand. Suggesting a change in provision, we knew, would be a challenge for many. However, what we could clearly evidence at this time, was that we were not doing anything particularly well and we had no evidence base of our own to suggest that what was on offer was having any impact on our families. Proving that we were doing something ineffectively turned out to be a good place to start! The Troubled Families initiative was telling us that some families were having contact with multiple agencies, addressing individual concerns. This piece of knowledge allowed us to suggest that whilst the initiative worked to address this multi-agency input, if we could encourage agencies to follow the same approach, families would at least be receiving consistent messages about their parenting. Representatives from the local authority, health, education and the voluntary sector, came together in a strategic working group to explore the different approaches and agreed to invest in one approach across the whole county.

Choosing the right approach

Shropshire's health visitors had recently been trained in the Solihull Approach, though they had had no capacity to deliver any parenting groups. Their enthusiasm for this way of working had led our school nursing service to follow suit and they had also begun to access Solihull Approach training. The local authority carried out a study of all available approaches and found that the Solihull Approach would be a cost effective approach to introduce at a time of budget cuts and would allow for our own train the trainer programme, which was appealing. The Solihull Approach team subsequently came to Shropshire and introduced us to their model. A local approach tried and tested in the West Midlands, by real people who had a face and were at the end of the phone, was a definite influence, when making the brave move to throw out all previous approaches and start afresh. The working group agreed the approach, and the first round of Foundation training was introduced in Shropshire in December 2012.

Training the workforce

Our initial priority was to train up our multi-agency workforce and encourage a shared language across the county. The Solihull Approach proved to be successful with our professionals supporting families across the county from day one. It had been a strategic decision to invest in the Approach at a managerial level; many practitioners were told that they would need to attend this new training and for those support workers in the local authority the decision was made to make the training mandatory. Human nature, as we know, means that people don't like being told what to do, particularly when their loyalties lie elsewhere and we knew that getting our own workers on board would be our first challenge.

To address this, the working group made the decision to train 12 multi-agency trainers in Shropshire, who were representatives from health, the local authority's Children's Services and the private sector. These trainers had all had previous training experience and vast experience of working with families to draw on. They were a diverse group of people who had not previously trained or worked together, but they quickly appreciated the Approach and became a team, sharing their enthusiasm with their own professional areas.

Teams became open to this new offer of training as it was being delivered to them by one of their own. It wasn't all an easy ride, several attendees at trainings came in with arms crossed, determined not to be swayed to a new approach when their loyalties lay elsewhere. However, the beauty of the Solihull Approach, we quickly discovered, was that it does not conflict with any other approaches. It values the practitioner's experience and knowledge, and simply offers a framework to their way of working. Since our first delivery of the Foundation training we have not received a single negative evaluation of the training. We have delivered the training in Shropshire to approximately 600 multi-agency professionals to date.

Over the years we have chosen to keep our training pool small. In this way we can quality assure our training, our trainers have the opportunity to deliver regularly and they are able to share and build on their experience of delivering training.

Introduction of parenting groups

As a first step, getting buy in from practitioners working on the ground was essential, before rolling out the parenting groups. This way, our workers would have an understanding of the Approach and what they were signposting families to, as well as being able to complement with the same messages in their daily roles working with families.

Although our focus in 2013 was the roll out of the Foundation training to our professionals, we did trial a few 'Understanding your child' parenting groups. Our very first group we delivered was a mix of identified 'troubled families', families on child protection plans and universal families who had simply shown an interest in improving their parenting. From the outset, the support that these families offered each other was humbling and we were confident that we had made the right decision to adopt the Solihull Approach in Shropshire. We have never looked back.

As mentioned in my introduction, Shropshire is a very large rural county, and this for children's services is often our biggest challenge. We do not have the ethnic diversity of our more urban neighbours and we consistently score lower than English averages for homelessness and unemployment. Our educational achievement rates are consistently above the national average, as are our rates for life expectancy.

This all paints a reasonably healthy picture. Shropshire is a beautiful county, with numerous conservation areas and listed buildings, attracting tourists from both home and abroad. In reality we have had to work with the same allowances per person from central government as our urban counterparts, and as driving from one end of the county to the other can take up to two and a half hours, this vast coverage has been one of our greatest challenges in supporting families. A worker will regularly drive for an hour, to visit a family for an hour, before returning to their base. Three hours out of a working day can easily be spent on one family, which in an urban model of working may take little over an hour. Delivering to groups of parents straight away offers us an economically sensible way of working. Introducing the Solihull Approach at the same time as significant government spending cuts, where the local authority was being faced with a significant number of redundancies to meet these cuts, meant that as a local authority we had to think creatively as to how to get this provision out to parents in localities.

Working with schools

We made the decision to work with our schools and encourage them to see the benefits for their families and to become involved in the programme of delivery. Schools know their families and know their localities. Shropshire has 152 state funded schools, 20 of which are secondary schools. The primary aged schools are split into 12 groups across the county. An initial offer was made to the 12 primary school groups and to all secondary schools to send representatives to access the Foundation training, followed by the Group Facilitator training. In the first year, 11 out of the 12 groups agreed and six of the secondary schools.

Since this time we have continued to roll out the training to schools and have delivered to 70 primary schools and 18 secondary schools. In recent years schools have also been faced with significant cuts in their budgets and many staff have moved on. In Shropshire, to enhance our offer and encourage on-going engagement with the parenting offer, we offer on-going support and training to schools.

Once anyone has trained as a facilitator in Shropshire we add them to a facilitators data base, and from this we send out termly newsletters, which offers news about our county delivery, and also any new research that might be of interest and relevant to our parenting offer. We also offer termly network/CPD sessions across the county, which provide an opportunity for group facilitators to come together and share their successes and their challenges. We always invite a guest speaker to come along and offer some additional training or share an area of knowledge that will benefit the group.

This network of facilitators has been key to keeping the parenting offer alive in Shropshire. Facilitators have formed relationships and support each other, as well as knowing that they can access training to benefit their professional development and have allowed for on-going relationships with our very small local authority parenting team, who are always accessible at the end of the phone to offer support and guidance. These great relationships with our schools have allowed us to offer universal parenting groups across the county, reaching far more parents than ever before, and in many cases preventing referrals into our targeted children's services.

Some of our schools have seen the impact of the course so significantly on behaviours of children that they have adopted the Solihull Approach as part of their induction programme for new parents. One of our infant schools in the busy town of Market Drayton, which has a high proportion of 'troubled families', invites all new parents of reception aged children to attend for a full morning during their child's first month of school; parents are invited into their child's classroom to meet the teacher and work with the child on phonics or maths to enable and encourage them to help at home with their child's learning and they attend an 'Understanding your child' workshop. Finally they are invited to stay for a school lunch with their child. This school then subsequently offers an 'Understanding your child' group, which is always then well attended. Parents' evaluations of the group are always glowing and parents who attend do not do so because they see themselves as bad parents, but because they see themselves as parents who want be the best parents they can be. This school is an example of how the stigma can be taken out of parenting support, by making it an offer to all parents. The parents, their children and the school all reap the benefits of this.

The head teacher of the school has said;

> The Solihull Approach has been one of the best courses that we have offered to parents in terms of making an impact for both the parents and the children. Parents can attend by choice and we are able to target parents who we feel will benefit from the course. That one parent has described it as 'life changing' speaks volumes.

And one parent wrote in her evaluation of a recent group;

> I have come out the end of it understanding that as parents, we make mistakes but we can fix it, apologise and move on without still carrying the guilt. Our children have their own amazing thoughts and feelings and it's not my job to manage those feelings but to teach my children how to manage them. I am so thankful to have this opportunity to learn this approach and wish the group was not ending as I am much happier and so are my kids.

Branding and coordination

On introducing the groups across the county we were keen to take the stigma out of parenting support. To do this we decided that we would flood the county with posters and information explaining that this was an offer for all parents. We decided that we should introduce our own branding to complement the Solihull Approach and make this a Shropshire offer, which would become recognised and trusted by all Shropshire parents. An art competition was run in a local primary school, and many budding young artists submitted entries with drawings of their families. The Shropshire Council parenting team had the honour of choosing the winning entry, and this artwork has headed our parenting campaign ever since; it has been used on posters, leaflets, websites, letter heads and emails. The parenting team has continued to coordinate the parenting offer centrally, keeping in touch with facilitators across the county, providing training, support and promotion of groups. This small central team has been key to keeping the offer alive and moving forward during some very economically challenging years.

Specialist groups

With our schools doing such a great job of picking up our universal offer of parenting groups, this allowed our local authority parenting team and other children's services practitioners, to focus on a more targeted delivery. We were regularly being told by our facilitators that our families with children with special educational needs and disabilities (SEND), were our most challenging families to support in our universal offer of groups. Although parents were always supportive of each other in groups and every family had their own individual issues, the element of appreciating what it meant to have a child with SEND was missing. These families also told us that they wanted a group specifically for them. With this feedback, we introduced a termly offer of 'Understanding your child' groups specifically for these families.

These groups have proven to be a huge success, and we have found that these families have benefited significantly with meeting other families who have some understanding of their situation. Many have gone on to support each other once the groups have finished.

One mum told us

> I have never received the support and understanding from my own family for my daughter, which I have received from the other parents in this group, they have thrown me a lifeline, and I no longer feel like I am on my own. I think maybe I have offered other parents some support also, which has made me feel like I have done something useful, I haven't felt that way for a long time.

We also found that some of the families with more complex needs, who might have been guided toward a group by their social worker or family support worker, in some instances could be a challenge in our universal groups. Being told that you should do something does not always sit well with our sensitivities and several parents would arrive feeling resentful and defensive. This persuaded us that we should offer targeted groups for families who were being supported by our children's services, facilitated by practitioners who were experienced in working with these more complex families, and again quickly we found that the parents' commonalities helped enormously in engaging parents to begin supporting each other.

Introduction of workshops

One of our challenges, particularly in our more rural communities has been and continues to be getting the numbers of parents together to run a group. We as professionals have seen the benefits time and time again, and parents who have attended and completed courses have been great advocates for us. However, sometimes there are still difficulties in engaging parents, particularly parents of teenagers. To address this, very early on we decided to introduce the Solihull Approach workshops.

For some, the workshop alone has proved to be enough for them. For many, however, it has encouraged their attendance at a parenting group. The teenage workshop in particular has also proven to complement our targeted work with families across children's services. Many parents of teenagers work, and struggle to commit to a 10 week group, and many are accessing targeted support across Early Help and Social Care. The workshop provides information about the teenage brain that both parents and professionals find fascinating. It does not offer parenting advice, but offers information in an entirely non-threatening way. Parents across all levels of need have found this workshop valuable, what they take away and do with the information is up to them. For many it allows them to view their teenagers a little differently and perhaps prioritise their challenges. For others, it allows

42   *Karen Ladd*

them to recognise that they do in fact need additional support and they choose to go on to attend a group.

Introduction of online courses

In 2017, we were thrilled to be able to offer the online 'Understanding your child' course to our families. This is another great tool which enables us to offer something to those families who are unable to access groups. This might be due to the remoteness of their location or due to other reasons of inaccessibility of the groups on offer, for example, work commitments. We made it clear across our children's services teams, that an online course should never replace a targeted intervention. We offer the online course as a universal offer to parents who are interested in being the best parents they can be and it should be promoted as such.

From the outset the course has been promoted through our Children's Centres, Family Information Service, health visitors and our schools. Although intended as a universal offer, several professionals have come back to us and shared that they have in fact chosen to use the online course as a tool to guide their intervention and have worked through it alongside parents, challenging their ideas and drawing out reflective discussion. Others have used the online course to give to partners who might be out at work and therefore unavailable to engage with the targeted offer of support and have been encouraged to use the course in conjunction with the targeted intervention to promote discussion within the family and shared messages. We know that the course has also been accessed by grandparents who are offering childcare to some of our targeted families. Purchasing the multi user licence has allowed us to promote and offer the course free of charge across the county to all of our parents.

Antenatal Solihull Approach

In 2016 we starting rolling out the Solihull Approach antenatal course, 'Understanding pregnancy, labour, birth and your baby', across the county. This had finally been agreed at a strategic level and was a co-delivery between our midwives, health visitors and Children's Centre support workers. Finally, we were able to say that we were offering a comprehensive parenting approach, from the antenatal period across all age ranges. Sadly, we have been hit hard with cuts in recent years, across the county's health services and Children's Centres, so, as in all other areas, sustainability of this programme has been a challenge. Three agencies working together, rather than one on their own, has allowed us to continue and again we made the multi-agency decision to purchase the multi user licence for both the antenatal and postnatal online courses. The offer of this online provision has alleviated some of the pressures of demand for the face to face group, which has allowed us to continue. Our midwives give out postcards at the time of booking, signposting the antenatal and postnatal courses. Our health visitors then give out a further postcard at the child's two year check to promote the online 'Understanding your child' course.

Parenting clinics

We have a very small dedicated parenting team as part of Shropshire Council's offer of Early Help. In 2017 the decision was made, that as well as offering targeted 'Understanding

Managing a large roll out of the Solihull Approach: Shropshire   43

your child' groups, the team would also offer 'Understanding your child' clinics at locations across the county. Instead of supporting in families' homes, where possible we encourage families to come for a clinic appointment.

These appointments are used in various ways; some may come as a one off to discuss a specific concern about a child's behaviour and access some support, whilst others come for several weeks. The parenting practitioners use the Solihull Approach to inform their direction of support. For parents who have completed the 'Understanding your child' course some time ago, it has been an opportunity for them to drop in and revisit some of the messages previously learnt and discuss their current parenting challenges. The clinics are well attended, and allow for wider access for parents across all levels of need.

We have had parents attend the clinics whose children have been removed and are in care and are working toward having them returned to them, parents on child protection plans and parents attending with grandparents who all contribute to the daily childcare in the home. We have had a GP attend who was struggling with their teenager and several professionals who have been struggling with the demands of work and parenting. Parents can attend anonymously if this is appropriate and there are no identified safeguarding concerns, or can attend as part of an agreed plan. We are proud that we are able to offer this as a universal offer to all parents.

Local evidence base

All of our groups and workshops are evaluated as prescribed by the Solihull Approach team, and we are proud to share these so they can be part of the Solihull Approach's evidence base. For our own purposes however, from the outset we have put our own evaluation process in place to enable a degree of measure of progress for all families completing a Parenting Group. We simply ask parents to identify two goals that they would like to work on during the group and also to measure, from zero to ten, where they are in understanding and managing their child's behaviour at the beginning of the group and again at the end. This has allowed us to build our own local evidence base and to consistently prove the worth of the parenting programme in Shropshire. In our yearly reporting since 2013, we have, without exception, reported over 98% of parents completing groups seeing an improvement in their understanding and management of their children's behaviours.

Conclusion

Multi-agency commitment to the delivery of the Solihull Approach programme has allowed us in Shropshire to promote a brand of parenting support that is recognised across the county. Parents are being introduced to the Approach during pregnancy, before they have even had the chance to experience the challenges of being a parent. They are hearing messages at this stage which we hope they will carry on benefiting from throughout their children's lives. If difficulties arise as their children get older and enter their school aged years, we believe that parents will not be frightened to join our 'Understanding your child' groups, as they will already have some understanding of what support the group will offer. As children become teenagers and the challenges change along with the young people's development, we hope that we can build on messages previously heard and that these will continue to make sense and support the understanding and management of developing behaviours. Ultimately, we hope that by supporting parents of children of all ages using the Solihull Approach, we will help shape our young people's experience of being parents themselves.

The voices of Shropshire parents

'Fab course really enjoyed it!'

'I have learned to believe in myself more.'

'The group has helped me to respect my children as individuals with their own needs.'

'It has been lovely to be amongst supportive, understanding parents.'

'I feel less frustrated and more in tune with my children.'

'Every parent should do this course!'

'The course genuinely helped me through the breakup of my marriage and taught me the best way to ensure the least impact on my son'

'I'm not the only parent in the world struggling.'

'I finally get why my kids behave like they do.'

'Being a mum is hard work, but actually I'm not that bad at it.'

'I now listen to my children and they listen to me, amazing!'

References

1. 2011 Census, Office for National Statistics © Crown copyright 2016
2. Office for National Statistics licensed under the Open Government Licence. © Crown copyright 2018

6 From small beginnings: the Solihull Approach in Northern Ireland

Averil Bassett

Introduction

In the following chapter, I aim to give a brief picture of the growth and development of the Solihull Approach in Northern Ireland (NI) during my employment with the HSC (Health and Social Care) Clinical Education Centre. My hope is to demonstrate how the small steps that were taken in 2010 have progressed to widespread integration of the Solihull Approach programmes throughout children's services. To achieve this there have been many levels of partnership, from the practitioners working closely with families to the strategists setting public health direction.

Acknowledgements

I want to acknowledge that this chapter couldn't possibly reflect all the great work that is current in Northern Ireland. The Solihull Approach is not just an approach to a way of working but also has a range of parent group programmes that are being delivered by Solihull Approach trainers with parents, foster carers and in schools, reflecting the diverse ways that it can be applied.

None of this would be possible without the dedication and commitment of the many individuals and groups I have had the privilege of working with. This includes practitioners and managers, Solihull Approach trainers, policy makers and all those who saw the benefit of this model and committed their time and effort to the vision of improving outcomes for children.

Solihull Approach Director and Manager

From the outset, I have worked closely with Dr Hazel Douglas, Solihull Approach Director, Mary Rheeston, Solihull Approach Manager, and the Solihull Approach office staff. Their practical support and friendship has been unequivocally generous and fundamental to progress. I took them at their word and contact them regularly for advice and 'containment'.

Background

Northern Ireland Solihull Approach programme delivery commenced in early 2000 by a group of enthusiastic practitioners. Their vision and delivery was to all disciplines working in children's services. The success they had in raising awareness of infant mental health through integration of the Solihull Approach was influential to developing regional direction.

46   *Averil Bassett*

Northern Ireland has a population of 1.8 million. There is a child population of 433,000 with approximately 23,000 births per year. It has an integrated health and social care system with five Trusts delivering health and social care to the population. Public health policy is to 'Give Every Child the Best Start in Life', recognising that what happens to children in their earliest years sets the trajectory for future outcomes in health and education. This is reflected in the 'Healthy Child Healthy Future: Universal Child Health Promotion Programme for NI (2010)' which is delivered to all children from birth to nineteen years.

HSC Clinical Education Centre

The Clinical Education Centre (CEC) is an 'in service' education provider constituted by the Department of Health NI (DoH) for the delivery of education to nurses, midwives and allied health professionals across the five HSC Trusts in response to identified education needs. The CEC Nurse and Midwife Education Consultants complete a teaching qualification and work closely with clinical practice across all parts of the Nursing and Midwifery Council Register. It is a CEC priority to work strategically with the DoH, the Public Health Agency and stakeholders in support of education for service development.

Being a member of the Healthy Child Healthy Future group was the conduit for the introduction of the Solihull Approach primarily, but not exclusively, to the health visiting workforce. It was identified as a programme that incorporated policy direction, was easily accessible, cost effective in its delivery and very importantly, recommended a theory to practice model. CEC annual programme planning included Solihull Approach requests from the Trusts. This ensured a planned number of programmes per year and a systematic approach to workforce development.

My introduction and journey with the Solihull Approach model began in the South Eastern Trust, where I completed the Solihull Approach foundation programme (as it became known in Northern Ireland) delivered by a social worker and family therapist. The programme content, which included the scientific evidence for early brain development and links with the parent carer relationship, integrated in a fresh way what I had aspired to in supporting parents as a health visitor. I could see straight away that this programme had the potential to increase confidence and skills and would be welcomed by practitioners.

It offered much more than great content. I found the delivery by the facilitators helped me to begin a journey where I could process my own childhood experiences and understanding of the parenting that I had both received and given. I remember describing the programme to a colleague as 'therapeutic'. I realised over time that this was containment and reciprocity being modelled and that the Solihull Approach trainers had integrated this into their teaching style.

Teaching the Solihull Approach foundation programme

The teaching methodologies in the two day programme are considerate of different learning styles and facilitative of reflective practice enabling practitioners to integrate the Solihull Approach model effectively into practice. With examples of good practice already in Northern Ireland, this became the programme of choice by the Public Health leads for practitioners delivering the Universal Child Health Promotion Programme to support infant mental health and parenting.

As a teacher, the Solihull Approach model was very meaningful as I recognised that nurses attending programmes are often 'full up' with anxiety and stress. Over time, it became an observable reality that the practice of containment creates a positive learning environment and reciprocity helps the teacher to think about the practitioners in a person-centred way. It's not a new phenomenon that practitioners come from busy practice settings and that their domestic lives are full of modern day stressors, but by practicing the skills of containment and placing a focus on 'looking after ourselves' there was a deeper level of engagement in the learning environment. I found this to be transformational in my role as a teacher.

Now with a number of years of experience in the delivery of Solihull Approach programmes, I have found the model to far surpass my early expectations. It is a huge privilege to support the development of practitioners in their personal and professional development. Evaluations of the programme are overwhelmingly positive. There have been many examples where practitioners, through the sharing of childhood or practice trauma, have recognised the benefit of containment as practiced by the Solihull Approach trainers. This level of practice development using containment has become recognised in teams and it is common place to hear the phrase 'I need containment'.

Solihull Approach Practice Sessions

Our small team of CEC Solihull Approach trained Nurse and Midwife Education Consultants quickly gained experience in delivery of the Solihull Approach foundation programmes. From the start, we had an agreement with managers that a minimum of four practice sessions were mandatory and integral to the foundation programme. The focus of these is on:

- the theoretical model
- subject discussion from the Solihull Approach Resource Packs e.g. First Five Years
- reflective practice
- demonstrating the use of containment and reciprocity through case studies.

Experience demonstrates that there is a better uptake of practice sessions when groups are kept together, as they have formed relationships on the foundation programme.

Practice sessions guidance

1. Practice sessions commence one month after the foundation programme and take place one month thereafter, with the aim that practitioners complete the 2 day foundation training and four practice sessions within six months.
2. There is a group agreement and containment exercise at the start of each practice session.
3. All participants agree to participate in reflective practice.
4. The facilitator's role is to support practitioners and link the key messages of the Solihull Approach model to practice examples.
5. A Post Practice Evaluation is completed by the practitioners to identify challenges and apply learning to future sessions.

48   *Averil Bassett*

6. Practitioners unable to complete four practice sessions with their group can complete these with another group.

7. A further two practice sessions per year is practiced in some areas.

8. The support of managers is fundamental to the delivery and embedding of the model.

Practice session facilitation was a new area of development following programme delivery. Instead of preparing a subject to teach, I was supporting the practitioners to provide an overview of their chosen subject from the Solihull Approach Resource Pack. We found that by giving them time to choose a subject that was relevant to their practice on day two of the programme and recommending that they deliver this in pairs with a case study, this created a commitment and an expectation of attendance at practice sessions.

Some of the greatest challenges to the Solihull Approach trainers come from practice sessions and yet this is where so much learning takes place, not just for the practitioners, but also for the trainers. Busy practitioners may feel resentful at travelling for a two hour session, especially if expectations are not made clear at the outset. Some don't feel comfortable at presenting to the group or may not feel that their case study example is 'good enough'. As a team, we have placed importance on sharing these challenges and discussing ways of practicing containment and developing facilitation skills.

This same challenge was also evident in the wider group of regional Solihull Approach trainers, shown in the results of a questionnaire on their experience of practice session delivery. CEC developed a Practice Session Facilitator's Toolkit that incorporated a structure, key messages from the model, session plan and a post practice session reflective evaluation. This has been used extensively by Solihull Approach trainers and is available free on the Solihull Approach practitioner website[1].

Train the trainers: CEC education and practice model of delivery

Traditionally a cascade model of training delivery has many advantages and challenges which are well recognised. Practitioners have a wonderful opportunity to share the application of the model with their colleagues. There are other challenges, not least that practitioners who are busy have little time for preparation. trainers can feel unsupported by an infrastructure that doesn't have protected time for role development. Their commitment in preparation may go unnoticed as it often takes place outside of working hours and is not included in their job description.

CEC Education and Practice Model

This afforded an opportunity for CEC to develop an education and practice model of delivery. I believe this is important for the professional development of Solihull Approach trainers both within education and practice. It adds a quality assurance and education governance to programme delivery and promotes sustainability through continuous development of new Solihull Approach trainers. To address these challenges, CEC developed the following pathway, promoting partnership and mutual respect, that recognises the skills and benefits that education and practice can bring to programme delivery.

Pathway following completion of Train the trainers

1. Solihull Approach regional trainer observes a further Foundation programme.
2. Solihull Approach regional trainer meets with CEC Solihull Approach trainer to prepare for programme delivery.
3. Regional trainer delivers the Foundation programme with CEC trainer.
4. Regional trainer delivers the practice sessions with CEC trainer (initially for support of skills development).

By 2017 all health visitors and nurses from children's teams were Solihull Approach trained. We had a cohort of Solihull Approach trainers (health visitors) working both within the public health teams and some Sure Starts. CEC was actively involved in the development of Solihull Approach trainers and the Solihull Approach was continuing to gain momentum across children's services. However, up until 2013 there was only one Trust that had extended Solihull Approach places to other disciplines and the voluntary sector.

Regional Infant Mental Health Planning Group (2013 to 2015)

The development of this regional group was instrumental in widening access to the Solihull Approach programmes for other disciplines. A Public Health Agency audit identified gaps in infant mental health training and inequity in access to Solihull Approach programmes. I made a proposal to the Public Health Agency outlining how CEC could assist partner agencies in their vision to increase infant mental health awareness programmes to both the statutory and voluntary sectors. The successful application secured funding for a coordination post and Solihull Approach programme delivery to meet the actions of the workforce development plan. This included the provision of Solihull Approach foundation programmes to over 300 practitioners and Train the trainer programmes for identified practitioners across disciplines.

Multi-disciplinary delivery was met enthusiastically by the team of CEC Solihull Approach trainers. As a Solihull Approach trainer, I could see clearly that one of the hidden outcomes was the respect that was generated within groups, through understanding different roles across the voluntary and statutory sectors. Practice sessions were rich with examples of using the model within different contexts, providing a forum for learning and informal supervision.

Regional Infant Mental Health Framework (2016)

The above plan became formalised as an Infant Mental Health Framework for Northern Ireland (2016). A workforce development action was to introduce the Solihull Approach to pre-professional qualification programmes. Some success has been achieved through a partnership arrangement with Ulster University, Public Health Agency, CEC and the Trusts, securing delivery of Solihull Approach by CEC for all specialist community public health nurses since 2013. This has been valued by the Trusts, as the students start to use the model from the outset of their practice and the students have attested to its value.

Early Intervention Transformation Programme 2015-2018

With each new development there are new challenges and rewards. An early intervention initiative led by the Public Health Agency provided the opportunity for CEC to deliver the combined antenatal foundation programme and antenatal parent group to 120 midwives per year for three years. The aim is to enhance midwifery practice through the focus on early relationships and the transformation of traditional parentcraft classes to group based care and education using the Solihull Approach antenatal parent education group for all first time parents. The feedback from both midwives and parents has been overwhelmingly positive and in favour of continuing to work in this way beyond the lifespan of the project.

Parents are finding increased support for pregnancy and birth with many maintaining relationships with their group members after the classes are finished. We look forward to the completion of Queens University Belfast research to demonstrate outcomes. Our initial evaluations show improved breastfeeding rates and confidence in decision making in the parenting role.

Following the success of delivery to midwives, a group of Queens University Belfast lecturers have completed the Solihull Approach Antenatal foundation programme. They are now in early planning stages for the integration of this into pre-registration midwifery programmes.

Regional Solihull Approach trainers forum

Northern Ireland has over 100 Solihull Approach trainers. They are an important group for continued delivery and sustainability, needing professional development, supervision and opportunities for networking to share their experiences of delivery of Solihull Approach programmes.

CEC has established an annual regional Solihull Approach trainers' forum Learning Event to provide professional development, networking and sharing of new Solihull Approach developments. This event is supported by our partners from the Public Health Agency and the Solihull Approach.

As awareness of the effectiveness of the Solihull Approach has spread, there has been increased interest and requests for Solihull Approach programmes across a range of sectors in Northern Ireland. A report was commissioned by the Public Health Agency to capture developments to date. It makes recommendations for growth and development and sustainability into the future. This has given hope for continued investment in Northern Ireland. I look forward to the next chapter...

References

1. www.solihullapproachparenting.com/making-it-happen/

7 The Solihull Approach in the antenatal and postnatal period

Mary Rheeston

The birth of a child should be a wonderful, life-changing time for a mother and her whole family. It is a time of new beginnings, of fresh hopes and new dreams, of change and opportunity. It is a time when the experiences we have can shape our lives and those of our babies and families forever.

National Maternity Review, 2016[1].

This is how we would all like to think about welcoming a new baby into the world. However, in reality, preparing to be a parent is complicated. In biological terms it should be straightforward, as we are genetically designed to reproduce the next generation and nature has built in a series of survival mechanisms in both the infant and mother. Infants are programmed to recognise the sound of their mother's voice in the womb and the smell of her breastmilk, they have reflexes such as rooting and grasping and will attempt to search out the human face that matches the most important voices they have heard throughout their time in the womb. The infant brain is only partially developed at birth to allow for further growth after birth, when it will adapt itself to the physical and emotional environment it is born into. Babies have a distinctive means of communicating, namely crying, that adults caring for the baby are genetically driven to respond to as part of the attachment process. That's the straightforward bit.

Where it gets complicated is when you add into the mix a parent's individual readiness either physically or psychologically to become a parent, their ability to adapt to changes in their lifestyle and relationships, cultural attitudes and stigmas around the concept of parenthood, messages around parent education, availability of support in preparing and experiencing parenthood, as well as coping with existing or new physical or mental health issues. Spiteri in 2013[2] concluded that the concept of preparing for parenthood is multifaceted and complex, with a number of contributing domains. Their suggestion was that, in order to address parents feeling unprepared, professionals should focus on the content and delivery of successful 'preparation for parenthood' interventions. Five years on from their exploration of the concept of preparing for parenthood, we have a deeper understanding of what those successful interventions might look like. There is increasing evidence that relationship based programmes are most likely to provide parents with the type of antenatal and parent education that has relevance in the real world of parenting[3,4]. We should not be surprised by this. As a human race the way we relate to each other, our development and the positive emotional outcomes and happiness we strive for are embedded in our relationships. In fact to borrow a phrase from the Solihull Approach team; 'It's all about relationships'.

The Solihull Approach has over the past twenty years evolved in its understanding and ability to provide helpful interventions and resources to parents and professionals. We have seen the overwhelming evidence emerge that confirms the importance of the antenatal, postnatal and early years of a child's life alongside the ups and downs of practitioners attempting to integrate critical messages from research into practice. Despite the privileged position we find ourselves in today, of having a greater understanding than ever before of what babies need to grow into healthy well functioning adults, health professionals can face conflicting challenges in providing the services that support the best outcomes for infants. New initiatives in the antenatal and postnatal period are arising and practitioners continue in their efforts to provide meaningful services to parents. Unfortunately, unless driven by strategic planning, public health policy or managerial direction, antenatal and postnatal parent education can be seen as a luxury rather than a vital contribution to the health of our nation. Together with a change in indicators for professional practice there is a growing concern amongst practitioners that at a strategic level there needs to be a recognition that professionals such as health visitors and other family workers can have an impact at community level in enabling parents as they transition to becoming a parent[5]. Having said that, practitioners continue to have hope that what they are doing will be recognised and are motivated in their conviction that their work will contribute to the emotional health of the present and future generations.

The Solihull Approach has long recognised the value of early intervention as a preventative mechanism and sees supporting parents' emotional wellbeing and their capacity to think about developing a relationship with their baby as they journey to becoming parents as a key factor. It is because of this that we have developed a range of trainings for professionals, groups for parents and online courses for parents that together offer the potential for a seamless progression of training, resources and interventions through preconceptual, antenatal, postnatal, childhood and adolescence phases. All trainings, resources, groups and online courses are underpinned by the Solihull Approach model of containment, reciprocity and behaviour management as a way of thinking about relationships between parents and professionals, supporting parent/child relationships and the content and delivery of information.

Preconception

As I mentioned earlier, early intervention is fundamental to our work and we are always keen to explore new territories. At the request of professionals we have developed a school course for young people around 14 to 15 years old called 'Understanding yourself and parenting'. It uses the Solihull Approach model and research to introduce young people, in a journey of eight sessions, to their own development, the emotional world of the baby and how important relationships are for them as young people, parents and babies. We piloted the course several times and invited feedback from the young people attending the course in school and they were generous and extremely honest in their comments. If it was boring they said so and in true Solihull Approach style (reciprocity) we tuned into their responses and changed it!

Antenatal

In the antenatal period we have adapted the Solihull Approach foundation training for professionals working with parents-to-be and new parents. The core model remains the same but the case examples and sections applying the Solihull Approach to practice are specific to supporting parents as they make the transition to becoming a parent. It is in this time leading up to having the baby and the weeks and months after the birth that parents most actively search out information and support. Antenatal education classes, or Parentcraft as they were known in the past, provide parents with one of the access points to what is generally considered a non stigmatised and acceptable way of gaining information about being a parent. The Solihull Approach antenatal group for parents 'Understanding your pregnancy, labour, birth and your baby' is part of a suite of groups that parents can access when practitioners are delivering them in their area. The five or six session group (we added an additional week to the original five session group at the request of midwives to cover practical care of a baby with a Solihull Approach 'flavour') is a relationship based group approach to antenatal education that integrates the traditional elements of pregnancy, labour and birth with enhancing the relationship between the parents and their baby.

An evaluation[4] of the group using data from pre and post measures completed by 26 fathers and 34 mothers (n=61) indicated that feelings of attachment in both mothers and fathers increased. There was also an increase in mothers' intention to breastfeed. In addition mothers' anxieties related to pregnancy, labour and birth decreased. Intention to stop smoking did not show a statistically significant change and so the section in the facilitators' manual relating to this has now been expanded and future studies will revisit this measure. The group is compatible with the UK Government document Preparation for Birth and Beyond[6] and operationalises the guidance contained in that resource. The Solihull Approach 'Understanding your pregnancy, labour, birth and your baby' also conforms to UNICEF's Baby Friendly Initiative[7] and can also be used alongside the Solihull Approach Peer Breastfeeding Supporter training.

Northern Ireland

Northern Ireland have selected the Solihull Approach foundation and antenatal group facilitation training to be a central part of the antenatal parenting programme provision in their exciting Early Intervention Transformation Programme (EITP) that brings together six government agencies and Atlantic Philanthropies, as part delivering a Social Change initiative[8]. ETIP is a jointly funded programme of early intervention that aims to equip all parents with the skills needed to give children in Northern Ireland the best start in life, support families when problems emerge and more effectively to reduce the risk of poor outcomes later in life. In preparation for the EITP they embarked on a process of consultation and research and the result was an innovative new approach to antenatal parenting provision.

Siobhan Slavin: NI Journey to Introducing Solihull Approach Antenatal Parenting Programme for First Time Parents (2018).

The Solihull Approach antenatal group is delivered alongside mother's clinical appointments at 16 weeks, 25 weeks, 28 weeks, 31 weeks, 34 weeks and 36 weeks.

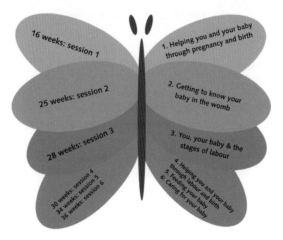

To date 350 midwives have completed the 2 day Solihull Foundation training and have completed pre and post training questionnaires. Results from the completed questionnaires show:

- 100% of midwives have increased confidence in helping parents to develop a positive relationship with their baby/child
- 92% of midwives have increased knowledge of brain development in the womb and the first three years.

Feedback from midwives facilitating the programme has been extremely positive:

> This has been a fantastic working experience. I feel I have grown hugely as a midwife and a facilitator during this time. There have been lots of ups and downs but there is nothing that I have experienced that I haven't learned and developed from. This is an ongoing process so my learning and development continues. I have come out of my comfort zone and will continue to do so. Seeing the women and their partners get so much from this programme and my contribution to it gives me great job satisfaction

There is an ongoing evaluation of data from parents attending the Solihull Approach antenatal groups and initial feedback from the first 350 parents is very encouraging. Parents reported:

- More confidence of becoming a parent. Confident about what to expect, Confidence of my ability to go through labour. Feel a lot more supported and confident.

- My approach to getting ready for the baby. Understanding needs of baby. Bonding. looking after baby. I'm now prepared a lot better for being a parent. Development of the baby. Keeping baby safe and confident. Feel more comfortable while talking to the baby. My feelings towards being a Dad.

- Plenty of information. Learnt a lot and have covered a great range of topics. Lots of practical advice about labour, pain relief. I have a better understanding of birth and labour signs.

- Great classes, great midwives, always a smiling face, [names of midwives] have been fantastic and are a credit to the health service. The support, advice and honesty have prepared my husband and I. Working in a small group has been very beneficial as the one to ones great. Thank you so much for everything.

Additional data collated in Northern Ireland had shown that 85% of first time mothers completed the programme and 75% of mums who had completed 'getting ready for baby' programmes (Solihull Approach) and given birth attempted breastfeeding. Over 90% of parents reported that they felt confident about feeding and playing with their baby most of the time. When asked if they could soothe their baby most of the time 87.92% reported that they could.

Postnatal

Following on from the antenatal period, postnatally most parents continue to be open to seeking information about caring for their baby. It is probably the last opportunity practitioners will have to offer groups for parents that do not have the stigma or reputation of parenting groups being only for parents with difficulties. Practitioners offering groups to parents beyond the postnatal time are often confronted with a deep seated feeling of resentment in our society that parenting groups are all about being told what to do as a parent. This is one of the reasons we have resisted calling Solihull Approach groups 'parenting groups'. We have opted for the phrase a 'group for parents' in an attempt to represent the sense of ordinariness that attending antenatal and postnatal groups has for parents. The Solihull Approach postnatal groups, both the universal Postnatal group (for the general population of new parents) and Postnatal Plus (for mothers and fathers experiencing postnatal depression or difficulties in their relationship with their baby), aim to create a non critical, relationship based, sensitive environment that encourages parents to think about the plethora of information from the perspective of their understanding of themselves and their baby. Topics such as crying, feeding and being separate from their baby are thought about with the aid of the concepts of containment and reciprocity before practical strategies are even contemplated. Managing parents' expectations in both the antenatal and postnatal groups is one of the important tasks of facilitators running Solihull Approach groups. We explain that the group will cover facts and issues such as crying and sleeping, but that the Solihull Approach group may feel different in the first few weeks as we lay the foundation for a relaxed and supportive experience of becoming a parent. Our experience is that parents respond positively to this approach and value the time given to them as people and not solely in their new identity as a parent.

Perinatal

Increasing attention and investment in the last few years has been given to the perinatal period, identified as the time between pregnancy and the first 12 months after a child's birth. There is an emphasis on prompt and geographically equitable access to care for mothers with mental health problems, as it is acknowledged that there is a pressing need to improve outcomes for the woman and minimise the negative impacts on the unborn or developing baby/child[9]. The Solihull Approach has a part to play in the ambitions of the perinatal element of the Implementing the Five Year Forward View for Mental Health[10]. A number of community perinatal mental health teams and perinatal services in the UK including Tameside and Glossop, South West Yorkshire, Northumberland, Tyne and Wear, Halton and others have received Solihull Approach training. In their training evaluations they reported that the training was highly relevant to their roles/team and one delegate said that it had been 'a game changer in many ways in the way to approach clinical work'. Another said 'the principles can be used in everything we do and are easy to use and implement in current practice'.

Online antenatal courses

Being responsive to the changing landscape of emotional health and wellbeing work has been an important component of the way in the Solihull Approach functions. It is built into our model of thinking. The digital age opens up new opportunities for supporting emotional health and wellbeing. Parents continue to value face-to-face relationships, but attending a group is not for everyone and some parents may not be able to attend a group for a variety of reasons. Consequently, we have also created online courses for parents that replicate the content of the 'Understanding your pregnancy, labour, birth and your baby', 'Understanding your baby' (universal) and 'Understanding your child'. They are not intended to replace groups where parents can meet in a group facilitated by a practitioner, but they can be a helpful thinking space so that parents can still choose to invest time in their role as a parent. Although online courses for parents do not have the advantage of actual conversations with other parents, we have created virtual parents who share comments about how they feel as a parent.

We have evaluated the online antenatal course and in doing so we were curious to know if they would have the impact that face to face groups do. An evaluation[11] of the online antenatal version 'Understanding pregnancy, labour, birth and your baby' found that the results showed a reduction of anxiety towards the pregnancy and birth, participants felt closer to their baby and there was an increased intention to breastfeed. These results replicated those in the evaluation of the Solihull Approach antenatal group for parents of the same name[4].

Conclusion

Our objective for mothers, fathers, babies, children and families is to create an environment that on a public health level can support emotional wellbeing for everyone. The antenatal and postnatal period is a pivotal starting point. The Solihull Approach offers a way of thinking and a shared language for professionals, parents, children and the general public and has already shown that it can communicate complex key messages from research to parents and practitioners. Our intention is to continue to passionately pursue our vision of everyone experiencing positive emotional health and wellbeing and meeting a baby's potential with empathy and excitement.

References

1. National Maternity Review (2016). *BETTER BIRTHS, Improving outcomes of maternity services in England.* https://www.england.nhs.uk/wp-content/uploads/2016/02/national-maternity-review-report.pdf

2. Spiteri, G., Borg Xuereb, R., Carrick-Sen, D., Kaner, E. and Martin, C.R. (2014). Preparation for parenthood: a concept analysis. *Journal of Reproductive and Infant Psychology, 32*(2), 148-165.

3. Department of Health (2011). *Preparation for birth and beyond.* https://assets.publishing.service.gov.uk/government/uploads/system/uploads/attachment_data/file/215386/dh_134728.pdf

4. Douglas, H and Bateson, K. (2017). A service evaluation of the Solihull Approach Antenatal Parenting Group: integrating childbirth information with support for the fetal-parent relationship. *Evidence Based Midwifery,* 15 (1), 15-19.

5. Hollinshead, J. and Christie, K. (2017). First steps to better outcomes. *Community Practitioner, 90*(9), 42.

6. Department of Health (2011). *Preparation for birth and beyond.* https://www.gov.uk/government/publications/preparation-for-birth-and-beyond-a-resource-pack-for-leaders-of-community-groups-and-activities

7. UNICEF (2018). *Baby Friendly Initiative.* https://www.unicef.org.uk/babyfriendly/

8. Department of Health (2018). *Early Intervention Transformation Programme.* https://www.health-ni.gov.uk/sites/default/files/publications/health/antenatal-care-education.PDF

9. NHS England (2018). *The Perinatal Mental Health Care Pathways*. https://www.england.nhs.uk/wp-content/uploads/2018/05/perinatal-mental-health-care-pathway.pdf

10. NHS England (2016). *Implementing the Five Years Forward View for Mental Health View*. https://www.england.nhs.uk/wp-content/uploads/2016/07/fyfv-mh.pdf

11. Shahid, A. and Johnson, R. (2018). Evaluation of an online antenatal course 'Understanding pregnancy, labour, birth and your baby' by the Solihull Approach. *The Royal College of Midwives*. Evidence Based Practice, 16 (3), 11-106.

8 IT'S A GIRL! (A mother's experience of the Solihull Approach antenatal group)

Terezie Leach

'Do you want to know the sex of the baby?' 'Yes,' we both said. 'It is a girl!' I still couldn't believe it! I was at the hospital having my 20 weeks scan, watching my baby on the screen as the sonographer described different parts of the baby's body. I was happy and worried at the same time. I was almost 35 years old. Never planned a baby so this was a bit of a shock for both me and my husband. It took us some time to adjust to the idea. The constant sickness did not help. I frantically started researching about everything related to pregnancy and birth.

My midwife mentioned to me about antenatal classes for first time parents. My husband and I were enrolled and looked forward to attending. There were evening sessions at the local hospital spread over 5 weeks with two midwives present. The class was full of first time parents like us, so I did not feel awkward.

The first lesson was about containing stress. I really needed this! Being anxious by nature I wanted to do anything to minimise the transfer of my anxieties to my unborn daughter. It was said that correct breathing can help tremendously during labour, but it is also a good skill to have in life to help cope with many day to day stresses. It was emphasised how important it is for the husband to learn the breathing as well so he can help during labour. At the time I didn't understand fully how important this was, but from then on I practised the breathing every evening and I felt it was helping.

The next week the midwives talked about stages of labour and the important role of a birthing partner. The midwife strapped a 'sympathy bag' (a bag with weights) on several partners (including my husband) in the group so they can try to imagine how heavy it is to carry a baby. She also asked them to try different birthing positions so they can sympathise when mothers are in labour. It was great fun, but I learned so much at the same time. After this session I was a bit more confident and felt reassured that I can do it!

In our next session we learned how to care for a new born baby: how to wash baby; all about nappies; and the benefits of breastfeeding. I had already heard how good breastmilk was for the baby, but after that evening I was determined more than ever to try it, as I came to the conclusion it is so much easier than bottle feeding: no need for sterilisation; no worries about the right temperature; and it is there any time my baby needs it with all the goodness needed at that time. And also, not to mention the money it will save us.

Our next session was walking round the birthing unit and delivery ward. As this was the hospital of my choice it was useful to see the delivery room and get to know the environment although my heart was pounding; a few more weeks and our daughter will be born here. What is she going to look like?

Our fifth and last session was all about the baby's brain. There's so much baby can learn even in the womb! We have been encouraged to talk and read to the baby, to play soothing music and sing. Not good at singing but will give it a shot! Maybe it is a good time to search in my head for all the nursery songs and rhymes my mother taught me when I was a baby.

All in all I really enjoyed my antenatal classes. I thought it was very professional but at the same time I found it reassuring. It educated me about things I never thought of before. I was a bit sad when the classes were over. Soon it will be action time! Will I remember the breathing?

I went into labour at 10pm on Sunday. The contractions were very irregular at first so I was able to sleep in between some of them. But towards the morning they were coming every 10 to 20 minutes. I started to time them and jumped on the ball to relieve the pain. At 8am I passed a bit of blood. I called the hospital and was told to come in. Surprisingly I was really calm and my husband too. We even managed to have breakfast and headed off to the hospital. We got there about 9am on Monday morning. My contractions were getting stronger and stronger. They put me in a room, the very one we viewed when touring the birthing unit. I couldn't believe how calm I was. A very kind midwife examined me and put me on a monitor, reassuring us that our baby daughter is slowly making her way out and will be with us soon! Now the breathing came in handy. I must admit at one point I thought it was too much and I couldn't take it anymore; the gas and air was not bringing any relief. In fact I thought the best pain relief was my husband's encouraging words and his breathing with me, especially when I was giving up. And we did it! Our baby girl was born at 13:09 on Monday! No words can describe the moment she was put on my chest, beautiful little baby girl! I do not even know how she found my breast, but she was sucking vigorously! She was calm and seemed contented. The unforgettable moment – the happiest I have ever been!

9 NO WAY! (A father's experience of the Solihull Approach antenatal group)

Jackie Leach

When I found that Terezie was pregnant I was distraught since we never planned to have any children. However, after the initial shock we started to warm to the idea.

Indeed, I was in denial. Only when I saw the 20 week scan and seeing a tiny heartbeat did I start to believe what was in front of me.

The antenatal classes were absolutely amazing. I was petrified and excited at the same time. Not only did we learn about the development stages of our daughter, we were told what to expect pre and postnatally. What gave us even more confidence and reassurance was the experience and professionalism of the two midwives delivering the antenatal classes. These classes were frank and to the point. Being our first child, we did not know what to expect. As a first time father my main concern was the wellbeing of Terezie and the baby. Having gone to all Terezie's appointments and all the antenatal classes I felt very much a part of Terezie's pregnancy.

On the day of our daughter's arrival I felt such a calmness. We prepared as much as we could have given what we had learned during our antenatal classes. What was particularly invaluable was the breathing exercises we had learnt. Indeed, at one point while Terezie was in labour I felt quite dizzy. Why? Because I was doing the breathing exercises with Terezie, and must have had an oxygen rush!

We arrived at the maternity ward at 9.00am. Our daughter was delivered just after 1.00pm. What I found exceptional was Terezie giving birth naturally without any pain relief (I say without pain relief because Terezie was given gas and air, but by the time she worked out how to use it our daughter was born). What made this possible? Throughout the whole time Terezie was doing the breathing exercises we had learnt in our antenatal classes. Also, when our daughter was born she was not crying. Again, we put this down to the fact that Terezie was calm throughout the delivery. We also made sure that during the term of Terezie's pregnancy our daughter was always in a calm environment. We cannot believe how calm and contented our daughter now is as a result.

What I found invaluable was being with Terezie constantly for the first 3 months of our daughter's arrival. If I could have had a year off work I would have done so. Being with Terezie for those three months gave me a priceless insight into what it is to be a mother. Indeed, we had decided from the outset that breastfeeding was the best start we could give our daughter. I was therefore able to support Terezie in this endeavour and Terezie was able to breastfeed our daughter in what at times seemed to be non-stop feeding. It was amazing to see Terezie's transformation during and after pregnancy. Terezie was able to thoroughly enjoy her pregnancy but especially once our daughter was born, Terezie was able to give her entire attention to our daughter.

I cannot believe what a dream and gift it is to have our daughter who is happy and contented. Again, because we appreciated what a gift and responsibility it is to have a child at what is for us relatively late stages in our lives, we were fully engaged and focused on our daughter even before she was born. Having the support and advice from our antenatal classes and our medical practitioners helped us to bring our daughter into the world and for this we will be forever grateful to all concerned in assisting us as a family.

10 Using the Solihull Approach in a therapeutic parent and infant unit in rural Australia

Vivian Lee and Georgina Timmins

Introduction to the Agnes Unit

The Agnes Unit (named after the Agnes River in Gippsland; all units at Latrobe Regional Hospital are named after a local river) is a parent and infant unit that offers a therapeutic, short term, residential treatment program. The Unit admits infants up to 12 months old and their parent/s, with capacity for five families (which can be with twins or triplets). It is part of the Latrobe Regional Hospital (LRH), and is physically located in Traralgon in the state of Victoria, Australia but services families from all across the Gippsland region. Agnes Unit opened in December 2014 and in its first three years had 331 admissions.

Victoria is the second most populous of the Australian states and territories, despite being geographically one of the smallest. Perhaps for this reason, it actually offers a relatively wide spectrum of emotional and mental health services for the range of difficulties that can occur in the perinatal period. This of course begins with, and includes, primary health (general practice) and the usual maternity services that will have contact with the vast majority of perinatal women and infants, hopefully beginning in the antenatal period or even preconception. These services can offer mental health screening, identify risk factors such as a history of mental illness, substance abuse or exposure to family violence and offer initial support and treatment, as well as coordinate referrals to other services. More vulnerable families may need access to enhanced (in addition to the usual universal) maternal and child health services. In Victoria, all maternal and child health nurses are highly trained professionals with triple qualifications in general nursing, midwifery and maternal and child health. Some non-government organisations (NGOs) may offer support services with a perinatal and infant focus. Families can also access private mental health clinicians, for example psychologists, mental health social workers, psychiatrists or psychotherapists from other disciplines. Many of these professionals can attract rebates through the Australian Medicare system, reducing out of pocket costs for the individual to access treatment. Publicly funded area mental health services can offer specific community-based support and treatment with a perinatal and infant mental health focus. The size and scope of these services will depend on the area. For example, in Gippsland, the publicly funded Perinatal and Emotional Health Program, also part of Latrobe Regional Hospital, has been in operation for eight years, offering community based assessment and short to medium term treatment for parents and infants struggling with mild to moderate emotional and/or mental health issues in the antenatal and postnatal period.

Whilst for the majority of families, community-based treatment will be all that is required, a subset will benefit from a residential or inpatient program. This may be due to the acuity and severity of parental mental illness, perhaps with escalation in risk to self or their infant. Alternatively, residential programs can offer unique observations of and direct work with infant issues, for example, around sleep and settling or feeding. Psychiatric parent and infant units, as first described by Main[1] have existed for over 60 years as a therapeutic entity. The state of Victoria actually opened its first unit at Larundel Psychiatric Hospital in 1983 and continues to have a high number of parent and infant beds relative to other Australian regions[2]. There is also a wide continuum in the different levels of care available. At the most acute end, there are the publicly funded, acute psychiatric parent and infant inpatient units that are open 24 hours, seven days per week and can assertively treat mothers with major mental illnesses including puerperal psychosis. Private hospitals also offer psychiatric care for the mother but at less acuity or they focus more on the infant's regulation (sleep and settling or feeding). Non-psychiatric early parenting centres offer joint day or residential stays for infants and their families that focus on parenting and infant issues. Some, in addition, can deliver specific parenting assessment and skill development programs through the regional child protection services.

Previously, all the residential or inpatient parent and infant units in Victoria were based in the metropolitan city of Melbourne. In recent years, the state government has committed to broadening existing services to improve access for infants, parents and families in rural and regional areas. As part of this expansion of services, three new residential units were opened in regional centres to enhance the capacity of the state-wide system. The Agnes Unit was the first of the three units to open.

About Gippsland

The Gippsland region is located in the south-east of the state of Victoria, the smallest and most south-eastern state of mainland Australia. Gippsland is to the east of Melbourne, Victoria's capital city. The traditional owners for most of Gippsland are the Gunaikurnai people, but the area was named by explorer and pastoralist Angus McMillan in the mid-nineteenth century after Sir George Gipps, governor of the colony of New South Wales at the time[3].

The area of Gippsland stretches from the outskirts of Melbourne's east across to join the New South Wales border in the far east and is bordered in the north by the Great Dividing Range and by beautiful coastline across the south, all up measuring about 42,000 square kilometres. Gippsland has the geographical diversity of rolling green (or brown depending on the time of year!) hills of farmland, bushland and cool-climate rainforests, a myriad of lakes, rivers and tributaries, gorgeous sandy beaches with clear blue waters (which includes the second longest beach in the world, the appropriately named Ninety Mile Beach), the mountains of the southern part of the Victorian Alps, many national and state parks and coal and natural gas reserves. The size of the Gippsland region is larger than the countries of Belgium, Switzerland and the Netherlands; similar to the size of Denmark;

nearly three times the size of the historic county of Yorkshire in the United Kingdom; and nearly twice as big as New Jersey in the United States of America.

Australia's census data from 2016 recorded that Gippsland had a population exceeding 271,000 people, and of these, over 15,000 were children aged between zero to four years, constituting 5.6% of the overall population[4]. Aboriginal and Torres Strait Islanders, Australia's first peoples made up approximately 1.5% of the overall population[4]. Gippsland's total population is comparable to the populations of the countries of Vanuatu, New Caledonia and French Polynesia and is remarkably less than the more densely populated countries of Belgium, the Netherlands, Switzerland and Denmark[5].

Gippsland is made up of six local government areas (LGAs): Bass Coast; Baw Baw; East Gippsland; Latrobe; South Gippsland; and Wellington. This is mentioned because each of these LGAs are of different sizes, geography, population, rurality and the like, and different services including health provision are provided in each of these municipalities. The Department of Health and Human Services of the Victorian State Government is responsible for funding public health services, including public mental health services in Victoria. However, the Gippsland Primary Health Network, an organisation of the Department of Health of the Australian Federal Government, also determines health priorities and services.

The Agnes Unit is located at the Latrobe Regional Hospital site in Traralgon (163 kilometres from Melbourne), which is situated in Latrobe: the second smallest of all Gippsland LGAs but containing the largest population (74,329 or 27%)[6]. However, LRH provides mental health services (both inpatient and community based) right across the Gippsland region and therefore families may be referred for care in Agnes from across the area.

A thinking framework for the unit

Agnes Unit is funded as a Monday to Friday residential unit offering short term, therapeutic treatment for infants, parents and families presenting with emotional and/or mental health issues of mild to moderate severity. Such a rural, residential, five day service is a first of its kind in Australia and perhaps the world. During its development phase, it was unclear what the demand would be like for such a rurally based sub-specialty service or what the referral pathways would look like. Careful thinking had to occur about what the purpose of the new Unit would be: who were we going to treat, how do we best do this, and what resources do we have at our disposal?

In developing the Unit, we knew that our target population would be families in the perinatal period. Being a five-day service, with the program starting on Monday morning and finishing by Friday afternoon, the parents and infants who present can be psychiatrically complex but not in need of continuous acute care. This kind of service actually addresses the needs identified in research on perinatal mental health issues. The literature shows that perinatal depression is extremely common, with as many as 19.2% of women suffering from a depressive episode during the first three months postpartum[7]. About 10% of fathers also suffer from perinatal depression and there is a moderate positive correlation with maternal depression[8]. Perinatal anxiety is also common but will require further research to estimate its exact prevalence, together with and separate to

66   *Vivian Lee and Georgina Timmins*

depression[9]. Meanwhile, postpartum psychosis, where continuous acute care will more likely be necessary, is much less common at 0.1% to 0.2%[10]. Importantly, there often appears to be a conflict in perinatal services (overt or often more subtle) of whether the treatment focus should be on the parent or the infant. We wished to create a service that would focus on the infant and parent-infant relationship in addition to parental mental health.

In thinking through how to best deliver effective treatment, we were aware that there is a long and rich history in infant mental health, which is backed by increasing quantity and quality of clinical and research evidence. Therefore, there was no need to try and create something from scratch. It was then a matter of distilling the available information – theories and ways of working, into a form that could be consistently distributed amongst staff.

A lack of sub-specialty staff in such a regional area was expected and this was confirmed when the original multidisciplinary team was being sought. Essentially, our experience has been that aside from the nurse unit manager, who was one of the four clinicians working in Gippsland's Perinatal and Emotional Health Program and the early career psychiatrist who is from child and adolescent psychiatry background, the original staff group had no specific experience in a perinatal and infant mental health service. However, we managed to find excellent staff with passion and interest. Some had invaluable experience in related fields such as acute inpatient and community based adult mental health, midwifery, paediatrics and maternal and child health (and therefore infant development).

Dr Julie Stone, an infant, child and family psychiatrist who had been commuting out to Gippsland from Melbourne to work with the local Child and Adolescent Mental Health Service (CAMHS) for most of a decade, was a senior staff member who was involved in setting up Agnes Unit. She believed that to create a truly therapeutic service, it needed to begin with thinking and the development of therapeutic practice. Dr Stone therefore put together a document, which she called: Thinking Framework – A Guide for the development of Therapeutic Practice within the Mother and Baby Unit. She did not need to create any new theories or ways of practice, but summarised existing knowledge from the field of infant mental health into an easy to understand piece of writing, that staff could read and learn from as an introduction to the perinatal and infant mental health work at Agnes Unit. The key information Dr Stone incorporated into this thinking framework included mentalization approaches[11], Attachment Theory[12,13] and the Solihull Approach[14]. The relevant Solihull Approach resource packs were obtained by our health service to support staff development prior to opening of the Unit.

The Solihull Approach has been particularly powerful and practically useful. The 'bottom-up' approach in the development of the model, where practice informs theory and theory, in turn, informs practice means that the Agnes Unit staff, mostly new to the field of perinatal and infant mental health, have been able to quite naturally grasp the integrated psychodynamic and behavioural theoretical concepts in the model and start using them in their practice. Their day-to-day clinical work with the parents and infants admitted to Agnes Unit then brings the theories to life, which in turn promotes reflective clinical practice. The cycle of practice informs theory, informs practice then continues.

Dr Hazel Douglas also generously supported the authors of this chapter (Vivian and George) to deliver the Solihull Approach 2 Day Foundation training as part of the original staff group's orientation to their work at the Agnes Unit. In addition to the Solihull Approach training, all staff working at Agnes Unit access individual supervision and participate in the team's weekly group reflective practice as part of ongoing professional development.

Experience of delivering the training

We (Vivian and George) have now delivered the Solihull Approach 2 Day Foundation training twice and are about to embark on this for a third time in mid-2018 (and very happily, our course is already fully booked!). The first group to receive this training in 2014 (as previously mentioned) was the entire initial multidisciplinary team of the Agnes Unit as part of their orientation, plus two clinical nurse educators from the LRH Mental Health Professional Development Unit. We were entrusted by our organisation to deliver the training at that time (and sorry Hazel – we had not even heard of the Solihull Approach model prior to reading the framework written by Dr Julie Stone). We enthusiastically joined together to plan how this could occur and how we could meet the looming deadline. In our favour was our ability to openly communicate and collaborate, write and complete long and comprehensive 'things to do' lists, as well as sharing strong clinical backgrounds and foundations in child development and attachment and working therapeutically with families. The Solihull Approach made sense clinically and was highly compatible with our beliefs, values and experiences, making the model immediately understandable and accessible.

A minutely detailed timetable was drawn up to guide proceedings, since we had never delivered any education together before as co-presenters, let alone ever delivered this particular training, and especially to a group of colleagues that we would have ongoing relationships with. To our credit, we believe both of us are conscientious, organised and set high standards for ourselves. Through the planning and delivery of this first course we positively discovered that we work in a very natural, complimentary and authentic manner together, a real-life 'dynamic duo'! The training days flowed well and included a very motivated, attentive and engaged audience, who provided really positive feedback such as:

'Like approach of not focusing on 'problem',

'Really like and identify with the model... creates a clear framework and look forward to implementing it',

'Have not felt so positive about my career in many years',

'Not a problem to solve – 'think with' the family',

'Awareness of infant's perspective',

'Gentle, less confronting way of working with families',

'When clients are listened to and understood, it can have a powerful impact on their insight and their behaviour and child's feelings/behaviour in turn'.

A time lapse of over three years occurred between the first and second training courses being run. This was unfortunately due to George battling a serious medical illness. Despite this, as described throughout this chapter, much work was still completed during that time. The Agnes Unit staff very successfully and positively implemented the Solihull Approach within their therapeutic practice, and the two of us underwent supervision with Dr Hazel Douglas to become fully accredited trainers of the Solihull Approach 2 Day Foundation training.

Late in 2017, an 'expression of interest' was sent out to targeted teams within the Latrobe Regional Hospital mental health service for the Solihull Approach 2 Day Foundation training, to be held over consecutive Saturdays in early 2018. Very positively, the course was filled quickly. We then regrouped to prepare for this training and make some necessary adjustments from our previous program. The audience this time comprised of a number of new Agnes Unit team members who had joined since the original orientation training was given (midwifery, nursing and social work disciplines were represented), as well as clinicians from the current Perinatal and Emotional Health Program, Mental Health Professional Development and Community Residential Care units. We again worked collaboratively and complemented each other in every way, both behind the scenes as well as in presenting and facilitating this training. Feedback was again overwhelmingly favourable and encouraging, as exemplified by:

> 'The information (whilst not new) provides a framework to work to and guide clinical interventions. Useful to avoid feeling overwhelmed with the complexity of stressed families',

> 'Listen, Listen, Listen',

> 'Reaffirmed what we do and why',

> 'Improved/enhanced focus on relationships and reason behind behaviour',

> 'I found this day very interactive and the trainers extremely knowledgeable',

> 'Having you both as presenters definitely made coming in on a Saturday 100 times more worth it'.

The two of us look forward to delivering this training again soon to continue sharing the Solihull Approach with others.

The treatment program

Over time, the Agnes Unit treatment program has of course evolved, with staff undertaking further training (including graduate certificates and diplomas in infant mental health), growing staff experience and confidence and helpful feedback from the families. One of the principles that has informed our practice from the very beginning and has remained since, is that we work with each family as unique individuals: there is no one-size-fits-all approach; we take the time to listen; we think together and try to understand what is really going on, with particular focus on the infant's socioemotional communication and the dyadic relationship, before offering any suggestions. This is very much the practice advocated by the Solihull Approach, where it begins with containment and reciprocity,

Using the Solihull Approach in a parent and infant unit in rural Australia 69

and any behaviour management strategies offered are informed by the first two concepts. Families are usually admitted for two to three weeks, going home on the weekend. This is still brief treatment, but allows time to get to know the family and work through things together without rushing.

The journey to Agnes Unit begins with the referral, which can be made by a community professional already working with the family, or it can be a self-referral. We find that for many perinatal families, things can quickly escalate and become overwhelming and then just as suddenly they can somewhat improve (especially after making the telephone call to Agnes Unit). Often, there is a lot of ambivalence about needing to access support, particularly residential, and there may be associated feelings of guilt and failure. Staff taking the referral and later offering an admission are acutely aware of this and do their best to help parents feel comfortable about accessing the service. Common presenting problems to Agnes include: for the infant, regulation issues which can manifest as sleep and settling, feeding, activity and emotional difficulties; and for the parents, adjustment or mental health issues, usually depression, anxiety, escalation of pre-existing personality and coping problems. The parent does not need to have a diagnosis or mental health history to access Agnes Unit.

Parents and infants are admitted (or return to the unit) on the Monday morning. For new families, they are oriented to the unit by an allocated staff member (who is usually from a nursing background, but may be our part-time social worker), and after they have had time to settle in, this same staff member spends time getting to know the family, including taking the family of origin histories of the parents, and learning about the journey of conception, pregnancy, birth and the infant's early experience. The staff member and family jointly formulate the presenting problems, putting them in context of predisposing and precipitating factors. They then, together, develop a treatment plan that focuses on both the parents' and the infant's emotional and mental health. Whilst mothers have usually been the identified parent seeking support, fathers and partners are actively encouraged to participate in the program.

Families are offered individualised therapeutic treatments. Over the course of an admission, this usually includes: individual support on the unit (for example, being listened to when the parent is feeling particularly overwhelmed or distressed, or having a staff member be there for support during difficult times, like settling the infant); psychiatric review; biological investigation or medication treatment if clinically indicated; and psychotherapy sessions, which may be individually for the parent, dyadic or commonly couple's sessions are also offered, all depending on the particular needs of the family. These treatments offer emotional and psychological containment for the parents (and system). This helps to make space in the parents' mind so they can better receive their baby's socioemotional communications and have capacity to contain their baby.

There is a focus on reciprocity, which, as per the Solihull Approach, describes the sophisticated interaction between the infant and parent where both are involved in the initiation, regulation and termination of the interaction[14]. For many overwhelmed parents who are struggling with a transition to parenthood marked by emotional and mental health struggles, a complicated pregnancy or traumatic birth, or a disconnected early relationship with their infant, being in a space like Agnes Unit offers an opportunity for

70   Vivian Lee and Georgina Timmins

them to 'be with' rather than 'do to' their infant without life's usual distractions. Staff model reading the baby's cues and encourage development of the parent's ability to read and respond to their infant's communications. Play between parent and infant is promoted at all developmental stages, with a focus on improving parental sensitivity and joint enjoyment.

Many parents come to Agnes Unit desperate for strategies, whether it is to help settle their baby to sleep, stretch out feeds, or get their baby into a more predictable routine so that family life can be less overwhelming. While we will try different things over the course of an admission with the family, the focus is very much on containment and reciprocity first. We invite the parents to think together about their current experiences and struggles, particularly in terms of the infant's underlying feelings, mental states and intentions. The connection and influence between how the parent feels and what the infant experiences then become evident. For the majority of parents, a better understanding of the context of struggles and the increasing connection with and enjoyment of their infant quite naturally help to shift things for the better. The strategies, which sit within the behaviour management part of the Solihull Approach, are then just tweaks of what is physically being done with the infant. The thinking and psychological shifts come first though.

In addition, a group program incorporating the concepts of containment, reciprocity and behaviour management is offered. Sessions may focus on parental mental health (for example, on the common problem of anxiety, with work on relaxation or mindfulness), the transition to parenthood, reflecting on family of origin experiences, or focus on sensory play, nursery rhymes, or even learning about broad concepts of Attachment Theory and how they apply to the current infant-parent relationship. Parents often find that hearing about similar struggles or experiences in other parents helps to decrease the sense of stigma and associated feelings of guilt or failure. Being encouraged to play and interact with their infants in fun and developmentally appropriate ways helps to increase dyadic joint delight and connection. In extreme situations, there have been parents who, due to their own early childhood neglect and current life chaos, have been introduced to reading, singing and playing with their infant for the first time.

Practitioners' experience of using the Solihull Approach

To work therapeutically with parents and infants is intellectually challenging and emotionally demanding. There is the danger of practitioners becoming overwhelmed if they are not being well supported. The subtle complexities inherent in this sort of clinical work are unfortunately not often well understood by people, even mental health clinicians. Therefore, it is crucial that there is a therapeutic framework to hold the staff and our thinking. Staff at Agnes Unit feel extremely positive about using the Solihull Approach in our practice. A few themes emerge in the feedback, including: how easily it can be understood by clinicians from diverse backgrounds; that it helps to develop a consistent approach in working with families; it supports parents to think through challenges; and importantly, it encourages everyone to think about the infant's experience.

As described earlier, only the nurse unit manager and psychiatrist had direct experience in a perinatal and infant mental health service prior to working at Agnes Unit. Staff have come from many diverse areas of practice, including, but not limited to adult mental

Using the Solihull Approach in a parent and infant unit in rural Australia **71**

health, midwifery, paediatrics, maternal and child health, child protection services and trauma counselling. While some of our staff have many years of clinical experience in their fields, others are just starting out in their careers, having had only limited experience in other areas of healthcare such as aged care. A common trait though has been passion for perinatal and infant work. Apart from the varied clinical backgrounds, our team members are also diverse in age and life experience. Agnes Unit has staff from every decade of life from our 20's through to 60's. What is wonderful about the Solihull Approach is the way it ties together multiple theories in a logical and comprehensive way and yet staff do not need extensive specialist experience to understand and work with the model. It inherently makes sense and the aspect of 'practice informs theory and theory, in turn, informs practice' becomes evident as the team, together, grows in experience and confidence. A staff member shares:

> The containment and reciprocity aspects WORK and they are relevant. The more I practice, the more meaningful the model is. When I explain the model to other learners I come into contact with, the look of interest on their face reminds me just how fascinating and rewarding this work is.

While diversity within the team adds richness and promotes growth, consistency in approach and practice is crucial when working with parents and infants. New parents in particular often report how frustrating and confusing it can feel when they have been given different advice by different people, especially when they are feeling emotionally or mentally vulnerable. The Agnes team therefore works hard to minimise inconsistency by focussing on offering a common way of thinking through issues and actively communicating how we are working with the families. No one is then working in isolation, and our individual observations and impressions are shared within the team to enrich our joint understanding of each family. The Solihull Approach helps with this process, by providing a joint platform and language for our thinking and communication. This is especially helpful when training new team members. The following is from a staff member who is early in her career:

> The Solihull Approach training has encouraged me to be more mindful of the interactions that are happening around me and also of my own interactions with others. It has encouraged me to really listen to the mothers, fathers and the infants and to think about what challenges they may be facing and what may be going on for them. By using the three concepts of the Solihull Approach; containment, reciprocity and behaviour management I am then able to encourage the parents to reflect on their own emotions and then we are able to think together about how this may affect the infant. By allowing the parents to express and acknowledge their own emotions they are then able to be contained as their needs have been responded to by staff, therefore they are then able to contain and respond to the infant.

What resonates with staff in using the Solihull Approach is the way it encourages and enables parents to think through challenges with their infant, rather than just learn techniques to 'fix' things. This is very empowering for the parents, in that it makes them the expert when it comes to their own infant. To facilitate such a psychological shift in the parent, from wanting to 'do' and 'fix' to being open to wondering about and understanding their infant's experience, staff have to shift in their own approaches too to model and parallel this process. A very experienced staff member from a midwifery background describes her work at Agnes most beautifully:

> When I enter a room and meet a mother and baby for the first time, and thereafter, I take the time to 'sit on my hands and do nothing' initially, if possible… to soak up the atmosphere in the room and the feelings being generated by the mother and baby. It is only after I have tuned in to those feelings that I can begin to appreciate, empathise, contain and assist the family in a way which will be beneficial and empowering.

This way of working, taking the time to listen, 'soak up', think together and understand, then encourages everyone to think about the infant's experience. The concept of reciprocity in the Solihull Approach focusses our attention on observing the infant's underlying feelings, mental states and intentions rather than seeing him or her as a passive recipient to which things are done. The infant can then come alive in the clinician's and the parent's minds:

> Thank goodness we now recognise that babies come into this world ready to socialise with eye contact, hearing, sense of touch and smell and are given permission to be in a relationship with their mother immediately. This recognition of 'the dance of reciprocity' is one of the most powerful observations I have made in my time as a midwife over the years, where we have actually given mothers this wonderful gift to share with their babies. This enables the mother to relax and enjoy her baby instead of something to be controlled at all costs, with rigid routines and long bouts of crying. The concept of 'spoiling the baby' is long gone hopefully.

Many parents describe to staff how during their admission to Agnes Unit they realise that their 'baby has a mind'. Their infant-parent connection deepens when the dyad are supported and given the space to participate in and enjoy their relational dance with each other.

The experience of parents and infants

Over the past three and a half years, working with hundreds of families, we have received overwhelmingly positive feedback. This has been through qualitative feedback forms we have collected, in addition to the heartfelt notes and cards we receive each week. Many families have commented that an Agnes Unit admission should be for all families in the perinatal period! It has been moving and humbling to see the psychological shifts that parents are able to make in such a short duration of time, and hence the subsequent positive changes in their infants. The containment, reciprocity then behaviour management approach has been effective with most families. It helps to first re-create space in the overwhelmed parent's mind, through their experience of being able to talk about and work through their difficult thoughts and feelings with help from staff. This process restores the parent's ability to think and they are then able to work through their challenges with their infant. Common feedback from parents is that they came to the Unit

Using the Solihull Approach in a parent and infant unit in rural Australia   73

to get help with settling their infant to sleep, but it ended up being so much more. One mother shares:

> My experience has been life changing. I came with the expectation of learning how to get my daughter to sleep and, with the help of staff, I managed to do some deep reflective thinking about my life and my choices, resulting in my whole family on the way to being more connected, communicating more effectively and building stronger relationships with each other. This experience has been invaluable to me.

Agnes Unit's focus on the infant and the dyadic relationship recognises that parental emotional and mental health is very much linked with the infant's regulation. It is uncommon that the infant can be well regulated if the parent is struggling, and vice versa. By allowing the parent space to think, connect (with their infant, partner or other significant people in their lives) and more effectively communicate, the infant usually also improves. This same mother also lets us know:

> [My daughter] has loved being at the Agnes Unit. Since being here she has become more settled, happier, is going longer between feeds and has started talking and laughing. From the first moment we stepped foot in the door she was shown kindness and love from so many people.

Promoting the connection between the parent and infant is crucial to our work, and this extends to the connection between the father or partner and the infant too. Our experience working with our rural Australian population in Gippsland has been that in families where the couple remains together (Agnes Unit sees a large number of single parent families, perhaps signalling their increased vulnerabilities), a 'traditional' role division has often been the case. This is where the father does not have much time off work to be with and grow confident with the baby and the mother takes on the primary caring responsibilities. This also means that not many fathers can participate in the full Agnes Unit program, despite always being invited. We really do our best to support the fathers to participate and feel included. For example, in her feedback, a mother describes:

> My husband visited once every week for the three weeks we were at the Agnes Unit. Each and every time he was welcomed and felt comfortable being at the Agnes Unit. Through his short stays he learnt to be more comfortable and connected to [our daughter]. And he was taught that even though he may not feel helpful, he is.

The transition to parenthood can be a very isolating time for some families. Parents are often reluctant to show how vulnerable they really are and the extent of their struggles. To acknowledge that they are not coping is usually associated with feelings of guilt and failure, and for some, even fear that this will mean their infant will be taken away. It is not uncommon for parents to look very much 'held together' and functional on the outside, while struggling within and on the edge of no longer being able to continue on. The advantage of a residential program is that it is harder to hold onto a façade for 24 hours each day and this can more quickly lead to acknowledgement of vulnerability and encourage self-reflection. When a parent becomes open to receiving help for herself, it

74   Vivian Lee and Georgina Timmins

also creates more resources within her to help her baby and this can facilitate their deeper connection. A mother gives a moving account of her journey at Agnes:

> I came to the Agnes Unit because I ran out of options. I could no longer manage it on my own any more. My five-month-old woke frequently, was difficult to settle and I had exhausted all my resources. I came here with a heart to accept help. Something I had never done before. I tried to maintain my outward appearance of 'got it together' but inside I was dying.
>
> Agnes gave me hope. They cared and they listened. After a couple of days I defrosted. I began to relax. The muddy waters began to clear. I was able to see that my daughter's 'sleeping problems' were a giant mirror to my own problems I had tried to muscle through. I cannot do it all. I need to let others help me. The more space and time I had the more obvious things became. The way I viewed the world was from a place of fear. How could a child settle when mum wasn't settled herself?
>
> After eight days at Agnes I was settling my baby, she looked into my eyes as she slowly drifted off to sleep. She was peaceful, she was content and she told me she loved me, and I loved her.
>
> I would never have resolved such deep unrest if it wasn't for Agnes. My problems would have compounded and created more in the future. Even if I can't fix something for my family, at least I can come from a place of peace and love and that is enough.

While infants may not yet have the words to so eloquently describe their experience at Agnes Unit, they are very much always at the forefront of our thinking and our work. Agnes Unit prides itself on its particular focus on the infant's internal world and the infant-parent relationship. Parental mental health, especially when there are deeper psychiatric struggles and even formal diagnoses, will always receive appropriate attention and treatment at Agnes Unit, but as part of this treatment the parent is also helped to remember their baby's experience in all of this. Most of the time, focussing on the infant also helps the parent to improve in their own mental state. During a family's admission, Agnes staff observe the infant's regulation, development, interactions with others and wonder about their internal world; and encourage the parent to do the same. Some of the most satisfying and memorable experiences for staff have been when we have worked with an infant, who has been withdrawn or delayed in their development as a result of the severity of the struggles in their family. To observe the infant as they come alive in their parent's mind, then in their interactions with the world and with people is very rewarding. It always amazes us how quickly infants can respond when provided with the right (thinking, emotional and physical) space.

Reflections

It has been a pleasure to be given the opportunity to reflect on and share our experiences of using the Solihull Approach for the training of staff and in our therapeutic practice with parents and infants at the Agnes Unit. The 'practice informs theory and theory, in turn, informs practice' element of the Approach comes to life over and over again. With increasing clinical experience with perinatal families presenting with unique stories of struggles, though often with common themes, the psychodyanamic, relational and behavioural theories of the Solihull Approach become more meaningful. What is exquisite about the Solihull Approach is that it offers a way of thinking that can be applied to clinical (and life) problems at any developmental stage and any level of complexity. Sometimes, the more complex the problems, the more relevant this way of working seems. And somehow, almost 'magically', something shifts in the clinician's and in the family's minds, and things become less overwhelming, can be thought about and then worked through.

Acknowledgement

We thank the families who have come to the Agnes Unit over the years, and the staff who have been so open to learning and have then used their knowledge, skills and sensitivities to help infants and parents. In particular, thank you to the parents and staff who have given us permission to use their feedback in this chapter.

Note: Solihull Approach training can now be accessed in Australia from https://www. helenstevens.com.au/solihull

References

1. Main, T. (1958). Mothers with children in a psychiatric hospital. *The Lancet, 272,* 845-847.
2. Buist, A. (2004). Mother-baby psychiatric units in Australia – the Victorian experience. *Archives of Women's Mental Health, 7,* 81-87.
3. *Australian Dictionary of Biography. Gipps, Sir George (1791–1847).* http://adb. anu.edu.au/biography/gipps-sir-george-2098.
4. *Australian Bureau of Statistics* (2016). Census QuickStats. http://www. censusdata.abs.gov.au/census_services/getproduct/census/2016/ quickstat/205?opendocument.
5. *World Population Review. Total Population by Country* (2018). http:// worldpopulationreview.com/countries.
6. *Australian Bureau of Statistics. Data by Region.* http://stat.abs.gov.au/itt/r. jsp?databyregion&ref=CTA2.
7. Gavin, N., Gaynes, B., Lohr, K., Meltzer-Brody, S., Gartlehner, G. and Swinson, T. (2005). Perinatal depression: a systematic review of prevalence and incidence. *Obstetrics & Gynecology, 106,* 1071-1083.
8. Paulson, J. and Bazemore, S. (2010). Prenatal and postpartum depression in fathers and its association with maternal depression: a meta-analysis. JAMA, 303, 1961-1969.
9. Ross, L. and Mclean, L. (2006). Anxiety disorders during pregnancy and the postpartum period: a systematic review. *Journal of Clinical Psychiatry, 67,* 1285-1298.
10. Sit, D., Rothschild, A. and Wisner, K. (2006). A review of postpartum psychosis. *Journal of Women's Health, 15,* 352-368.

11. Fonagy, P., Steele, M., Steele, H., Moran, G. and Higgitt, A. (1991). The Capacity for Understanding Mental States: The Reflective Self in Parent and Child and Its Significance for Security of Attachment. *Infant Mental Health Journal*, 12, 201-218.

12. Bowlby, J. (1980) *Attachment and Loss.* New York: Basic Books.

13. Ainsworth, M., Blehar, M., Waters, E. and Wall, S. (2015). *Patterns of attachment: A psychological study of the strange situation.* New York: Psychology Press.

14. Douglas, H. (2012) *Solihull Approach Resource Pack: The first five years. Cambridge:* Jill Rogers Associates.

11 The Solihull Approach and Peer Breastfeeding Supporter training

Mary Rheeston, Elaine Kindred-Spalding and Amy Sadler

The benefits of breastfeeding an infant are well documented for both the mother and baby. Breastmilk nourishes babies, providing all the necessary nutrients needed for healthy development, together with the unique protective properties of antibodies that defend the baby against infection. Breastfeeding promotes bonding between mother and baby and reduces the mother's risk of breast and ovarian cancer, type II diabetes and postpartum depression[1]. However, taken in isolation, the knowledge that breastfeeding is a fundamental building block for health has not been sufficient to engage the majority of women in the UK to breastfeed. Factors such as cultural attitudes, intergenerational patterns of feeding, marketing of formula milk products and breastmilk substitutes, as well as inconsistent levels and types of support available to breastfeeding mothers have all had an influence on breastfeeding rates.

While decades of interventions and promotion by professionals and campaigners have made some progress in changing infant feeding practices in favour of breastfeeding, progress has been slow. Figures from Public Health England's 2016/17 aggregated rates were 44.4% compared with 43.8% in 2014/15[2,3]. Data for Scotland appeared slightly more improved at 41% in 2016/17 from 38% in 2014/15[4,5]. Rates in Northern Ireland in 2014/15 were recorded as 37.9% at six weeks and Wales recorded exclusive breastfeeding in its 2010 Infant Feeding Survey as 17% compared with 23% in England[6]. Drawing direct comparisons between breastfeeding rates for Northern Ireland and Wales with England and Scotland is challenging as the method of data collection in each country varies. Having said that, data from the UK as a whole has rates far below those that would be expected in a developed country. In comparison to the UK, Norway, a country held as a positive example of a breastfeeding friendly nation, has rates of 71% at six months; significantly higher than the UK as a whole, where rates have been shown to be as low as 34%[7].

There are a range of interventions that have been designed to support breastfeeding mothers to improve breastfeeding outcomes and support from peers is one service that has gained popularity over the last twenty years[8]. Mothers supporting mothers in childbirth, breastfeeding and childcare is not a new phenomenon. However, as the structure of our society has changed, more formal and organised initiatives have arisen in an attempt to counteract the ebbing of family support networks that were once the norm after having a baby. Peer breastfeeding support is commonly thought of as support provided by a mother who has breastfed, but is not a relative and has received some level of training. An early definition by Dennis[9] was that peer breastfeeding support was;

> A specific type of social support that incorporates informational, appraisal (feedback) and emotional assistance. This lay assistance is provided by volunteers who are not part of the participant's family or immediate social network; instead, they possess experiential knowledge of the targeted behaviour (i.e., successful breastfeeding skills) and similar characteristics (e.g., age, socioeconomic status, cultural background, location of residence).

Initially peer breastfeeding supporters were volunteers and unpaid. As the role has evolved its status has changed and there are now some organisations that have created a paid peer breastfeeding supporter job role in addition to volunteers. Breastfeeding mothers and professionals value peer support greatly and it is identified by UNICEF Baby Friendly Initiative (BFI) as a mechanism for supporting and improving services[10].

Research shows that breastfeeding peer supporters are an effective mode of support for a variety of reasons. However, evidence of this type of peer support is fragmented and it has been difficult to compare individual programmes[8,11,12]. Peer breastfeeding supporter training and services are often developed locally and very few have a theoretical basis, most focusing on the process of change. In addition, training and supervision differ in content and process[8]. One of the strengths of the Solihull Approach is that it has a robust theoretical structure that underpins all trainings and resources including peer breastfeeding supporter training, supervision of peer supporters and their interactions with families. This can facilitate strategic planning as well as the operationalisation of services. For example, the Solihull Approach programme of parent support can be implemented in groups and one to one work from the antenatal period, postnatal stage and throughout childhood to 18 years. The Solihull Approach model offers a theoretical framework comprising of three well established concepts of containment, reciprocity and behaviour management[13]. By using this way of thinking as they support parents, peer supporters and practitioners are able to support the emotional wellbeing of the mother so that she is better able to process strong feelings that may feel overwhelming at times. This can in turn free space in her mind to think about her interactions with her baby that can include both the emotional and practical aspects of breastfeeding.

When the Solihull Approach Peer Breastfeeding Supporter training was initially developed in 2003, both volunteer mothers and professionals involved in the training faced many issues that some practitioners continue to struggle with in the present day. When the first peer breastfeeding supporter training was conceived, breastfeeding mothers were not only in the minority, they were almost invisible. There were strong intergenerational attitudes supporting bottle feeding and a lack of facilities allowing mothers to breastfeed outside the home. The Sure Start (later known as a children's centre) in Chelmsley Wood, based in a housing estate built in the late 1960's to accommodate the overspill of Birmingham residents, had made significant efforts to create a breastfeeding friendly environment. Local child health clinics were available to mothers, but there was a reluctance by families to access services. At that time the area was defined as a deprived neighbourhood and in a 2018 report Chelmsley Wood was rated in the bottom 20% of deprived areas nationally and displayed many of the related health outcomes that accompany deprivation[14]. In 2003 the opinion amongst professionals and parent volunteers keen to develop breastfeeding support was that unless the culture and attitudes towards breastfeeding shifted, no amount of public health messages would increase breastfeeding rates.

So the first Solihull Approach Peer Breastfeeding Supporter training was developed with a focus on communicating a culture to the local community of supporting the feeding relationship through reciprocal and responsive interactions between mothers and babies. The peer breastfeeding supporters, midwife, health visitor and breastfeeding counsellor in the Sure Start team believed that supporting that relationship would be a key driver in promoting a breastfeeding relationship. All involved felt strongly that while breastfeeding knowledge and skilful application were important, at the heart of everything was a mother and baby in a relationship. Practitioners and volunteers wanted parents, mothers, fathers, partners and families, many of whom had never seen a baby breastfeed, to have a place where they could be curious and talk about feeding in a non judgemental and open way.

The Solihull Approach theoretical model had already been used to underpin practice and services in Chelmsley Wood Sure Start and across the Solihull Borough[15]. It therefore seemed a natural step to integrate the concepts of containment and reciprocity into the design of a peer breastfeeding supporter training. Peer breastfeeding supporters recognised the importance of delivering evidence based information about the technical aspects of breastfeeding. However, it was felt that being equipped to offer emotional support to mothers and families was equally important. A six week course was designed and piloted with a group of mothers who had breastfed their babies, lived in the local area and were volunteers at Sure Start. The experiences and feedback from the Solihull Approach peer breastfeeding training courses allowed the training to evolve, although it is interesting that the overall structure and general content of the training did not change. Amendments were predominantly timings and notes for facilitators based on learning from delivering the course. The peer breastfeeding supporters then began to attend the baby group being run in the centre and were supervised by the midwife involved in the training.

Over the following ten years a growing number of practitioners have delivered the Solihull Approach Peer Breastfeeding Supporter training across the UK. In Solihull, strategic planning, commissioning and changes to the Sure Start programme and children's centres resulted in the responsibility for promoting breastfeeding in Solihull becoming the remit of an infant feeding coordinator in Solihull. The Solihull Approach 2 Day Foundation training and peer breastfeeding training continued to play a significant part in the range of trainings offered to volunteers and practitioners. The infant feeding team and the Solihull Approach team continued to exchange experience and learning which allowed the training to remain current. For example, time was allocated for trainers to discuss competency frameworks and assessment criteria for peer supporters if these had been developed locally and information was updated and amended to be compliant with the Baby Friendly Initiative[10].

An impressive team of peer breastfeeding volunteers, paid peer breastfeeding supporters and professionals in Solihull have worked with enthusiasm and passion to attain BFI accreditation using the Solihull Approach model and peer breastfeeding training as core components in their planning. They reported that the strong theoretical model, shared approach and emphasis on emotional support were seen as a valuable contributory factor in obtaining BFI accreditation.

As mentioned earlier in the chapter, increases in breastfeeding rates have moved slowly and it is sad to say that infant feeding teams nationally still face many of the issues that the early developers experienced.

> When deciding whether to breastfeed, or considering whether to stop, mothers tend to talk the issues over with close friends and family. Unfortunately, in the UK, many mothers' social networks have been substantially drained of positive breastfeeding experiences by a history of healthcare practices that have tended to work against decisions to breastfeed and by a wider social context in which breastfeeding is not seen as part of everyday life. Mothers, sisters and friends who want to help can find themselves at a loss.

> Trickey[16].

Breastfeeding peer support fills this gap in knowledge and support and it has been proven that through peer support, women can develop skills and confidence in breastfeeding which has a positive impact on breastfeeding duration[17].

Being a breastfeeding peer supporter is perceived as being akin to being a well informed friend (although the friend/supporter distinction discussed below is important). The motivation to volunteer is often based on a desire to help others and the chosen activity is heavily influenced by factors that meet the personal needs and goals of the individual[18]. Thelwell[11] interviewed breastfeeding supporters, asking about their experience of using the Solihull Approach model and also found that motivation for volunteering included a strong expression by volunteers of wanting to help others. A peer supporter stated her motivation was;

> To help other mums in the same way breastfeeding cafes and peer supporters supported me.

And another said;

> as nice as volunteering is for other people it (the peer breastfeeding role) kind of gives you a purpose sometimes, it gives you confidence and it makes you feel good at some things that you wouldn't necessarily have been good at.

Of course motivation is a great starter, but becoming an effective peer breastfeeding supporter requires skills and knowledge acquired through training and supervision to be applied in a sensitive way and also keeps both breastfeeding mother and peer supporter safe.

The development of the peer breastfeeding training pays careful attention to the emotional transition volunteers need to make to become an effective peer breastfeeding supporter. An important part of the training course is to convey the message that the peer supporters will be listening and supporting as a peer supporter, not a friend. For example, there may be advice and information they would give a friend that would not be appropriate as a peer supporter. The process of transition from peer to peer supporter can take time and is one of the reasons the course is spread over six weeks. It offers peer supporters time to reframe how they see themselves in the role and the trainer opportunities to support and assess the readiness of volunteers. Within the training, the topics of confidentiality and boundaries are sensitively woven in, with consideration given to their placement within the course. The framework of the Solihull Approach once again underpins this process. We are interested in how peer supporters feel and how they perceive their role, as well as helping them understand that they are representatives of an organisation and expected to provide up to date and evidence based information when they are volunteering or working as a paid peer supporter. Greater breastfeeding knowledge is acquired through the Solihull Approach Peer Supporter training, but it is the listening skills and understanding the importance of providing a containing experience for the mother and baby and family that the training focuses on.

In addition there is a special emphasis on supervision, as supervision is an essential aspect of the peer breastfeeding training and volunteer role. During the training, supervisors work on this extensively and continue after the training has been completed. The Solihull infant feeding team feel this is the most important aspect of peer breastfeeding support. Peer support is more about the human factors, making a woman feel important, that someone is listening to her and responding with kindness and respect.

One of the authors (Elaine) describes her experience of delivering the Solihull Approach Peer Breastfeeding Training:

> Passion, dedication, oxytocin, 'working with love', job satisfaction, making a difference, memories forever, mums come back with subsequent babies, emotional, important, grateful, listened to, sharing, feelings.
>
> I have been involved in writing and updating the Solihull Approach Peer Support training. It is good to see how the peer supporters develop during a course, thinking about the responsibility of their role, listening as a peer supporter rather than a friend or fellow mum.
>
> I have held many peer support training courses over the last nine years and it is lovely to see how passionate and enthusiastic the mums are to learn more about breastfeeding, the Solihull Approach, being a peer supporter and supporting other mums and families. The mums bring their babies and children to the training, which can be a challenge for the mums and the trainers; however, this is how they usually volunteer in our breastfeeding cafes so it can be good practice for all. In the past we have had a crèche in a next door room, which helped with noise levels and concentration, but also had its limitations in that sometimes it was the first time a mum had left her baby with someone else so often containment started there and this could take time. Learning (and delivering training) can be difficult in this environment, particularly as mums are thinking about their baby at all times (and sometimes older children if they come along too). The trainers are putting the Solihull Approach into practice during the training, by modelling containment, reciprocity and behaviour management. We provide refreshments, a warm welcome, comfy seating, toys for babies and toddlers and make sure that all the mums feel they are in a safe environment where they can discuss and share their knowledge and experience.

Elaine Kindred-Spalding

82   Mary Rheeston, Elaine Kindred-Spalding and Amy Sadler

In Thelwell's thematic analysis[11] of Solihull Approach peer breastfeeding supporters experience, it was evident that there was satisfaction with the training and it had enabled supporters to use the theory in their interactions with mothers and families. A peer supporter who had attended the training said:

> So you understand it and the theory's there in your head… And I think your confidence only increases once you do it, once you've been with the women and you know that it works and you've seen it in practice working. And then it makes you feel like actually, all this stuff I've learnt does really work, because I've actually seen it work!

As well as the Solihull Approach way of thinking being integral to supporting parents, the model has also been embedded in the way many teams function. When used to its full potential the Solihull Approach can add to shared values and promote a vibrant and cohesive mutual culture that is emotionally supportive for all staff and volunteers.

One of the authors (Amy), a midwife who trains peer supporters in her role as an infant feeding advisor, describes how the Solihull Approach has impacted on her work:

> It isn't possible to compartmentalise how the Solihull Approach is used within my role. I feel that it is intrinsic to my role and to myself as a compassionate human being. The Solihull Approach is so embedded in my work that it works unconsciously. A huge aspect of my job is containment; the feeding issue may not be the main concern (although it seems that way to the woman when we first meet) but she is so 'full up' with other issues that she may think if she can just fix this breastfeeding issue then everything will be better. Part of my role is to listen, truly listen to what she is saying and help her make sense of it. I don't give prescriptive advice (unless required for a medical reason), I make suggestions and the woman is then empowered to make her own decisions. This partnership in care also means greater engagement and increased patient satisfaction. This in turn means greater job satisfaction for me as I can see the difference made and the feedback the team receives proves that the women are immensely grateful.
>
> Amy Sadler

In many areas where peer breastfeeding supporters have been trained in the Solihull Approach, breastfeeding cafes have been set up and this is the case in Solihull. As part of the course in Solihull, peer supporters spend time in breastfeeding cafes to gain experience where they observe interactions between professionals, trained peer supporters and mothers or families attending the breastfeeding cafe. Peer supporters are often nervous about what they might be asked and anxious that they may not know the answer. The professionals who supervise the learners always impress on them that their main role is to provide a containing experience for mothers and listen, before addressing any reported breastfeeding issues. Experience within the breastfeeding cafes is that they often find that once mothers feel contained and have had a chance to talk and be listened to, they discover their baby's behaviour may be completely as expected and they leave feeling reassured and much happier, without a 'breastfeeding issue' needing to be 'fixed'.

The Solihull infant feeding team is fortunate to have paid peer supporters who were all mums in their breastfeeding cafes in the past. They completed the Solihull Approach

The Solihull Approach and Peer Breastfeeding Supporter training   83

peer breastfeeding supporter training delivered by the infant feeding team and then volunteered in the breastfeeding cafes run across the Solihull borough. Experience of running breastfeeding cafés in Solihull has taught the team that they are best facilitated by at least two staff, ideally more. Containment is the most important component of thinking when setting up a breastfeeding support group. Mothers attending may arrive feeling overwhelmed, so having more than one person in the breastfeeding café can mean individual attention can be given to a mother if necessary.

In addition to the emotional experience of attending the cafe the physical environment can also help or hinder a positive emotionally supportive experience. Simple factors make a difference such as: how the room is set up; whether the door needs to be answered leading to interruptions in a conversation; whether mothers come in to the room with easy access; whether there are drink making facilities, etc.. A typical breastfeeding cafe in Solihull runs something like this. Two volunteers welcome and make drinks for mothers and family or friends who accompany them. Volunteers will have been trained to understand the importance of providing a containing experience; two trained Solihull Approach peer breastfeeding supporters will listen and talk with mothers creating a relaxed and friendly environment. In addition, one paid peer supporter or specialist midwife always attends and supervises the session. When mothers arrive, after the warm greeting they receive, the peer breastfeeding supporter will have a general discussion about 'how she is doing' as part of a quick triage that enables the volunteer to decide who the most appropriate person for the mother to speak to will be. For example, if the mother has a breastfeeding issue such as a basic latching on difficulty or is perhaps a little tearful, because she is struggling with night time feeds, a volunteer breastfeeding peer supporter will engage in a sensitive supportive interaction with her. If the issue is more complex, such as more intense breastfeeding concerns or postnatal depression, she would be seen by the specialist midwife or paid peer supporter with extended experience.

During the session, the aim is that each mother will receive an experience where she is able to be listened to, so that her emotions and experiences feel less overwhelming and she is able to think more clearly and feel better able to manage her breastfeeding problems. Many mothers say they leave with a sense of relief. Some say this is because they have endured a feeling of isolation, of being a breastfeeding mother in a bottle-feeding culture before they came to the group. Some say it is because, as breastfeeding mothers, they have found an environment where they can say 'for once, we are in the majority'[12].

The Solihull Approach informs the culture of the group and in addition to the embedding of containing experiences, the theory of reciprocity supports how the rhythm of the session develops and enhances peer supporters' understanding of breastfeeding itself. The dance of reciprocity describes the rhythm of interactions and can also be useful to peer supporters and professionals in thinking about the structure of the session. When the Solihull infant feeding team talk about how they approach the beginning of the group, when mothers arrive, they use the Solihull Approach concepts to provide a language for describing their observations, experiences and thinking. For example, they know that the initial steps in the dance of reciprocity (initiation and orientation) can be crucial for establishing smooth predictable patterns and they apply this to the breastfeeding cafe.

They understand that the first minutes of the group may feel chaotic and so their aim is to move the heightened emotional temperature into a slower, calmer and more relaxed phase that will eventually prepare mothers for the end of the session. After the session when a team reflect on a particular breastfeeding cafe experience the dance of reciprocity can reveal important information that can be used and taken forward into future groups.

The use of the Solihull Approach as a model of thinking for peer breastfeeding support is, as far as we are aware, unique. The strong robust theoretical model has a well established history of promoting emotional wellbeing and venturing into the field of breastfeeding support has shown it to be equally as productive. Mothers and families who are supported by peer supporters trained in the Solihull Approach peer breastfeeding supporter course consistently refer to receiving emotional support. Using the model in their thinking allows peer supporters to apply the knowledge they have gained about breastfeeding in a timely and appropriate way. Mothers recognise the qualities in the Solihull Approach trained peer supporter. For example, a mother who attended the group said of the paid peer supporter 'It's not all about her story, and she'll jump in with advice, which is brilliant, but she doesn't take over, she just listens and lets me offload… and she seemed very interested at the time'[12].

Peer breastfeeding supporters who are volunteers can be a noticeably mobile population of volunteers who may 'dip in and out' of volunteering as their children grow and more babies arrive. Experience and knowledge as Solihull Approach peer breastfeeding supporters led some to pursue a career in caring and supporting breastfeeding mums and they often say they would do their job for free if they could (as they once did as volunteers). All peer supporters say they love their job, as they get so much back by way of gratitude and also in seeing mothers gain confidence and babies thrive. This expression of personal gain in being a peer supporter emerged as a prominent theme in Thelwell's study[11]. Peer supporters reported that they valued the positive feedback from mothers and enjoyed working as a peer supporter. The local Solihull peer supporters and professionals have developed a close supportive team and have said;

> it is wonderful when a mum returns with subsequent children and tells you how long they breastfed their previous child and that you were the one who helped this happen. It is always very apparent how important this is to all mums.

References

1. WHO (World Health Organisation) (2018). *Ten facts about breastfeeding.* http://www.who.int/features/factfiles/breastfeeding/en/

2. PHE (2017). *Official Statistics Breastfeeding prevalence at 6-8 weeks after birth (Experimental Statistics) 2016/17 annual data Statistical Commentary (November 2017 release).* https://www.gov.uk/government/statistics/breastfeeding-at-6-to-8-weeks-after-birth-annual-data

3. RCM (2018). *New Breastfeeding statistics for England.* https://www.rcm.org.uk/news-views-and-analysis/news/new-breastfeeding-statistics-for-england

4. ISD (2015). *Breastfeeding Statistics Scotland Financial Year 2014/15.* http://www.isdscotland.org/Health-Topics/Child-Health/Publications/2015-10-27/2015-10-27-Breastfeeding-Report.pdf

5. ISD (2017). *Financial year of birth 2016/17.* https://www.isdscotland.org/Health-Topics/Child-Health/Publications/2017-10-31/2017-10-31-Infant-Feeding-Report.pdf

6. NIA (2017). *Breastfeeding: Attitudes and Policies.* http://www.niassembly.gov.uk/globalassets/documents/raise/publications/2016-2021/2017/health/0917.pdf

7. National Assembly for Wales (2012). *Infant Feeding Survey.* https://gov.wales/statistics-and-research/infant-feeding-survey/?lang=en

8. Ashmore, S. (2017). Breaking down barriers. *Community Practitioner,* 90(3), 49-50.

9. Dennis, C., Hodnett, E., Gallop, R. and Chalmers, B. (2002). The effect of peer support on breast-feeding duration among primiparous women: a randomized controlled trial. *CMAJ,* 166(1), 21–28.

10. UNICEF UK (2013). The evidence and rationale for the UNICEF UK Baby Friendly Initiative standards. https://www.unicef.org.uk/wp-content/uploads/sites/2/2013/09/baby_friendly_evidence_rationale.pdf

11. Thelwell, E., Rheeston, M. and Douglas, H. (2017). Exploring breastfeeding peer supporters' experience of using the Solihull Approach model. *British Journal of Midwifery,* 25(10), 639-646.

12. Tan, M., Rheeston, M. and Douglas, H. (2017). Using the Solihull Approach in breastfeeding support groups: Maternal perceptions. *British Journal of Midwifery,* 25(12), 765-773.

13. Douglas, H. (2018). Solihull Approach Resource Pack: the *first five years.* Solihull: Solihull Approach Publishing.

14. Solihull Observatory (2018). *Solihull People and Place.* http://www.solihull.gov.uk/portals/0/keystats/solihullpeopleandplace.pdf

15. Barlow, J., Kirkpatrick, S., Wood, D., Ball, M. and Stewart-Brown, S. (2007). *National Evaluation Report: Family and Parenting Support in Sure Start Local Programmes.* http://www.ness.bbk.ac.uk/implementation/documents/1550.pdf

16. Unicef (2017). *Breastfeeding in the UK,* https://www.unicef.org.uk/babyfriendly/about/breastfeeding-in-the-uk/

17. Hoddinott P., Chalmers M. and Pill R. (2006). One-to-one or group-based peer support for breastfeeding? *Women's perceptions of a breastfeeding peer coaching intervention.* https://www.ncbi.nlm.nih.gov/pubmed/16732780

18. Clary, E.G., Synder, M., Ridge, R.D., Copeland, J., Stukkas, A.A., Haugen, J. and Miene, P. (1998). Understanding and assessing the motivation of volunteers: a functional approach. *Current Directions in Psychological Science.* https://www.jstor.org/stable/20182591?seq=1#page_scan_tab_contents

12   The Solihull Approach Postnatal group 'Understanding your baby'

Mary Rheeston

Introduction

Postnatal groups have been in existence for decades, with the aim of guiding and supporting new parents during a time of transition. If you had a baby in the 1990s and 2000s you could most likely expect health visitors in almost every local child health clinic to run a series of six postnatal group sessions free of charge. Although organised independently by different health visitors, the topics covered in groups were similar across the board. They invariably included information about sleeping, feeding and weaning (now referred to as 'introduction to solid foods'), going back to work, first aid, cot death (now referred to as 'sudden infant death syndrome') and play and development. In addition, a discussion about mothers' emotional health ranging from 'feeling down' to postnatal depression was often included at some point. The vast majority of postnatal groups would have been classified as 'universal' in today's terms and aimed at the general population of new mothers, either first time mothers or mothers with older children. A lesser number of more specialist support groups were offered for mothers experiencing postnatal depression, facilitated by health visitors or voluntary/charity organisations with a particular interest in supporting mothers experiencing mental health issues. Universal postnatal groups generally involved the same parents, almost exclusively mothers, together with their baby attending each session from when babies were around six weeks of age. Mothers who went to postnatal groups expressed a view that they would like fathers to be given the same information that they received but often this was reliant on the mother passing on leaflets to fathers provided by health care professionals[1].

Access to groups commonly followed an invitation from a health visitor or marketing of groups through posters displayed in local child health clinics or GP surgeries. Mothers, like those today, were motivated to attend a postnatal group for a variety of reasons; many sought to meet other mothers with new babies and hoped to find a support network in an unfamiliar social world of which they had little or no experience. They valued sharing birthing and parenting experiences with other mothers and found it reassuring to talk with mothers going through similar times that they were. It was often the case that mothers, as a consequence of attending a postnatal group, went on to develop long lasting friendships with other mothers[2]. Very few, if any, of these groups were evaluated. Most were designed by local health visitors using their understanding of child development, behaviour management, government guidance on breastfeeding and weaning and training that highlighted the importance of supporting women's mental health, especially in relation to postnatal depression[3].

Fast forward twenty years and the landscape of postnatal groups has changed. The idea of attending a postnatal group continues to appeal to new mothers and to fathers. However, the availability and access to this type of universal service has dramatically altered. Postnatal groups are still in existence, but their numbers are drastically reduced and many are either 'one off' sessions or are facilitated by health visiting team support staff or children centre workers with health visitors attending sessions requiring specific knowledge, for example about breastfeeding and introducing solid foods. In addition to NHS groups, some voluntary sector organisations run free groups and there are groups where parents pay to attend, such as National Childbirth Trust (NCT) groups. Postnatal groups for women experiencing postnatal depression are also offered in some areas by health visitors, children centre workers, voluntary or charity organisations. A small number of areas have built the provision of postnatal groups into their commissioning process. For example, in Solihull, health visitors run both the Solihull Approach postnatal universal and targeted groups as part of their service delivery and the overall public health strategy. Midwives in Solihull run the Solihull Approach antenatal group 'Understanding pregnancy, labour, birth and your baby' and a range of different practitioners deliver the Solihull Approach 'Understanding your child' for parents of children aged one to 18 years.

Applying the Solihull Approach model

The Solihull Approach has developed two versions of a postnatal group, both referred to as 'Understanding your baby'. One is a six week group for parents for universal delivery, whilst the Solihull Approach Postnatal Plus group runs for eight weeks and is designed to support mothers and fathers experiencing postnatal depression or difficulties in their relationship with their baby. Both postnatal groups have been created so that parents, partners, grandparents and those caring for the baby can attend the group. The Solihull Approach postnatal groups are based on the Solihull Approach model and this is threaded through both the content and process of the groups. Each of the postnatal group programmes aim to support parents and their baby by bringing together the Solihull Approach theoretical framework, knowledge from research and practice and over ten years of Solihull Approach experience of delivering parenting groups for parents.

Although 'Understanding your child', the first manualised and evidence based[4,5] Solihull Approach group for parents, developed in 2006, the idea of using the Solihull Approach to underpin the structure and thinking of a group for parents may have originated in postnatal groups run in clinics in Solihull shortly after the Solihull Approach was created. When the Solihull Approach began in 1996 health visitors using the model applied the three concepts of containment, reciprocity and behaviour management in their one to one work with families with young children. The focus was around parents seeking support for concerns about their child's feeding, sleeping, toileting and/or behaviour difficulties[6]. As health visitors integrated the Solihull Approach theories into their wider practice they began to experiment by using the Solihull Approach model in different aspects of their work. Soon health visitors reported that they not only used the Solihull Approach in specific or complex circumstances, but also realised that its structure formed the basis for

88   Mary Rheeston

everything they did[7]. Anecdotal reports from health visitors using the Solihull Approach in Solihull in those early days were that in postnatal groups the model gave them a way to think creatively about how to deliver information about, for example, sleeping. They saw the potential for the Approach's application beyond one to one work with families and strongly believed it could enhance the experience of parents attending a group.

health visitors were also gaining a better understanding of how to support the mother/child relationship through a range of interventions. A health visitor running a postnatal group at that time described to colleagues how she tried out the newly coined 'Solihull Approach' in a weaning session. Instead of the focus of the group being about providing current weaning and feeding information based on the COMA report[8], she talked with parents about how they themselves felt about food and how this might impact on their experience of introducing pureed food (the first phase of introducing solid foods to babies at that time) to their baby. She went on to explore what they already knew about their baby's feeding signals and what this might mean. After she had finished the session she was very excited by how engaged the mothers had been. She described to other health visitors in the office how invigorating and different the session had felt and she suddenly exclaimed 'Oh I completely forgot to tell them about how to puree food and when to wean. Oh well they went away happy. I can do that next week'.

As a health visitor at that time I also totally changed the way I presented weaning sessions, to include containment and reciprocity. My experience was that prior to using the Solihull Approach model in the session, the first and last question mothers always asked was 'how do you know when to wean?' Later I realised that after using the model to inform the session mothers no longer asked the question. They focused more on reading their baby's cues and grew confident in their knowledge of their baby, so that they could judge how to apply the factual information they were given to suit their own baby.

These anecdotal examples of change were part of the early shift in thinking that many health visitors experienced. A qualitative evaluation of health visitors' experience of using the Solihull Approach[7] revealed that the combination of the three well established theories could have wider application than its original use in single pieces of work for feeding, sleeping, toileting and behaviour problems. The thoughtful practice amongst health visitors that emerged as a result of being introduced to these theories was strengthened by the ongoing interest of Hazel Douglas in practitioners' work with families. health visitors and other professional groups engaging with the Solihull Approach have displayed imagination and enthusiasm in trying something new and this has allowed them to incorporate their skills and knowledge and give fresh meaning to what they see in their everyday practice. The Solihull Approach offered a language and freedom of thought to further develop practitioners' work and in the case of health visitors their public health role in affecting the emotional health and wellbeing of the families they were working with, as well as the next generation.

The current Solihull Approach postnatal groups, the Postnatal and the Postnatal Plus, are the result of many years of development, practice and evidence gathered in working with parents in a group setting. They bring together professionals' experience of delivering groups for parents using the Solihull Approach model at their centre, a deeper understanding of ways in which to support the parent/child relationship and feedback from professionals and parents who have attended the pilot postnatal groups. Feedback and experience from Solihull Approach groups for parents has informed a belief that making education about caring for a baby relevant and meaningful for parents is most effective when portrayed through a parent's relationship with their infant.

Interestingly, the themes covered in postnatal groups over the decades have remained constant, probably because fundamentally babies and parents themselves have not changed. What is perhaps different about the Solihull Approach in addressing these elements of parenting is that it uses the concepts of containment and reciprocity to help a parent understand and 'feel' their baby's needs (both physical and emotional). Activities and facts contained in the Solihull Approach postnatal groups are presented sensitively, so that parents have an opportunity to process how they feel about a topic as well as absorb its details. It would be easy to offer parents a schedule for getting their baby into a sleeping or feeding pattern and on paper this may look highly plausible, but the Solihull Approach is more interested in how an individual parent/child relationship moulds itself around such areas of development. For example, if we forget to ask a mother or father about their experience of sleep and what it means to them, we may be omitting an important component that could help a parent construct a personalised story to support their decisions in the way they apply general advice and care for their own baby.

Both the Solihull Approach Postnatal and Postnatal Plus groups are called 'Understanding your baby' as the postnatal groups each endeavour to provide an environment where mothers and other adults caring for the baby have space to think sensitively about their relationship with the baby. Parents may come to a postnatal group because they wish to understand the needs of their baby and develop a positive relationship with their infant, even if this is not easy at the time of attending the group. By creating two distinct groups we are acknowledging that the capacity of mothers and fathers experiencing postnatal depression to respond to their infant in a sensitive way can be impaired[9]. The Postnatal Plus group aims to offers a specific intervention to improve maternal and paternal confidence and promote emotional wellbeing.

The subject matter covered in both postnatal groups is the same. However, the method of delivery, description and time allocated to some areas within the postnatal groups is different. In the Postnatal Plus group, communication and crying is covered over two sessions instead of one session in the Postnatal group. Sam Giles, a health visitor who has run Postnatal Plus groups, has observed that 'containing parents' feelings so that they can appropriately deal with their baby's feelings is important, especially if parents themselves are feeling full up and are not always able to recognise when their baby is struggling'[10]. There is more time allocated to thinking about being separate from their baby and the ending of the group. These are areas that may cause parents with postnatal depression increased concern or anxiety. Consequently, subtle changes made to activities and timings are woven into the Postnatal Plus group in a way that provides sensitive processing time for the mothers and fathers in the group. Although the Postnatal Plus group is eight weeks in comparison to the universal group's six weeks, it is not just the case that the Postnatal Plus group has two extra sessions. The adaptations and thinking are spread throughout the manual and this has meant that it has been necessary to produce a facilitator's manual for each of the postnatal groups. See below.

Postnatal (Universal) group

Session 1: Understanding your and your baby's feelings

Session 2: Understanding your baby's brain development, communication and crying

Session 3: Understanding your baby's rhythms and developing healthy sleep patterns

Session 4: Understanding your baby's feeding

Session 5: Understanding your baby: Play and development

Session 6: Understanding your baby's childcare and moving forward: the next steps

Postnatal Plus group

Session 1: Understanding your baby: helping you think about how you and your baby are feeling

Session 2: Understanding your baby's brain development and communications

Session 3: Understanding your baby's communication: Crying

Session 4: Understanding your baby's rhythms and developing healthy sleep patterns

Session 5: Understanding your baby's feeding

Session 6: Understanding your baby: Play and development

Session 7: Understanding your baby: Being separate from your baby

Session 8: Understanding your baby: Review and moving forward

Running the groups

The training required to deliver the postnatal groups follows the pathway for all Solihull Approach group facilitation training. This includes facilitators completing the Solihull Approach 2 Day Foundation training that introduces practitioners to the Solihull Approach. They would then be expected to understand and apply what they have learnt about the theoretical model into their practice before completing a one day Group Facilitator training day. The training route has been carefully considered as it is important that practitioners have substantial understanding of the model that underpins all aspects of the postnatal groups. The concepts of containment and reciprocity are essential to the quality of how facilitators run the groups, deliver the information and support parents throughout the sessions.

When reflecting on her experience of using the model as a framework for thinking and the resources available to run a group, Sam Giles pointed out that 'containment is a big element throughout the groups, we contain the parent so they can contain their baby'. She also said that she felt supported by having the group facilitator's manual; 'the manual's basic structure is well laid out and there are extra bits of facilitator notes if you need it'. As part of the parallel process we aim to provide a containing experience for facilitators in their use of the facilitator's manual. In addition to facilitator notes we have included a facilitator's evaluation sheet in the manual. Sam reflected that she has found the evaluation sheet helped her by allowing time to think about what went well or what she needed to look at a bit more before the next session. The training and resources enabled her to feel contained as a facilitator and that in turn allowed her to create a

The Solihull Approach Postnatal group 'Understanding your baby' 91

safe, containing environment for parents. Her experience of running the Postnatal Plus group was that she particularly liked the slower pace of the Postnatal Plus group for those parents who might need 'a little more advice and support'. She describes how 'knowing the information is evidence based and woven throughout the programme enables you to draw on elements of the Solihull Approach that allowed parents to feel contained as well. It gives you confidence to pass it onto parents'. She also reflected that there are challenges to running postnatal groups, in particular engaging parents who might not normally be vocal in a group, but that the group allows time and safety to discuss things and be involved. For example, the design of some activities enables parents to talk about a topic without necessarily talking about themselves. When asked what she felt parents found most helpful about the Solihull Approach postnatal group she said that it was the interaction with other parents, the containment and access to professionals for information. She said that there could be struggles, but there was also a massive benefit to parents and that the Solihull Approach can be applied to all aspects of parenting.

Evaluation

Evaluation of the postnatal groups is encouraging. Findings from a pilot study of both postnatal groups delivered in Islington in 2014 revealed positive and helpful feedback from parents[11]. Parents who attended groups expressed views that the group helped them understand their infant children. A mother commented that the group 'really improved my understanding of my son and I was able to empathise more.' Another mother said that 'it definitely helped my confidence and I would tell other parents to go'. When asked what parents could suggest to improve the group they highlighted that it was important that fathers are included.

The issue of fathers attending postnatal groups is longstanding and in relation to the Solihull Approach group is more associated with the timing of groups rather than its suitability for fathers. We include fathers as part of the Solihull Approach groups and the online courses. A mother commented that she felt 'it was a shame at times my husband couldn't be there even though he has the handouts' and suggested a group could be run on a Sunday. Practitioners are constantly searching for solutions to the issue of making groups accessible for fathers. The most common difficulties are the flexibility of practitioner's work patterns and access to buildings. Another option that could be made available to fathers is for them to be offered access to the Solihull Approach online postnatal course so they can access the same information and thinking as the parent who is attending the face to face group.

Preliminary data collection using pre and post questionnaires and parent evaluations from each session is ongoing. Early data from qualitative feedback from parents attending both groups is encouraging. Parents in the universal group have commented that they feel more confident. In the Postnatal Plus group when parents were asked what had changed, several parents reported that they understood their baby more and could accommodate their baby's needs better. As with other Solihull Approach groups, we have included a parent evaluation in the facilitator's manual at the end of each session. This can be helpful to practitioners as they have reported the pictorial evaluation works for everyone with any level of literacy and is simple and easily used. In addition, because each session is evaluated it allows facilitators to pick up on things that went well together with things that could be improved as the group progresses, rather than waiting for one overall evaluation.

Conclusion

As we gather together an increasing evidence base for the Solihull Approach groups we are encouraged by the positive outcomes, but what is most endearing is how either attending a group as a parent or delivering the groups to parents affects people on a personal level. Parents appreciate the relaxed time they have to think about being a parent and professionals who run the group get a great deal of satisfaction.

Sam Giles sums this up by saying that she gets 'most satisfaction from running the group from start to finish. Seeing the progress of parents and feeling confident, feeding back their home activities with others and the joy it produces and pride of sharing those things with parents and facilitators.'

References

1. Saunders, J. (2009). *Parents' experiences of a new baby group.* http://dera.ioe. ac.uk/2705/1/Microsoft_Word_-_PLR0910027Sanders2.pdf

2. Deave, D., Johnson, D. and Ingram, J. (2008). Transition to parenthood: the needs of parents in pregnancy and early parenthood. *BMC Pregnancy and Childbirth.* https://bmcpregnancychildbirth.biomedcentral.com/ articles/10.1186/1471-2393-8-30

3. Schrader McMillan, A. S., Barlow, J. and Redshaw, M. (2009). *Birth and beyond: a review of the evidence about antenatal education.* London: Department of Health.

4. Bateson, K., Delaney, J. and Pybus, R. (2008). Meeting expectations: the pilot evaluation of the Solihull Approach Parenting Group. *Community Practitioner,* 81, 28-31.

5. Johnson, R. and Wilson, H. (2012). Parents' Evaluation of 'Understanding Your Child's Behaviour', a parenting group based on the Solihull Approach. *Community Practitioner,* 85(5), 29-33.

6. Douglas, H. and Ginty, M. (2001). The Solihull Approach: changes in health visiting practice. *Community Practitioner,* 74(6), 222-224.

7. Douglas, H. and Whitehead, R. (2005). health visitors experience of using the Solihull Approach. *Community Practitioner,* 78(1), 20-23.

8. Department of Health (1994a). *Weaning and the weaning diet: report of the working group on the weaning diet of the Committee on Medical Aspects of Food Policy.* London: HMSO.

9. Murray, L., Cooper, P. and Fearon, P. (2014). Parenting difficulties and postnatal depression: implications for primary healthcare assessment and intervention. *Community Practitioner,* 87(11), 34-38.

10. Giles, S. (2018). Personal communication.
11. Walker, L. (2014). *Evaluation of the Solihull Approach Post Natal Parenting Group in Islington 2014: A Pilot Study.* (Unpublished).

13 The Solihull Approach: a children's centres perspective

Louise Moreton

How my journey with the Solihull Approach began

I think my earliest recollection of a reference to the Solihull Approach was from a discussion I had with a colleague who was the lead for training and family learning programmes at a local Sure Start project in Warwickshire. I remember my colleague was referring to previous experience she had working within a neighbouring local authority practice which she considered to have been particularly beneficial for parents.

Several years later in Birmingham, when I met a local midwife who had recently been on Solihull Approach Foundation training, I was reminded of this earlier conversation and the impression left by the positive regard my former colleague had expressed. The midwife was equally impressed with her experience and explained that the NHS Trust she was employed by were having Solihull Approach training for all their community midwives. In future the traditional Parentcraft sessions would be replaced with Solihull Approach 'Understanding pregnancy, labour, birth and your baby' courses, although we preferred the strapline 'Journey to Parenthood'. As two facilitators would be required, the proposal was to work in partnership with children's centres and for practitioners from these organisations to co-deliver with midwives. I was delighted with the opportunity to get involved, and so began my journey as a Solihull Approach practitioner.

Getting started

I began my career in Early Years in the mid 1990s, but also had the good fortune to work for several years for a large children's educational charity. This taught me the importance of family learning and also how to plan and deliver adult education. I found these were valuable skills as I became involved in children's centres, where the emphasis was on engaging families to improve children's outcomes through early intervention. Like others engaged in this sector I have observed numerous strategies, parenting programmes, courses and interventions designed to support families; a lot of very good work has been achieved under the guise of children's centres. However, when I was properly introduced to the Solihull Approach I definitely experienced that 'light bulb' moment. I think it is important to recognise that the Solihull Approach is more than just another series of parenting programmes; it is more holistic and should be applied throughout all areas of work. In order to be able to deliver the Solihull Approach courses effectively, it is necessary first to identify with and embrace this way of working; to experience first hand what is meant by the 'Solihull Approach'.

To become a Solihull Approach practitioner requires first accessing one of the Foundation courses. The training is the beginning; this provides the theoretical background and understanding of the Solihull Approach framework. It covers the three concepts of containment, reciprocity and behaviour management and how they are intrinsically linked. To fully appreciate the Solihull Approach you must then apply this knowledge to your own practice. By being able to explore and recognise where elements of containment and reciprocity are present in your own work and seeing how these may influence behaviour management, you are then ready to continue.

Solihull Approach antenatal parenting: Journey to Parenthood partnership with midwives

The first Solihull Approach antenatal parenting group I co-facilitated was in 2013 and after nearly five years of delivering the course I have never tired of it or ceased to enjoy the experience. Initially I was working with two midwifery teams, each with an allocated midwife to co-deliver the course. Over time it was not always possible for the same midwife to be present every week but the midwife team managers committed to providing support to ensure the parenting programmes continued. Ideally the same two facilitators should be present each week, but it is possible to run it successfully if there is one constant person delivering in each session. From experience, I would advise when initially setting up this service that the same two facilitators work together in the beginning until well established. Then, if one service is struggling because of staff levels or increased workload it is possible for someone else to step in with confidence.

I have been fortunate to work with some amazing midwives over the years. One midwife I know who qualified in the late 1980s confided in me that she really did not like doing Parentcraft. She described standing in front of a group of expectant parents and talking 'at them' for two hours in an attempt to impart as much information as possible; she dreaded being asked to deliver sessions. However, she thoroughly enjoyed facilitating the Solihull Approach sessions, so much so that she would actually volunteer to deliver them. Being able to interact and spend time with expectant mothers and fathers, helping them to prepare for parenthood in this way brought to life the passion she still has for her profession. Her experience and feelings about this way of delivering parent education has been echoed by so many of her colleagues. This positive opinion is also shared by many of the expectant parents as can be seen in the feedback typically received at the end of each course:

> 'Amazing job & very welcoming. Make everyone feel involved and relaxed. Pregnancy does not seem as scary now as everything explained wonderfully' (Jul 2015).

> 'Really impressed with the classes. Very well structured' (Aug 2016).

> 'Thank you for your fantastic work. I have recommended ante-natal classes to everyone who's having a baby' (June 2017).

> 'Enjoyed the sessions – informal and informative' (Sept 2017).

'Thank you for making the antenatal classes fun, putting my mind at ease (and for all the yummy cakes!) (Sept 2017).

'Really enjoyed the last 5 weeks' (Nov 2017).

Preparation

On a practical note, I soon discovered it was easier to coordinate delivery of the courses from the children's centre. Providing leaflets for the midwifery teams to give out enabled them to promote and encourage expectant parents to book onto a course at the children's centre. The children's centre receptionists were trained to be alert to any expectant parents who rang but appeared anxious, to ensure they received an early call back to go over any concerns. Otherwise, I would ring the week before the course started to go over the details and answer any questions. The importance of providing emotional containment begins before the start of the first session!

The Solihull Approach Antenatal Facilitator's Manual contains all the necessary guidance, 'lesson plans' and supporting materials for running these sessions. In addition, having the extra equipment in the Antenatal Resource Bag also aids delivery.

Whilst always encouraging fathers-to-be to attend I have been mindful that sometimes they may not be involved. I would usually propose that mothers-to-be may wish to bring a 'birth partner' with them but explain that coming on their own was equally okay. I would also suggest that they may wish to have someone else attend with them for support; often other family members or close friends would come to the groups. Many expectant fathers have attended the groups, with positive responses:

'I've been able to be involved in this part of the pregnancy' (Feb 2016).

'Bring my partner and I closer through doing this together' (June 2017).

Why five weeks really are necessary

On a number of occasions the question has arisen about the length of the course and a preference voiced for a four week option. I understand this can be attributed to the old Parentcraft courses, which traditionally ran for four weeks, or sometimes it can be to do with planning rosters. However, the benefit of having the five weeks is undeniable. To shorten the course would mean losing time spent on containment and reciprocity. It is my opinion that this accounts for participants being so positive about the groups. It is this vital preparation, prior to the sessions on labour and pain relief, which forms the basis for expectant parents' increased emotional resilience and confidence.

During the first session participants are asked 'How do you feel today?' and given a handout of a 'Feelings Map'. I usually ask everyone to think about the journey they have been on already and consider how they have felt since first discovering about being pregnant. Although the time for feeding back takes longer, it also allows for past emotions to be acknowledged which may have been suppressed. As facilitators there is a chance to model containment and often this is mirrored by participants with demonstrations of empathy. Also for fathers-to-be this is often the first time they have the freedom to express their feelings.

'Got to know each other sharing knowledge and experiences' (Oct 2014).

'The group was great and the staff team were brilliant! Felt very happy and comfortable with them and never felt bad once with what could be perceived as a silly question' (May 2015).

'Very helpful because at first I was very nervous about being a parent' (Aug 2016).

'Very helpful. Not terrified. Grateful' (Feb 2018).

Attachment with the unborn baby

The second session allows time to focus on the development and attachment with the unborn baby. There is an opportunity to watch The Baby Brain DVD. This is a good time to observe the expectant mothers' reactions, especially to the baby smiling. Normally the participants instinctively smile in response, often nudging or looking to partners to share this experience. Occasionally there may be someone who does not react as would be expected, this may signify underlying issues with the pregnancy, worries or negative feelings. I would always discuss such behaviour with the midwife present; there might be an opportunity to speak privately to ascertain if there are particular difficulties being experienced. We would also consider alerting the woman's own midwife. I have always explained at the start of the course that the midwife or I will be available to speak to privately during the break or at the end of each session if needed; the chosen venues have been considered in order to facilitate this.

'Feeling like its normal to feel the way I do regarding my baby' (June 2017).

'Helped me think about my baby rather than being pregnant & feeling uncomfortable!' (Sept 2017).

Labour and pain relief

By the time the group reaches sessions three and four, when labour and pain relief are explored in detail, the concepts of containment and reciprocity have already been introduced through earlier activities. It is easy to remind participants to reflect upon what they have already learnt that will help support them through this part of their journey into parenthood. There is an opportunity for expectant parents to consider what their babies will be experiencing at this time. They also reflect on their own roles and it is a good opportunity for fathers-to-be to work together for some of the activities.

'Enabled me to learn. Bonding with others. Support for my partner. Confidence in parenthood' (Nov 2016).

'Knowing what might happen – good + bad. Being prepared. Loved it!' (Nov 2016).

'Understand more about parenthood, about the baby's growth, what I need to do as a dad' (Oct 2016).

Preparing for after the baby is born

Throughout the course participants are encouraged to prepare for the postnatal period and for what becoming parents entails, including decisions to be made, for instance, about feeding choices. This is where children's centres are in an ideal position to offer information about further services and support. The evaluations completed at the end of the course show how parents-to-be feel more confident about the postnatal period. When asked about what attending the group has meant for them, replies typically include:

'Really enjoyed this group and I've really got a lot out of it! Feel like I've learned a lot and feel a lot more confidence and reassured about the experience. Lovely group and made lovely friends! Thank you' (May 2016).

'Feeling better prepared for birth ... more confidence to try breastfeeding, shared experiences with other expectant mums. Both me and my husband enjoyed the classes and found them really insightful. Would definitely recommend to other expectant mums' (Nov 2016).

'I also feel there is a lot of support out there after the birth' (Sept 2017).

'A chance to meet other mums, learn about parenting and something to look forward to each week' (Sept 2017).

Solihull Approach postnatal: 'Understanding Your baby'

Ideally children's centres should be able to provide universal postnatal parenting groups, such as 'Understanding Your Baby' and invite participants of the antenatal groups to attend. This six week course covers baby's feelings, brain development, communication, healthy sleep patterns, feeding, play and development as well as exploring childcare options.

Unfortunately, there was not capacity to provide this within my service. However, I was interested to learn of the eight week Postnatal Plus version which had been developed and could provide targeted support for those with relationship issues with their babies and mothers with postnatal depression. I spoke to health visitor colleagues who were equally interested; Solihull Approach forms part of their student training so it is a familiar model and is embedded in health visitor practice in Birmingham. Fortunately, the health visitor team manager was supportive of the idea, if it could be organised on similar terms as the antenatal groups were with midwifery. I would be responsible for the publicity materials and co-ordination. It was agreed participation in the groups would be by referral, for mothers experiencing 'low mood' with babies up to 9 months old. The groups would be limited to a maximum of eight babies with mothers and I would co-facilitate with one of the health visitors. There was also provision potentially for partners.

With referrals made by midwives, health visitors, social workers and children's centre staff, the Postnatal Plus groups have been delivered on a termly basis with excellent results. I have found that by the fourth session it is possible to see a distinct improvement in participants' emotional wellbeing. The feedback from those who attend supports this and from the referrers who are able to observe for themselves the positive impact.

Postnatal course structure

Like the antenatal groups, the postnatal groups also start by asking parents how they are feeling and to consider who can be helpful in supporting them now. The 'Feelings Map' activity is used and again allows mothers to open up. I always explain that it is okay to 'pass' if anyone does not feel happy to share, but as yet no-one has ever done so. I do believe it is very important to be able to set the right tone before introducing this activity. Parents are also encouraged to consider how their baby may be feeling and helped to think about their relationship with their baby. The session finishes with an outline of ways to relax, including mindfulness.

Two experienced facilitators are needed to ensure the group is delivered smoothly. The facilitators are able to model the Solihull Approach with the babies and often provide support for mothers by entertaining their infants so mums can have a drink and piece of cake! Hot drinks are served in this group as part of the structure of the sessions with health and safety being addressed at the start; a discussion was held prior to the groups starting and it was felt that this was an essential part of providing a 'containing' environment. In addition, I have found it helpful to have the room available for up to an hour before the session starts for mothers who arrive early. In some instances, part of their perinatal mental health issues means that being able to leave the house sooner, or arriving at a destination early, can alleviate heightened anxiety.

The second session provides information on baby brain development, which assists with parents getting in tune with their baby.

The course then moves onto communication, with understanding and responding sensitively to a baby's crying before parents' introduction to the 'Dance of Reciprocity'. I consider this to the 'light bulb' moment for most, with a noticeable improvement in parents' attunement and their ability to recognise and respond to their baby's rhythms.

The remainder of the sessions deal with feeding, sleeping, development and play before addressing how parents experience being separate from their baby, how this might feel and then thinking about their own needs in relation to support for the future. Childcare options are explored before time for reflection on what has been learnt and how parents would like to develop their relationship with their baby in the future.

Steps can be considered for the group to continue independently which is often expressed by participants as a natural progression in the network of support they have established. I sometimes find this is a natural development during the course and a group may be supported to 'get together' outside of the weekly sessions.

There are various themes which emerge from the evaluations and feedback at the end of the course. When asked what has changed or been learnt from attending the groups, often there is an association with increased confidence:

> 'Has boost my confidence being a parent' (Dec 2016).

> 'I learnt that a lot of problems I thought I couldn't solve I will be able to do' (Nov 2017).

> 'I think this group is a great confidence and support network for mums struggling. It helps with questions that you have, worries that arise and if you're doubting yourself' (Dec 2016).

'I'm stronger than I knew and understand support I have' (Mar 2017).

'Confidence in my daughter after attending the group has increased tenfold' (grandmother attending with daughter and grandson, Nov 2017).

'There are lots of people that suffer with postnatal depression, more than you think, and I am normal' (Nov 2017).

The groups also provide information and advice:

'More knowledge about weaning, introduction to Solihull Approach' (Jun 2017).

'I have learnt how to understand the different stages of development and I feel a lot better about myself and meeting other moms' (Nov 2017).

'New/recent research about weaning. Understanding more what my baby needs/ wants when they cry/smile etc.' (Nov 2017).

Networking and support is an important part of each group:

'Sharing experiences helped understanding' (Dec 2016).

'Understanding my feelings and actions are normal' (Mar 2017).

'Got me out of the house, made new friends' (Jun 2017).

'It's given me something to look forward to each week' (Nov 2017)

'I always leave the group feeling good' (Nov 2017).

The improved relationship, bonding and attachment experienced is undeniable:

'Given me a better understanding of my baby and me' (Dec 2016).

'That each baby is different and it's OK!' (Dec 2016).

'Better understanding of babies needs' (Mar 2017).

'How to accommodate my baby's needs. To trust instincts more' (Nov 2017).

Model developed for children's centres

Over the last few years my work has led to the development of a model for children's centres for Antenatal and Perinatal Parent Education and Breastfeeding Support. There has been funding from NHS England to replicate this model in other areas of Birmingham to help improve perinatal mental health. The importance of using the Solihull Approach framework is clearly reflected in my model and addresses national guidelines for effective local infant feeding services[1].

Antenatal and Perinatal Parent Education & Breastfeeding Support Model

Solihull Approach for breastfeeding support

In 2016 several local mothers, who attended the breastfeeding cafes I had set up, expressed interest in becoming volunteers to provide support for other mums. Due to an absence of local breastfeeding peer supporter training at that time, and with the support of my manager, I contacted the Solihull Approach team regarding their Peer Supporter training manual. As a result, I ran three courses the following year for breastfeeding mothers to train. They were joined by several children's centre staff from both my organisation and from another children's centre.

Since my own experience has shown the Solihull Approach to be an excellent model for supporting women struggling with breastfeeding, I was confident about choosing the Solihull Approach Peer Breastfeeding Supporter course.

Due to a lack of crèche provision the babies attended the training sessions as well. This was sometimes challenging, as by the time each group ended every baby was either crawling or walking! However, in the real world of breastfeeding cafes and breastfeeding support home visits, babies are always present and often accompanied by other siblings. Therefore, I felt this was a good experience for those training. However, if there is an opportunity to have another facilitator from midwifery or health visiting to co-deliver the sessions, I would strongly urge others to take advantage of this.

As usual, the materials and 'lesson plans' in the Solihull Approach Manual were of excellent quality. The feedback from those who attended was very positive despite some of the challenges:

> 'Very good course. Thank you for this opportunity and to be able to gain these new skills and knowledge, be able to offer support to new moms, offer containment' (Mar 2017).

> 'Excellent training and support to become a support to others' (Mar 2017).

> 'Very good course, found it highly beneficial towards my job role and professional development. Thank you' (July 2017).

102   Louise Moreton

'I will set up my own breastfeeding support cafe and support all the families (mothers) to support breastfeeding' (July 2017).

'I will use what I have learnt in breastfeeding cafe to help support other moms. Excellent course, very useful information' (Nov 2017).

Solihull Approach and students

I believe it is incredibly beneficial to have students involved with the Solihull Approach courses; it gives them a wonderful opportunity to experience first hand the effectiveness of this way of working. Student midwives have been a fairly regular addition to my antenatal classes, but I have also been asked if student health visitors, and more recently student nurses, can attend the various Solihull Approach groups. A first year student nurse on community placement with a local health visiting team attended the third session of a Postnatal Plus parenting group and afterwards wrote this:

What I enjoyed about today's session:

- Great support for all mums
- Never a judgemental word
- Sharing of information works really well i.e. new thing your baby is doing, why are they crying, how do you feel when they cry
- An opportunity for babies to play in a quiet environment plus for other mums to have a bit of a break!
- Having a structure for the session enabled us to get through certain topics in a calm, comfortable environment.
- Today has been a great opportunity as a student nurse to talk to mums about their experiences on a one to one basis in an informal place.
- Being able to observe babies and their development has been really interesting.
- As a community based support group, it works really well, to share concerns with others
- Thank you.

Student Nurse (May 2017)

More recently I received feedback from one of the student midwives who had attended several of the antenatal sessions I facilitated:

As a student, it was an invaluable experience in allowing me to relate what I had learnt in lectures to practice and also expanded my knowledge … it also highlighted the importance of listening to what women and their partners say and allowing them to interact during the session. This is an important observation that will carry through to all aspects of my midwifery studies.

…The sessions were very informative and interesting. However, Louise did not overload the women and students with information. She allowed everyone enough time to process the information we were given and if anyone had any further questions she was happy to help.

Student Midwife (Feb 2018)

Conclusion

I am passionate about my work and believe that becoming a Solihull Approach practitioner has enhanced my practice as well as providing a great deal of job satisfaction. I know that by sharing my experience and knowledge I have enabled many others to develop greater understanding and fulfilment, including parents and their children, volunteers and professional colleagues. I would recommend the Solihull Approach to everyone associated with children's centres as well as to any parent or parent-to-be. The ability to deliver Solihull Approach programmes in partnership with midwifery and health visiting colleagues is of benefit to parents and professionals alike. As our local health visitor team manager is fond of saying, 'it's all about outcomes for children' and with the Solihull Approach this is most certainly achievable!

Reference

1. Great Britain. Public Health England. (2016). *Commissioning Infant Feeding Services: a summary.* https://www.gov.uk/government/publications/infant-feeding-commissioning-services (Accessed: 10 October 2016)

14 The Solihull Approach and schools

Rebecca Johnson

Introduction

Schools are in a unique position in the UK of universalism, which means they connect with (almost) every child in the UK between the ages of four to 16 years. This is both their strength and their vulnerability as they are seen as a gateway for all manner of important agendas. Far from wishing to add to the list of initiatives or objectives by introducing another set of 'techniques', the Solihull Approach team recognised that the theoretical framework could be helpful for supporting the work that happens day in and day out in schools to support pupils with the pre-requisites for learning; feeling safe; cared for; and calm enough to learn. Many practitioners in the first decade of the Solihull Approach recognised this too and would say quite regularly 'you need to offer this in schools'.

In the first ten years of the Solihull Approach's development, it had been well established with health visitors and school nurses and the Resource Packs had been written, piloted, revised and professionally published. Individuals employed by schools started to attend the trainings and they reiterated the idea that the model had something to offer that would help schools.

By 2011 there had been a precedent for the culture of an organisation to be shaped by whole multi-disciplinary staff teams being trained in the Solihull Approach. The value of training everyone from the receptionist through to the managers had been demonstrated in Sure Start teams in the preceding years. For example, reception and child care staff had altered the way they greeted parents as they came into the centre and had been able to be mindful of the parents' experience of coming somewhere new and of both the child's and the parents' experience of separation during crèche sessions.

Whole School Training

The suggestion had been made that it would be similarly beneficial for the Solihull Approach 'way of thinking' to be available for whole schools. However, it was apparent that releasing staff for the 2 Day Foundation training was going to be a prohibitively big commitment for most schools. Schools in England, Scotland, Wales and Northern Ireland have five 'inset' or 'in-service' training days spread over the academic year, often at the beginning or end of school holidays or weekends. Therefore, an adaptation was made to the Foundation training to fit the training into a 9am to 3pm day with a twilight follow-up session two weeks later for example at 3.30-5.30pm. The usual limit of 12 delegates per training was reviewed and the benefits of whole group culture shift was weighed against the risk that a large group of delegates would prove unwieldy for reflective discussions and strong 'theory into practice' learning. The working group involved in developing this training consisted of teachers specialising in emotional, social and behavioural difficulties within a Specialist Inclusion Support Service, a school nurse and educational psychologist together with Hazel Douglas, Child Psychotherapist and Clinical Psychologist, and Mary Rheeston, Health Visitor, from the Solihull Approach team. This group considered the fact that delegates would know each other and share an organisational culture, and felt that training could be delivered to the whole staff group. The training was piloted, refined and re-piloted in the usual way.

At the time in England, there had been an initiative launched by the UK government's Department for Children, Schools and Families (DCSF) (subsequently replaced by the Department for Education (DFE)) to help schools focus on the links between learning, attendance and behaviour and the wider context for a child, in particular their emotional and social skills'. This had been packaged as the Social Emotional Aspects of Learning (SEAL)[1] in 2000. It consisted of a whole school approach that was taken up by at least 90% of primary schools and 70% of secondary schools in England. SEAL focused on five 'broad social and emotional aspects of learning: self-awareness; managing feelings; motivation; empathy, and social skills'. The Solihull Approach provides a framework for understanding how these skills evolve in children and young people from infancy onwards. It also helps professionals think about how to foster them within their relationships with both adults and children in the present. In a sense it operationalised the SEAL agenda and this was reflected in the adaptation of the Solihull Approach Foundation training for schools, known as 'Whole School training'.

The idea was to train everyone on the payroll from the caretaker and mealtime supervisors through to the headteacher and governors. Initial trainings were with unlimited numbers of staff, but over the years the learning has been that the maximum is a group of 50 with smaller groups for the twilight sessions, which involve more group discussions, with each facilitator taking a group and possibly splitting into further smaller groups if additional facilitators can be identified. In addition, some schools provide the full 2 Day Foundation training for particular staff within the school, such as those with a pastoral responsibility or learning mentors.

The programme covers brain development, containment, reciprocity and behaviour for learning (in line with SEAL) with an emphasis, as always, on putting the theories into practice. As with the 2 Day Foundation training, homework consists of an observational exercise and an invitation to apply the theories in a work context. Follow-up sessions two weeks later focus on feeding back from the homework and using delegates' own observations and practice examples to illustrate and consolidate understanding of the Approach's core principles. Training is supported by the School Years Resource Pack and, since 2016, a Supporting Information Booklet for each member of staff. For more about this, see the chapter on schools by Cheryl Valentine.

Solihull Approach training is also available as an Early Years Foundation training for schools and Early Years settings with nursery staff. This two day group training, accompanied by the First Five Years Resource Pack, integrates the Early Years Foundation Stage curriculum (UK) into the Solihull Approach model. It is a 10 hour training over two five hour sessions.

106 Rebecca Johnson

Research

Kent, in the South East of the UK, had been home to a successful cascade of the Solihull Approach training to over 2500 multi-agency practitioners, and over 100 managers, funded by the Local Authority and NHS Primary Care Trusts. Research was then undertaken to explore the impact of the Whole School training on school staff[2]. The training was delivered over three twilight sessions, with agreement from the Solihull Approach head office, to teachers, the headteacher, support staff and administrators. Training was then augmented by six subsequent support sessions delivered with a group of interested staff.

Data was collected before training and six months after the final support session from two primary schools. School A received the Whole School training, School B acted as a control for comparison. The study looked at teachers': anxiety; burnout; compassion, satisfaction and fatigue; self-concept, and teacher efficacy.

Quantitative statistical analysis found that six months after training, teachers in School A showed a statistically significant increase in satisfaction with their helping role, self-esteem, and teacher efficacy scores, as well as a decrease in feeling burnt out/stressed. The teachers at School B who did not receive the training only showed an improvement in teacher efficacy over the period.

Thematic analysis of qualitative interviews with seven staff members who had received the training captured their views on what they found useful. The themes were: being offered a framework that underpinned all aspects of the work they do; the focus on the relationships, not only with pupils, but with teachers, support staff and parents as well; and the focus on well-being and its link with learning.

> There's somebody in my class who joined quite recently, quite challenging behaviour. And as well as very firm boundaries I have used the reflecting back to him how he is feeling and erm, yeah it's worked... It's enabled him to calm down and be more reflective himself... ...'it's helped me to think twice' so I think that's rather good[2].

Face-to-face group and online course for parents

One of the recommendations from the SEAL programme was that greater engagement with parents/carers should be an essential component of any future initiative in the area of social and emotional skills development in schools. One of the biggest barriers to improving the social and emotional aspects in schools under the SEAL initiative was the 'influence of the parents and their models of behaviour outside of school':

> I wonder how much some of them are missing out on it at home'; 'A lot of children will have not had that background at home and this is where it becomes very difficult, when you talk about terms like empathy and self-awareness and thinking about other people, it's quite difficult[1].

The Solihull Approach schools offer includes a structured, evidence based, quality assured (CANparent Quality Mark) face-to-face 10 week, two hours a week, group for parents based on the Solihull Approach model, called 'Understanding your child's behaviour' or, increasingly 'Understanding your child'. Training to deliver the group consists of the 2 Day Foundation training plus a one day Group Facilitator training. Facilitators, who work in

The online version of 'Understanding your child' became available in 2013 and consists of 11 modules taking 15 to 20 minutes each.

pairs to deliver a group, must have a manual each. This group has been delivered in many community venues, including schools, by a range of practitioners including education staff. For more about this, read the chapters by Karen Ladd and by Cheryl Valentine.

The online version of 'Understanding your child' became available in 2013 and consists of 11 modules taking 15 to 20 minutes each.

The evaluation of SEAL identified that attempts to engage parents may not have been well received in some of the schools:

> I think some of our parents wouldn't be that understanding - they would think it would be a direct attack on their parenting skills'; 'We had to be careful because we didn't want to seen to be patronizing the parents[1].

School Multi-User Licences for the online course enable schools to offer the online option to parents free of charge and is specifically aimed at a universal, whole school community in order to normalise parental learning and self-development. This offer can help to bridge the gap between initiatives taking place in schools and the home environment. It also contributes to dismantling the stigma of parenting groups because it is clearly for every parent, whereas programmes have traditionally been offered to families in complex situations and have therefore become associated with families in difficulty.

Uptake of the online courses in schools depends heavily on the active involvement of the school in promoting the courses. When a 'trusted voice' known to parents writes personally to the school community to recommend the course more parents sign up and progress through the course than in schools where the information has simply been added to a website or newsletter. The choice of words is critical in sensitively describing the course and its potential benefits to all families, from those who are simply curious, and want to be the best they can be, to those dealing with more challenging circumstances.

The initial evidence for the online course is good. Data provided by the first 115 parents completing the course and the measures, indicated statistically significant increases in self-reported closeness and decreases in conflict in parents' relationship with their child(ren)[3].

Many parents have appreciated the courses. For example:

> Seriously impressed that the kid's school have subscribed for all parents/relatives of pupils to access the Solihull Approach online course. It's all about recognising emotions in yourself and your child and understanding how they impact upon behaviours rather than the old fashioned praising of good behaviours and ignoring of bad. It acknowledges that perceived bad behaviours need attention too as the cause may be stress/unhappiness/anxiety and those things shouldn't be ignored but supported.

> The key to reducing 'bad' behaviours is understanding your child as an individual and their emotional triggers and how you can work with them to manage them. Hooray! Thanks St Nicks... you've save me £40 and reassured me that I'm using the right approach. It's online, just 11 modules that you listen to/watch approx. 4/5 days apart and is VERY informative. Wowzer! It feels like a 'one small step for man' moment! ...There's a section about child development 0-3 years at the start and it says stuff I didn't know even though I've studied it about babies turning their heads away to make neuron connections ...sooooo good.

> Jen Hopkins, parent, Alcester.

'Really enjoyed this course! Best £39 I've ever spent!'

'This has been a really valuable experience that in a way will impact on many aspects of my life.'

'This course has been an absolutely invaluable gift to me. It has and will change so many aspects of my life. I am undoubtedly a better parent and more rounded and fulfilled person as a result. Some aspects have literally been like 'Eureka' moments to me! I WISH I'd known all this years ago.'

'The Solihull Approach course I did made it clear parents don't need lessons: daily life throws us enough of those. What we need is the space to step back and observe our children. We need some structured guidance to help us reflect on all the factors that make them behave the way they do; some developmental, some circumstantial.'

'I have found the online course very useful. Now, I take time to think more during difficult situations and during arguments with my kids.'

'It doesn't work all the time but bit by bit, we are working towards a less confrontational household!'

'Loving the parenting online course, excellent!!!!'

Workshops for parents

Schools can also offer a two hour workshop to parents of either young children or adolescents. These are available in the form of a manual to be delivered by a member of staff who has undertaken the 2 Day Foundation training and ideally the Train the Trainers one day course. The workshops have been used as a way to generate interest in, and introduce parents to, the idea of the group for parents 'Understanding your child', and can be used as stand-alone sessions on brain development for parents of adolescents, or brain development and reciprocity to parents of young school children, toddlers and babies. There is more detail about this in Karen Ladd's chapter.

Course for pupils

The Solihull Approach has always been driven by the prevention agenda. Initially the focus was on early childhood, then as it became established, opportunities presented themselves to work with midwives. The antenatal training and resources were developed. What a great way to influence the quality of relationships from birth! However, to be truly preventative why not go back even further to the preconception population? Hence the establishment of a Solihull Approach course for young people aged 14 to 16 years, 'Understanding yourself and parenting'. It is all about relationships, including couple relationships, the emotional needs of infants and new parents and of course their own re-configuring brains. This training was designed around the format of existing lessons slots and is presented in the format of nine lesson plans, which can be delivered by those who have completed the 2 Day Foundation training and a Train the Trainers one day course.

Some areas have been even more creative and have found ways to share the concepts of containment, reciprocity and emotional self-regulation with even younger pupils, for example in the last years of primary school, and you can read about this in the chapter by Jacklyn Purdon.

Conclusion

The Solihull Approach team have now developed a range of resources for schools to support learning through supporting emotional health. The resources are for teachers and other staff in schools, for parents and for pupils. We hope you enjoy reading about people's experiences of using these resources.

References

1. Humphrey, N., Lendrum, A. and Wigelsworth, M. (2010). Social and emotional aspects of learning (SEAL) programme in secondary schools: national evaluation. Research Report DFE-RR049. https://assets.publishing.service.gov.uk/government/uploads/system/uploads/attachment_data/file/181718/DFE-RR049.pdf pp.54.

2. Hassett, A. and Appleton, R. (2016). Understanding your pupil's behaviour: a pilot study from two primary schools in Kent. http://create.canterbury.ac.uk/15228/#hVMd9QidDCyVz0GS.99

3. Johnson, R. (2018). 'Improvements in parenting achieved with innovative online programme: Preliminary evaluation of 'Understanding Your Child – Online' (UYC-OL) A Solihull Approach course for parents and carers'. *Educational and Child Psychology,* 35(1), 40-50.

15 Solihull Approach Workshops for parents

Karen Ladd

Many parents struggle with the idea of attending a ten week group, particularly if they have no experience or idea of what the group may offer, or how it might be of benefit. One way of introducing parents to the Solihull Approach is by the offer of a workshop. Both of the Solihull Approach workshops; for Parents of Young Children and for Parents of Adolescents, are a useful tool in providing the flavour of an 'Understanding your child' group. To suggest to a parent that they might need some support in their parenting, for many, can perhaps be a most insulting suggestion, after all as parents aren't we supposed to know what we are doing? The beauty of the Solihull Approach workshop is that it really isn't about parenting, it provides information which supports our understanding of children's behaviours, related to their age and development. This is a far more comfortable offer to make to a possibly already struggling and demoralised parent.

The Workshop for Parents of Young Children offers an understanding of early brain development and the importance of reciprocity and relationship. The Workshop for Parents of Adolescents offers a look into changes in a young person's brain during puberty, which allows the exploration of some of the additional challenges that many of our teenagers experience. Neither workshop comments on poor or good enough parenting, but simply offers parents the opportunity to understand better the parent's role in supporting their child, through times of development. The workshops offer no suggestion of judgment, simply information. What the parent takes away from this is entirely up to them.

The workshops, we have found, have had several different uses. We have used the workshops in areas where our engagement numbers for groups have been low. Offering a workshop has spiked people's interest in understanding behaviours related to development in their children, which has, for some, encouraged them to go on and attend an 'Understanding your child' group. For others, the workshop has been enough to think about their own children and to be a little more understanding. A mum of a teenager said at the end of a workshop 'I can't believe I am nagging him all the time about his messy room, when he has all of that going on in his brain, poor kid, I really need to back off.' The same mum reported back several weeks later that her relationship had improved massively with her son, it wasn't perfect and they still had their fights, but she had really learnt to pick her battles and focus on what was important. Her son had appreciated that she had backed off, they were communicating better with each other and the house was generally calmer and a 'nicer place to be'.

Some of our primary schools have started to offer an 'Understanding your child' Workshop for Parents of Young Children as part of their induction offer to new families whose children are entering reception. This is made as a universal offer and therefore begins to normalise the offer of parenting support, as well as introducing parents to our ongoing offer of 'Understanding your child' groups. Other primary schools have taken the same idea and begun to offer the Adolescent Workshop to parents of their Year 6 pupils (ten to 11 years old) as part of the offer to support the transition to secondary school. As both of the workshops are very clearly offered to all parents, this is helping us remove the stigma attached to parenting support.

On occasion, workshops have been used to complement an 'Understanding your child' group. Often with groups only one parent attends; this might be due to work commitments or childcare arrangements. Where these parents engage well with the group, they often express that their partners would benefit from the group support, and they would benefit from their partners shared knowledge to support the changes that they might be trying to implement at home. Some facilitators have chosen to offer a one off workshop for the partners of attendees. The feedback we have had from these is always positive, with couples reporting that they are more supportive of each other as a result and more willing to listen to each other's ideas and work together to understand and manage their children's behaviours. Some who have attended these workshops have gone on to attend a group.

The workshops have been used creatively to support the development of specific groups. An example of this is with childminders, who have engaged with our children's centres and asked for some developmental opportunities. They have found the workshops both informative in terms of their own learning, but also insightful in further understanding the children in their care.

We have also delivered the workshops to grandparents, which has been a real pleasure. Grandparents bring such a wealth of experience. However, giving them the opportunity to understand brain development, when the majority would have had no access to this level of understanding when they were raising their own children has prompted many to reflect on their views of parenting.

We found with the introduction of the Adolescent Workshop that professionals were signing up alongside the parents that they were supporting. We certainly did not discourage this, but have also added the Adolescent Workshop as part of our offer of professional training. Several secondary schools have asked us to deliver this workshop to their staff, and their engagement and enthusiasm has been surprising.

One teacher approached the facilitator at the end of the training and said that she was retiring shortly, having been in teaching for 40 years, and in that time she felt that the information about the teenage brain shared in the workshop was the most useful thing that she had learnt in her 40 years; she wished so much that she had heard it all when she had been starting out and felt that she might have been a far more sympathetic teacher had this been the case.

Some teachers have also reported that they have reflected on their teaching approach with teenagers, particularly with those with additional needs to throw into the mix. One reported back that they have allowed their pupils a little more time to think and respond to questions and believes that this has had an impact in the classroom. Of course, many of the professionals attending these workshops are also parents and the majority of feedback that we have received has been related to their experiences with their own children.

The beauty of the Solihull Approach workshop is that it is non-threatening and therefore accessible to parents at all levels of need and this in itself, our facilitators would agree, makes it a pleasure to deliver.

16 Ravenswood Primary School: a school's experience of teaching children the Solihull Approach

Jacklyn Purdon

In Ravenswood Primary School, Scotland, we follow the motto 'teamwork makes the dream work'. The belief that through collaboration we achieve success is one of our underpinning values and at the heart of everything we undertake. Fully implementing the Solihull Approach in Ravenswood could therefore only be achieved if all stakeholders were involved. This required the full cooperation and active engagement of staff, pupils and parents alike.

Our whole staff underwent Solihull Approach training on an in-service day. Teaching staff, clerical staff, additional support needs assistants, classroom assistants and janitorial staff all participated in the training and collaborative working. Our in-service training was led by both current and former headteachers at Ravenswood.

Training highlighted the impact the Solihull Approach had compared to standard health visitor practice in the pilot evaluation study[1]. This reflected how the Solihull Approach could dramatically address behaviour problems in young people, something we wished to address as part of our school improvement. All staff responded extremely positively and agreed to implement the Solihull Approach throughout their day to day role in the school, whilst also recognising a need for the Approach in our local school community.

A collaborative strategy for planning the 'next steps' enabled staff to recognise that several of the initiatives and practices that had already been introduced into the life of the school overlapped with the guidance outlined in the Solihull Approach. This provided a natural platform for engaging the children in this new approach to our daily interactions.

The senior management team analysed staff responses and utilised common threads between our current practice and the Solihull Approach. As a result, the links between our current practice and the Solihull Approach became evident and we used this as the basis for planning our Solihull Approach activities for the benefit of the children.

As a management team, we selected three elements of our current practice that would support the integration of the Solihull Approach into our school. Each member of the senior management team planned and delivered separate workshops for the senior and infant departments. The three workshops comprised of:

1. The dance of reciprocity and teamwork.
2. Containment and the growth mindset.
3. Behaviour for learning and Relax Kids.

The children in Ravenswood are already arranged into three 'house groups' and age appropriate departments. The infant department is comprised of five classes from Primary 1 to Primary 3 and the senior department, also five classes, ranges from Primary 4 to Primary 7. The children attended a workshop within their house groups to ensure a cross section of ages, stages and family backgrounds. Each member of the senior management team led workshops for each house group in turn.

Our acting headteacher also led an informative introduction and gathered pupil responses in the plenary with all children in each department present. Support staff, including classroom assistants and additional support needs assistants, rotated activities with the children in order to support their learning by modelling appropriate behaviour and helping them learn the language associated with the Solihull Approach. These workshop arrangements, working as a department instead of just a class, ensured a consistent methodology was delivered across the school. This enabled the children to understand that the Solihull Approach would not only be used within the classroom, but throughout the school.

Our acting head teacher took responsibility for planning and leading the introduction to the Solihull Approach and a workshop linking the dance of reciprocity and teamwork. Within this workshop, the children undertook various team building activities to utilise the language associated with the Solihull Approach and actively follow the dance of reciprocity in a meaningful context.

Ravenswood @RavenswoodPS · Jan 11
We know that the dance of reciprocity is important to help everyone feel valued. 🐦 We can even repair ruptures with confidence! @SolihullAproach

Our acting principal teacher for the senior department planned and delivered a workshop based on containment and its link to the idea of a growth mindset[2]. The focus of this workshop was the growth mindset book 'Beautiful Oops'[3], where the children learned that mistakes are not a negative outcome but instead a learning opportunity from which we can improve. The children read the book and helped staff to turn spilled paint blotches into something beautiful.

Ravenswood @RavenswoodPS · Jan 11
P1-P3/4 made Miss Elliott SO proud today! 😊 We learned all about containment and how important it is to help each other develop a growth mindset. ❤️⭐ @SolihullAproach #teamworkmakesthedreamwork

Ravenswood @RavenswoodPS · Jan 11
P1-P3/4 learned all about containment as part of the @SolihullAproach today! 😊 We know how important it is to help each other and work together. Great job everyone! 😊 👍

Our acting principal teacher for the infant department planned and delivered a Relax Kids workshop in order to support the further exploration of behaviour for learning. This workshop focussed on the idea that we are in control of our own behaviour and can regulate our emotions in order to facilitate learning in school. The Relax Kids workshop (a training in child relaxation already adopted in the school) followed the seven elements of movement, play, stretch, feel, breathe, believe and relax. The focus of the workshop was on the elements breathe, believe and relax in order to train the children in self-regulatory behaviour.

Ravenswood Primary School: teaching children the Solihull Approach

Ravenswood @RavenswoodPS · Jan 11
Primary 1 - Primary 3/4 felt so relaxed during the final stage of our "Be Brilliant" Relax Kids sessions. We left with a better understanding of the behaviour management aspect of the Solihull approach too
@SolihullAproach @relaxkids

Ravenswood @RavenswoodPS · Jan 11
Primary 4/5 - Primary 7 participated in Relax Kids sessions with Miss Purdon today. It helped us to understand the behaviour management aspect of the Solihull approach @SolihullAproach

The children from each department had an extremely positive experience in each of the workshops and gave extensive feedback during the plenary session. They have also continued to use the language associated with the Solihull Approach throughout their day to day activities, such as, 'you have ruptured my dance' or 'thank you for that containment'. Comments from the feedback plenary session included: 'I can use the dance of reciprocity in class and in the playground'; 'I know how to stay calm if I get angry'; and 'I won't cry if I make a mistake, mistakes are beautiful'.

We will continue to monitor progress in the implementation of the Solihull Approach throughout the school. We also plan to engage parents in the Solihull Approach by delivering further family workshops, as well as continuing to hold 'stay and play' events so that staff can model behaviour and responses.

Our Solihull Approach journey has just begun at Ravenswood Primary, but our settled environment, positive ethos and willingness to embrace innovation and new approaches to learning and teaching show that we are on the right path.

References

1. Milford, R., Kleve, L., Lea, J. and Greenwood, R. (2006) A pilot evaluation study of the Solihull Approach. *Community Practitioner*, 79(11), 358-362
2. Dweck, C. (2015). Carol Dweck revisits the growth mindset. *Education Week*, 35(5), 20-24.
3. Saltzberg, B. (2010). *Beautiful Oops*. New York: Workman Publishing.

17 Delivering Solihull Approach training in primary and secondary schools in North Lanarkshire Council

Cheryl Valentine

'Solihull Approach training should be standard for all teachers, support staff and early years' practitioners!'

This is a statement I hear regularly when delivering Solihull training to education staff, and the reason being....because it works!

North Lanarkshire Council (NLC) have invested heavily in a multi-agency programme to deliver the Solihull Approach 2 Day Foundation training, the Whole School training and the 'Understanding your child' parent programme. The main focus has been to create a multi-agency workforce with shared knowledge, language and skill in supporting the emotional development of children and encouraging attuned relationships between parents and children.

As part of this programme and in line with the Scottish Attainment Challenge[1], the NLC education department is currently developing a nurture training programme for all schools to close the poverty related gap in attainment of pupils. A key part of this programme is the Solihull Approach training and the Solihull Approach 'Understanding your child' parent programme. The main aim is that all schools in NLC will participate in Solihull Approach training for staff and that they will deliver the 'Understanding your child' programme for parents. This, as you can imagine, is no small feat! With a workforce of thousands, it will take time to realise this ambitious aim. It has also been a journey of learning and we have adapted the process of delivering the programme to schools in response to learning from our initial testing. We have used the Quality Improvement model[2] to measure the impact of the training and identify changes that could lead to improvement.

We embarked on this journey over three years ago in March 2015 when we responded to requests from some very forward thinking primary school headteachers to deliver the training to their entire schools on an in-service training day. This was well received by the schools who engaged and it was decided to extend the training to identified schools whose catchment area was within the highest deprived areas of North Lanarkshire. Due to the number of schools involved, and the fact that whole school teams could only be released for training on in-service training days, it was decided to test delivery of the training to schools in groups, i.e. two smaller schools being trained together. We learned very quickly from this test! Our three key learning points were:

1. It is much better to deliver to schools individually, due to the number of staff (too many in one training session becomes unmanageable and restricts discussion). The chemistry between the participants changed when more than one school were trained together. When schools are trained individually, there is more discussion about specific aspects of their school and staff seem more comfortable to contribute to discussions.

2. Some schools were not 'ready' for the training or it did not fit into the school improvement plan for that year, thereby using up very valuable time on the in-service day that could have been used for another priority. We have now changed practice and schools are asked to complete a self evaluation 'nurture audit' to assess readiness to engage in the training. This has resulted in schools being more motivated and keen to engage in the training when the timing is right for that school and not because they are being directed to participate!

3. The training is most effective when one of the facilitators has experience of working in an education setting. We found that when the facilitators included relevant examples of Solihull Approach in practice in a school setting, it gave participants relevance and context.

Over the course of the Solihull Approach programme in NLC, we have increased our capacity to deliver the training and now have trainers within NLC who regularly deliver the training to both multi-agency groups and also to whole school teams. Nineteen of our trainers have a background in education and can provide a wealth of examples of how the Approach can be embedded into school life.

I have trained participants in multi-agency, all primary staff and all secondary staff sessions. I consider it a real privilege to share Solihull Approach training with others.

Solihull Approach is part of a huge movement in Scotland around ACEs, nurture and attachment. The Scottish government have a new working group tackling child trauma and attachment. It is a great time to be part of this work. I say at the beginning of training that the Solihull Approach underpins this work and gives participants the opportunity to hear about the research around brain development, containment and reciprocity and then gives us a lens to look at children's behaviour. Our aim is to get children to a place we can teach them and then – teach them!

Mary Cruickshank, Head Teacher/Solihull Trainer.

An evaluation of the early phase of the Whole School training was carried out by NLC Psychological Services in July 2016. Fifteen schools were involved in the evaluation. It was conducted by asking the staff at each of the schools about their understanding of how relationships affect behaviour, the importance of relationships on brain development and how well they think they understand their pupil's behaviour. The questions were asked before and after the training to gauge how attitudes have changed as a result of the training. The questions asked participants to rate each question on a scale of one to ten, one being low and ten being high.

The results (see below) clearly show that the Whole School training improved staff's understanding of how relationships affect behaviour, the importance of relationships for brain development and how well school staff understand the pupil's behaviour.

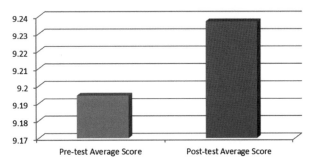

How do you rate your understanding of how relationships affect behaviour?

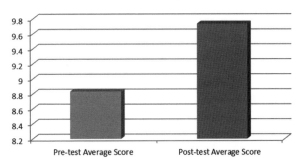

How do you rate the importance of relationships for brain development?

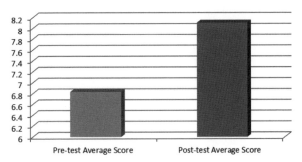

How well do you think you understand your pupil's behaviour?

The teachers gave very positive feedback, commenting on how they would use what they had learned from the training in their role. Here are some examples:

'I have thoroughly enjoyed the course and have learned many things which will be of great benefit in the teaching/learning process.'

'Reciprocity is essential with teacher/child. Allowing the child to 'lookaway' is facilitating their processing, and the importance of containment.'

'I will use containment within daily interactions.'

'Fantastic training course, I have benefitted both professionally and personally.'

'I will try to contain relationships with staff, pupil and parents, making sure I repair relationships after they have been ruptured. I will also give children time to process.'

'I will be more patient and understanding.'

'I will ensure the approach is consistent within our school, that we are all singing from the same hymn sheet.'

'Thank you for a containing course.'

Several headteachers have taken the time to write and share the initial impact of the training.

Thanks for a wonderful course yesterday. I was certainly glad to have been yesterday as I was meeting with a recently bereaved family this morning. It was quite an interesting situation as, when I'd asked some class staff to come along and meet up with the parents, another professional asked if the meeting could be delayed until the class staff had given her feedback on the work of the class. I found myself using parts of the model to explain why we needed to respond to the parents' needs first and then have the meeting with the staff.

Following discussion on containment, this school decided to use photographs of parents to help to contain the new Primary 1 children (four to five year olds) starting school.

I'd just like to say thank you very much for our training on Monday. The staff have all said how much they enjoyed it. I have noticed many of them addressing children in a different way, and some have already done their homework! The photo of the family in P1 has had an immediate impact too. One teary wee one was delighted to have his picture and carried it around all day. They are all on their desks. I think we will Velcro them down so that they can lift them if they want. Also we have allowed teddies or comforters in - something we would never have done without the training. This has helped the P1s to settle. The staff are also considering their expectations of pupils and whether they are really fair.

What a positive difference your training has had on the experiences of the children in our school and the ethos in our staff. We are all looking forward to the follow-up session.

It is clear from this evidence that the Solihull Approach has relevance and great benefit for school staff.

There was lots of learning from our early delivery to the primary schools. We held a trainers evaluation meeting in April 2017, when we discussed what has worked well and what we could improve or change.

What worked well?

The facilitators felt in general very positive about their experience. There was particular emphasis on the benefit of delivering the section on brain development. They also made the point that the training is best delivered when the environment of the school is right, i.e. when the school have completed the nurture evaluation and are in the right place with a good ethos to take it forward. They commented that it is also useful when the facilitators are from different backgrounds; this encourages networking, learning from each other and can enhance the experience of the participants. However, it works best when one facilitator has an education background, as they can share personal and relevant examples of the Solihull Approach in practice.

There was recognition of the importance of the senior leadership team in the school attending, as their role is crucial in taking the Solihull Approach forward within the school.

What could improve?

We recognised that some of the power point slides refer to SEAL, the English emotional learning framework. Although Scotland has a similar approach to helping children and young people develop emotionally, the language and framework is different. We change this to refer to the Scottish framework 'Getting it Right for Every Child'[3] and the 'Curriculum for Excellence'[4] to give local context.

As previously mentioned, it was recognised that the training experience is not as effective when delivered to more than one school team. The numbers can be too large, creating more of a 'lecture type' session and inhibiting the valuable discussions and reflection that is needed to think about the theory in practice.

We found it difficult to secure dates and times for the follow up session. We have now easily addressed this and changed the pre-training process by asking the headteacher to identify both dates before the training. Staff engagement in the follow up sessions have been variable; this could be due to the time of day they tend to be (usually 3.15-4.30pm). Staff are tired following a busy day and on some occasions the follow up day is too long after the initial full day training. We have addressed this by encouraging the schools to identify the dates as soon after the initial full day as possible. However, this is not always easy to secure due to other commitments that the school has. It is recognised that schools have many demands on them with new initiatives being introduced, each with high importance! There is however, not enough time at this session to fully explore all the aspects on the programme; we are now looking at a programme to further support schools in being reflective about how they are applying the principles of the Solihull Approach on an ongoing basis.

There was much discussion about the model of delivery and the consensus of opinion was that the multi-agency 2 Day Foundation training gives participants a better experience as they can network with and learn from colleagues from other services. There is however value in schools training all their staff at the same time; this allows discussion on how it can be embedded into daily practice and allows change and improvement to be implemented more quickly.

Due to the number of different 'nurture' initiatives currently being encouraged in NLC, we felt it important to show how they all link. We now describe the Solihull Approach training programme as being a base layer, a foundation for other programmes e.g. Video Interaction Guidance, Five to Thrive.

We also recognised that our secondary sector colleagues would benefit and applied for funding through Scottish Attainment Challenge funding to extend the programme from the primary sector to include the secondary sector. This was successful and a new, ongoing training programme for secondary schools began in March 2018. We used our learning from the initial training for primary schools to inform how we deliver the training for secondary schools and held a consultation event for senior leadership staff in secondary schools in December 2017 about the best delivery model for their sector. The new programme for secondaries was based on their feedback and our prior learning.

The model we are currently testing is that we are providing an ongoing programme for all secondary schools in NLC. The training consists of a two day training programme that individual staff can access. Schools have been placed into clusters of four to five schools. Each cluster can nominate two to three staff from their school and one colleague from a partner service. The aim is to maintain a multi-agency attendance. The training sessions are therefore not too large, with a maximum number between 14 to 16 participants, thereby encouraging discussion in a similar way to the 2 Day Foundation training model. Headteachers were asked to send staff who already have 'nurturing' approaches to their work; this was to capitalise on the early adopters with the hope that they will take positive messages back to colleagues! We are hopeful that we can also offer training for school departments (faculties). Some of our schools arrange internal cover for whole departments to attend training together. This is a model we are hoping to test imminently August 2018 and means we do not have to cram training into the in-service training days.

Participants attending the training each receive the 'Understanding your pupil's behaviour' Supporting Information Booklet. Each school receives the School Years Resource Pack and a copy of the 'Course for Young People; Understanding yourself and parenting' manual which enables Solihull Approach trained staff to deliver a nine session course to pupils.

We have made a few minor adaptations to the secondary sector training. Instead of the section on barriers and enablers that we cover on Day two of the 2 Day Foundation course, we have introduced a SWOT analysis (strengths, weaknesses, opportunities and threats). This allows participants to think of the challenges and opportunities for not only their personal use of the Solihull Approach in school, but also from an organisational perspective. We aim to share this information with the headteachers of our secondary schools to enable them to plan how best to embed the Solihull Approach in practice within their secondary school.

Feedback

The evaluations of the secondary training to date show that participants feel that the course is highly relevant to their role and that they intend to use what they have learned in their work at school. One of the participants said that their school should tear up their 'Managing Behaviour' policy as they need 500 different ones; one for each child! Some of the other comments include:

'I have learned about awareness, observation, understanding and looking at the bigger picture.'

'I will spread the word and start to drip feed all the concepts and practices amongst staff as well as use it myself.'

'It was great to hear other people's point of view and ideas of the course. There was a good spread of experience. The training was delivered excellently.'

'I will be more aware of the behaviours that are being displayed and also changing my interactions.'

'Excellent training, very useful and extremely relevant.'

'I have loved this training, it makes so much sense and I have had lightbulb moments. I have recommended this to colleagues.'

'I will think....there is a reason for behaviour displayed.'

As previously mentioned, we are currently delivering the training to staff that are mostly in a pupil support role in the school and already have nurturing practices. Some of them have indicated that some colleagues may find aspects of the Solihull Approach (namely responses to behaviour) more challenging to their own practice. We, as facilitators, will take this into consideration as we progress through the training programme and have already experienced situations where the concepts of the Solihull Approach have resulted in professional discourse. The response of course is...containment!

A trainer's experience

It is not only the participants who benefit. As trainers, we have learned lots from delivering the courses.

I have learned a lot to take back to my own setting and enhance my own practice where I am headteacher. I find the training very interesting as no two groups are ever the same. I am gaining confidence in handling people who have very different views from myself, an example of this being the person who told me that she disagreed with my statement that no parent ever sets out to be a bad parent, she said she thought some parents had a baby to get benefits. I was able to put my side across and hoped that I could win her round over the time I was working with her. (Not sure I did... although she asked me at the end if the training was being rolled out to all schools!) Cheryl talks about winning hearts and minds and that's exactly what we try to do. We cannot win them all.

126   *Cheryl Valentine*

I find the training exhausting, but this may because I am passionate about it and the impact it can have on professional and personal development. I tell participants that they will find it will change their professional and personal relationships! Sharing stories of your children is also demanding mentally. We take these children home in our hearts and it is mentally tasking discussing them, albeit anonymously. I tell the group about my background in schools and our recent HMIe report. This helps set my authenticity as a trainer.

I ask teachers to think about their reputation in the school community, what will people say about them in years to come? Were they soft? Were they effective teachers? Did they care about the children in their care?

I often share the story of 'Oscar' following the work on brain development. I use post-it notes and Maslow's hierarchy of needs. I then ask participants to name things a parent does to ensure the child's needs are met under each of the headings. I then ask them to place them on a wall like bricks. I share the story of Oscar whose needs are not met fully and I rip each post-it in half or toss it away completely. At the end we discuss this child's 'firm foundations' – or lack of them! We discuss how this child will fare alongside the others in P1. This activity is based on the work of Jenny Nock. I then talk about the idea of the child who seems to be 'three days late' as James Docherty described himself on starting school. He was the child of an alcoholic mother and abusive father.

The idea that a child has no control over its brain development is important to stress to participants. See the child not the behaviour. Children are showing distressed behaviour not bad behaviour.

In the session on containment I give examples of how we are containing children, staff and parents every day. I share the idea that we have changed our handling of meetings with parents to make them much more containing experiences. This includes our transition events. Sally Solihull and the balls is a very powerful way of explaining containment and it was fascinating on a secondary training session when a young female teacher was cradling the doll and soothing it while we explained the tasks. When the balls were placed on her the rocking stopped. She was unaware of this!

In the secondary sessions we have used a child and a text book and the balls – this is again a powerful way of showing how a child can be full up.'

Mary Cruickshank, Headteacher and Solihull Approach trainer.

Teaching the Solihull Approach to pupils

Many schools have introduced their own initiatives as a result of attending the training. This headteacher describes how she has used some of the Solihull Approach theory and delivered it to her Primary 7 pupils (ten to 11 year olds).

I have taken my P7 through the programme for the past two years. I brought a parent of a P7 pupil in to help me plan the programme. I told her if she wasn't happy with any aspect we would take it out. She did not ask for any part to be removed!

The programme sat within a focus on health and wellbeing and included our God's Loving Plan sex education unit.

We also had soup and scone making lessons and hygiene sessions including a hairdresser coming in and washing hair and a beautician who did manicures.

Brain development: the children were fascinated by this, they watched the Brave New World DVD[5] and were mature in their attitude throughout.

They were very engaged by the slides about both baby and teenage brains. This session sparked a lot of discussion and children were going home and speaking to their parents about it.

A child came to me at the end, I asked if he was okay, he told me his mum was an alcoholic and he wondered if he was like the child in the slide. I was able to reassure him that he was such a lovely child that it was obvious that he had been nurtured and loved by his mum. This is something to think about when doing the training with kids. I would be very careful about which groups I was doing the training with.

The containment session I worked as a drama session giving the children scenarios where they were either the parent or the child. The children playing the part of the parents were hilarious and were able to imitate their parents to a 't'! They loved the drama part of this and were able to work through scenarios. They showed great empathy as parents and learned some strategies to use with their parents! They got the idea that containment was a tool they could use. I used the Sally Solihull doll the first year but didn't feel children got the idea of the containment aspect.

Reciprocity: this tied in well with the work above. The children enjoyed the discussions in this session and were fascinated by the dance of reciprocity. The section on rupture and repair was really useful and stimulated a lot of discussion about how we dealt with conflict in schools.

I didn't use the behaviour for learning session with the children.

The final part was a parent event. The children prepared soup and scones for the parents. They watched Brave New World and the children did a very simple PowerPoint presentation on what they had learned. Parents were very impressed with the work and because the children were presenting we had a decent turn out of parents.

Mary Cruikshank, Head Teacher.

One of our secondary schools decided to test the 'Adolescent Brain' workshop with parents... and include the young people! Two sessions were provided in March 2018. Here are the results:

128 *Cheryl Valentine*

The main questions were around three areas:

1. Can the teenage workshop for parents be delivered to parents and teenagers together?
2. Do parents gain a greater understanding of the teenage brain?
3. Do teenagers gain a greater understanding of the changes in their brain?

We predicted that the workshop could be adapted to enable teenagers to attend *with* their parents thereby increasing understanding of the teenage brain in both parents and their teenagers.

We collected evaluations at the end of each workshop; 19 parents/children attended the first group and 16 parents/children attended the second group.

In general, participants felt that the workshop was relevant for them, although the group with the slightly older children found it most relevant. This could be due to the fact that the older children were approximately 12 to 13 years old and the teenage changes had started!

The key learning identified by participants included understanding brain development and the impact on behaviour i.e. the difficulty in reading facial expressions, changes in sleep patterns, how to stay calm, understanding risk taking. One response noted 'it will get better!' When asked what changes they would make, the responses show a more attuned response from a parent's perspective. These included being more patient and understanding, arguing less and being more positive. The young people recorded that they would like to try some strategies to help them, e.g. 'get more sleep, turn off phones, turn off Xbox at night, tidy my room and it's OK to be ME!'. Additional comments include:

'I really found this very interesting.'

'The presentation was amazing!'

'I enjoyed the class, very informative.'

'Very enjoyable and informative, good to spend time with Eva and have fun.'

'Thought the presentation was terrific. I would put this on to all parents as part of the Transition Programme.'

'Great mixture of information and tasks.'

'It helps us teenagers understand what we are going through, thought it was great.'

'Try not to flip my lid as much as my teenagers.'

'Great workshop, enjoyed it very much. Highly recommend to other parents.'

'Although we know these things, it is really relevant and interesting to have it put clearly.'

'I found it really helpful.'

'A great approach, hopefully it will be presented to all staff.'

'Would be really useful for pupils – especially select/identified groups.'

'Very well presented, interactive and interesting, appreciated free link so can read further.'

'This should be part of first year enrolment for pupils and parents.'

'Good presentation and lots of useful knowledge.'

'Well presented and enjoyable.'

'Well delivered and timed course.'

'Very good and informative, thank you.'

'Interesting and informative.'

The facilitators noticed that the sessions appeared to be very well received by parents and teenagers, who engaged well. The second group had some P7 pupils, several of whom are not yet in the teenage phase, therefore some of the content on brain development was not thought to be as relevant. It was felt that the length and pace of the workshop was good and that the numbers attending was just right, because any more may inhibit engagement and discussion.

As a result of attending the workshop, several parents are going to access the online course for parents and six have signed up for the 10 week 'Understanding your child' parent group to be provided next term.

As a result of this initial test, the school plan to continue with another workshop in the new term.

Conclusion

It is evident that all of the Solihull Approach training undertaken gathers great momentum as the enthusiasm of the participants filters through to other colleagues. We are still only at the beginning of the training programme and I predict that Solihull Approach training will not be a passing fashion in education but will become a core approach adopted by all practitioners. Why? Because it works!!!

References

1. Scottish Government, Cabinet for Attainment and Skills (2015). *Scottish Attainment Challenge.* https://beta.gov.scot/policies/schools/pupil-attainment/

2. The Health Foundation. *Quality improvement made simple.* https://www.health.org.uk/sites/health/files/QualityImprovementMadeSimple.pdf

3. Scottish Government (2017). *Getting it right for every child.* https://www.gov.scot/Topics/People/Young-People/gettingitright

4. Scottish Government (2004). *Curriculum for excellence.* https://www.gov.scot/resource/doc/226155/0061245.pdf

5. *Brave New World.* In 'Baby it's You: the first three years' DVD. Available from www.solihullapproachparenting.com

18 Implementing the Solihull Approach in the Scottish Fire and Rescue Service

Cheryl Valentine

'What can Solihull Approach training offer to the Scottish Fire and Rescue Service?'

This is a question that I am asked on a regular basis by colleagues who know and use the Solihull Approach within a family based context. To be honest, if you had told me five years ago that I would be delivering Solihull Approach training to firefighters I would never have believed it...me...a head of a family learning centre in North Lanarkshire Council?!

This exciting journey began in 2015 in the locality of Cumbernauld, North Lanarkshire. At this time, I was on secondment to deliver a Solihull Approach multi-agency training programme for practitioners across North Lanarkshire. The council had been investing heavily in the Solihull Approach, providing training for a range of multi-agency professionals including health professionals, early years staff, teachers and community workers. Around the same time, one of our family learning centres in Cumbernauld (Kildrum) was working in partnership with the Scottish Fire and Rescue Service (SFRS) to promote home fire safety visits; a service offered free of charge where firefighters visit homes to assess for fire risk and offer advice, support and free smoke alarms. Through discussion between the very forward thinking station manager in Cumbernauld (Gordon McGuire) and the family learning centre staff, it was identified that Solihull Approach training may be beneficial for firefighters, not just when carrying out home fire safety visits, but in their general role when engaging with the public and responding to situations where people have experienced stress and/or trauma.

A new partnership between North Lanarkshire Council and the SFRS began with an initiative to 'test' if the Solihull Approach can benefit the SFRS. Five pilot 2 Day Foundation trainings were planned and delivered over the summer of 2015 to operational crews in Cumbernauld Fire Station. We used Quality Improvement methodology[1] to plan, review and measure the impact of the training.

The initial objective was:

> To increase fire service personnel's knowledge and understanding of a relational approach to support early intervention for families and promote community engagement with the service.

Implementing the Solihull Approach in the Scottish Fire and Rescue Service   131

Our aim was:

> By August 2015, all firefighters in Cumbernauld will have a greater understanding of the Solihull Approach and be able to link this to their role as a result of the Solihull 2 Day Foundation training.

Early discussions between the station manager and Solihull Approach facilitators predicted that firefighters will have mixed responses to the training; some may find it difficult to relate the Solihull Approach to their practice. We felt that containment and reciprocity would be the main theories that they would be able to link to their role. The station manager predicted that the Solihull Approach would validate current community engagement policies and link to 'Getting it Right for Every Child'[2] and Children and Young People (Scotland) Act 2014[3]. In hindsight, this was a very innovative project and ahead of its time. A movement began across Scotland in 2017 promoting awareness of Adverse Childhood Experiences (ACEs)[4] to ensure services are trauma aware, but SFRS started this work 2 years earlier!

What happened when we ran the courses?

There was lots of learning from the very first course. It was quickly apparent that firefighters are very forthcoming with their thoughts and opinions as we had lots of very good and honest feedback!

The course was delivered in the fire station to 'on duty' crews which ensured that all firefighters within each group could attend. However, this did not come without some interruptions as the crew were operational! The station manager managed to release some of the crews from duty for the training by using other crews to cover, but this was not always possible. This meant that some of the courses were disrupted as the crew had to respond to call outs. This is all in a day's work for the fire crew. However, as facilitators we found it difficult to stop and start when they returned. On a positive note, the fire service are a very welcoming organisation and are well known for their generous hospitality; the participants and facilitators were very well fed!

Over the five courses delivered, 32 out of 47 firefighters completed the two day training; five firefighters attended Day 1 only. Not all firefighters were trained due to shift commitments and absences.

Most firefighters thought the training was interesting, especially those who are parents themselves. However, a few raised concerns that they were being asked to take on 'social work' roles. This is partly due to the climate within SFRS and the current review of their role; the fire service is promoting more of a community focus with multi agency engagement and as with any change, there can be some apprehension.

Certain aspects of the training were very well received, especially the section on brain development which the firefighters found not only very interesting, but also helpful when faced with some of the more vulnerable adults and when responding to adolescents in the community. Some of the firefighters felt this provided them with a greater understanding of some of the issues experienced by people in the community and this resulted in them being less judgemental. One firefighter wrote on his evaluation form that a key learning point of the training was 'junkies have stories to tell'. Although not politically correct language, this shows that the training has had an impact on the firefighter's attitude towards people in the community struggling with addiction issues.

When asked about the relevance of the training, 74% of firefighters felt that the training was quite useful to highly relevant, 26% felt it of little use to limited value (see graph below).

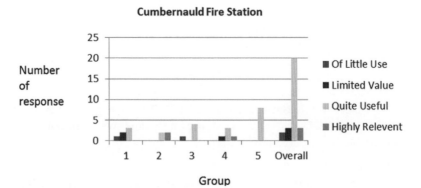

The comments and feedback from the initial group were taken on board and used to adapt training delivery for the following sessions. Some of these comments include:

> 'Relevant to the workplace, the community and domestically.'

> 'Course was well presented, it will benefit most firefighters in general life and should benefit all in the workplace when dealing with people at incidents; PDIR and HFSV.'

We learned that better pre attendance information was required and would give a greater understanding of the training and help alleviate some of the concerns and miscomprehension about the training. Some slides on how the Solihull Approach links to Scottish policy framework were added to the beginning of Day 1 to give relevance and context. This resulted in firefighters being more open to engage from the start of the training programme.

Another key learning point was that the original training programme focuses primarily on the relationship and interactions between parent/adult and child. This emphasis made it less relevant to SFRS and was altered slightly to include interactions in general between two people, using relevant examples from firefighters practice i.e. their engagement with the public. One participant wrote:

> 'Well presented training, Day 1 training could incorporate more examples of adult/adult interaction relevant to fire service roles.'

In discussion with Dr Hazel Douglas, some of the activities were adapted in response to the feedback on evaluation forms and verbal responses, for example, the 'Conor' DVD was replaced with a more relevant film outlining the impact of ACEs. We also adapted the observation activity that participants are asked to do between Day 1 and Day 2 to ask them to relate containment and reciprocity to their role at work. Here is one example that a firefighter reported on Day 2.

Implementing the Solihull Approach in the Scottish Fire and Rescue Service   133

I was to visit a young firesetter who had thrown a firework in Motherwell Town Centre, injuring a young girl.

I arrived at the house and was greeted by the young boy's parents, who had separated at the time.

They continued to talk over each other as the young boy sat between them, blaming this blaming that. I never really listened to what they were saying as I was there for the young boy and for his benefit. So I just butted in and asked the young boy `so how do you feel about it all?' He looked surprised and startled as if 'is someone actually interested in what I think?'

The parents then became silent as the young boy answered me saying: 'I feel terrible about what I done, was very silly of me to do that.' I then explained all the consequences of what could have happened through to the girl being permanently disfigured and him having a criminal record. The young boy then opened up. I am thinking he is not usually asked for an opinion, just told what to do or say and not listened to.

The Solihull training gave me the confidence to talk to that young boy and make him feel important, letting him express how he feels, it wasn't about what his parents thought, it was about him and his feelings.

David Jackson, Crew Manager.

Overall the feedback from the firefighters who attended the training stated that the Solihull Approach is relevant and useful for certain aspects of the firefighter role. The evaluations show that as we as facilitators adapted and improved each of the five courses in response to comments and suggestions, there was greater identification with the firefighter role. These included: home fire safety visits; PDIR (Post Determined Incident Response, that is, responding to the public following significant incidents such as a house fire); school visits; and trauma care at accidents. Community safety advocates felt it was useful to relate the approach to their general interactions with youth in the community and when supporting young firesetters. In general, firefighters felt that they would respond with more compassion, care and understanding when responding to traumatised people at incidents; being more aware of aggression as a reaction to stress and recognising the importance of containment.

During the training, the facilitators raised the issue of the firefighters' emotional wellbeing, especially after responding to a traumatic incident where there was serious injury or loss of life. Whilst it was acknowledged that there is emotional support and counselling available within SFRS, there was lots of discussion about how the firefighters tend to support each other to recover. The stick diagrams used to show when parents and practitioners feel emotionally 'full' proved particularly useful to give the visual example of how the parallel process of containment can work within SFRS. There were also lots of jokes about how they need to cuddle each other more!

The training had an additional positive impact that had not been predicted. Firefighters expressed more confidence to respond to concerns regarding child and adult protection.

134   Cheryl Valentine

This had previously been a concern as some firefighters felt uncomfortable in making a referral or did not feel it was part of their responsibility. One firefighter wrote that the training provided him with:

'...more confidence to justify adult and child referrals.'

Through the presentation on 'Getting it Right for Every Child' and the course content on the emotional impact of stress and neglect on children, the firefighters understood more about their responsibility to pass on concerns and showed a greater understanding of vulnerable individuals in the community. However, concerns were raised from several of the groups regarding the lack of feedback from partner agencies (mostly social work) after a referral for a child or vulnerable adult had been made. The firefighters described this as 'unfinished business' with no closure although this does appear to be improving.

Another area identified as needing better planning and support is the fire service presentations and visits made to schools. The firefighters felt that they are often not well planned and the resources and films used are not always appropriate, that is, the same video is used for upper secondary pupils as for younger primary pupils. This has been identified as an area for improvement.

It is apparent that firefighters use containment and reciprocity regularly in their work, but did not name or recognise this prior to the training. The overall impact on individual firefighters has been significant. Many of them have noted how they can use the approach in practice:

'I will use the training when dealing with children and adults at both incidents and visits/presentations.'

'I will endeavour to look at the bigger picture at incidents and home fire safety visits regarding the welfare of both kids and adults.'

'I will spend more time on observation in different circumstances, listen more.'

'I will have more compassion when dealing with vulnerable members of the community.'

'It will help me serve the community better.'

'I will be more aware of others needs and feelings.'

What happened next?

As a result of the success of the five pilot courses, it was agreed to present the results to the fire service area management team where there was discussion on how to scale up the training programme, including training firefighters to deliver the training to their colleagues. In addition, the station manager recognised that whilst we provided training for SFRS personnel on the practical elements of their job, such as home fire safety visits, there was potentially a gap that the Solihull Approach could fill to ensure that firefighters had the appropriate 'soft skills' to provide an appropriate range of responses to the complex needs of service users. Here is an extract of his experience of the Solihull Approach:

Implementing the Solihull Approach in the Scottish Fire and Rescue Service 135

The Scottish Fire and Rescue Service continues to evolve but our corporate vision of 'Working together for a safer Scotland' won't change. By working collaboratively to deliver Solihull to our operational firefighters and specialist Community Action Team staff we have taken massive strides to achieve that goal. Our children are our future and if only one intervention or emotional attachment results in a positive outcome then the results can grow exponentially.

We know we can't deliver alone. We can help in small ways but we need effective tools to do so and we need the support network behind us. That's what this initiative has brought. There are other activities the service is involved in across the country and every one adds a small piece of the jigsaw. We may not see tangible results for a generation but we needed to start somewhere.

I try to bring the Solihull Approach to bear in all my working and personal life whether it's supporting my three sons and my family, working with vulnerable persons or dealing with the effects on my firefighters of a traumatic incident.

I believe the SFRS is in a unique position in society to impact internally and externally. We are still a highly valued service which people reach out to in their time of need. I sincerely hope I never need to apply any of these skills ever again, but I know that if I do, then I am equipped to do so thanks to this body of work.

Gordon McGuire, Station Manager.

At this stage, there was an increasing interest in the Solihull Approach in the SFRS. In support of this work, and due to the positive results from initial testing, the SFRS youth engagement officer (Alistair Macintosh) became interested in how the training could be extended to other sections of the service. Here is his experience of the Solihull Approach:

Hopefully not sounding too evangelical, but the Solihull Approach training opened a window to a whole new world for me and way of viewing that world. I have been involved in work with young people for over 30 years and it changed the way that I engage not just with young people but colleagues and family.

Previously I was 'Joy' from the film 'Inside Out'. If I came across someone who was distressed I would, with the best of intentions, try and cheer them up to divert their thinking or worse would avoid contact with them thinking that they would 'appreciate the space'. I now understand the importance of supporting someone to contain their emotions and help them to self-regulate and also the importance of reciprocity to build bonds with people and help explore their feelings and the influence that these two simple steps can have on future behaviour. It has helped me put a context on Adverse Childhood Experiences and the importance of attachment not just in early years but throughout the life cycle.

Now that I understand the process and how my feelings can impact on it I am able to manage my own behaviour which has made me a better youth worker, colleague and father and consequently improving my own mental health and stress levels. I have gone on to develop my understanding further and have become a Solihull Approach trainer, helping pass the skills, knowledge and understanding on to Fire and Rescue personnel across Scotland.

Alistair Macintosh, Youth Engagement Officer.

Alistair was able to quickly see the benefit of delivering Solihull Approach training to prevention and protection personnel in the fire service, including community safety advocates and community firefighters. He predicted that this would give them the skills to effectively engage with members of the public. It was agreed to use the learning from the pilots in Cumbernauld to develop and deliver two further national pilots to 'prevention and protection' personnel.

The national pilot courses were delivered at the National Training Centre in Cambuslang and the training facility in Perth. Over the two courses 21 personnel attended, including watch managers, community firefighters and community safety advocates. Of those attending, all (100%) rated it either highly relevant (94%) or relevant (6%) to their work; this is an increase on the previous courses delivered. When facilitating these courses, it was evident that these participants could more easily relate the Solihull Approach to their role. This is partly due to the fact that they work more with individual people and respond to referrals from other services.

Additional comments made by prevention and protection participants supported the premise that this training should be extended nationally and include all community roles within the wider fire service. Comments included:

'The training was very well delivered...I think this training should be mandatory and delivered early to CFF's/CSA new in post. Thank you!'

'A fantastic course that will benefit all in the Fire Service if it is rolled out nationally.'

'Will use Solihull in all my duties with my job but also to give support to colleagues.'

'This course provided skills/behaviours every day. Often I feel after training I struggle to use it daily. This has provided me with skills to use in both life/work.'

'A very worthwhile course that sits well within my role.'

'It has made me look back at situations good and bad and now I can improve for the future.'

'Absolutely loved the course. Got so much from it.'

'Excellent course with good input from trainer...good to see that I'm doing the correct techniques when engaging with people.'

A key finding of both pilots was that this training was relevant to all aspects of engagement and not restricted to engaging with young people. SFRS personnel also identified that it would enable them to better support each other when working with complex and emotive issues. Facilitators became more skilled in delivering the course, collecting more relevant examples of using the Solihull Approach in the SFRS at each course and also as our understanding and knowledge about SFRS as an organisation increased.

Following the success of the pilots in North Lanarkshire, the local senior officer was successful in a funding bid to the Early Years Collaborative to create a temporary post for up to 12 months to deliver more training, both locally in North Lanarkshire for operational firefighters and nationally for prevention and protection personnel. A seconded Community Safety Advocate (Lynn Sweeney) is now in post and is enthusiastically developing and delivering the training programme across Scotland. Lynn's passion for the Solihull Approach is evident in her work.

Having spent 4 years as a Community Safety Advocate within Scottish Fire and Rescue I have seen too many families who have been affected by domestic violence, drug, alcohol misuse and poverty. Every time I go into a home either to carry out a safety check or to work with other agencies to try and make the family safe from fire, I always felt that we were only putting a plaster over the problem not getting to the root. I could see that the issues were being passed onto each generation and no matter how many times we went to back to visit things always seemed to stay the same.

Every Thursday I would go into the prison to speak to the new inmates and see the same faces back time and time again. The men would receive training, support and be given hope, but when they were back outside nothing had changed for them and they would end up back in the same place. Although the Solihull Approach didn't solve the problem, it helped me to look past the behaviour, the conditions in which they lived and see that unless we support families and assist with the parenting skills then the cycle would never be broken. How do you know how to support your child emotionally if you have never been shown this from your parents? How do you help to be a buffer for your child at times of adversity when you are dealing with your own issues and have no one to contain you?

I also recognised through Solihull that behaviour is a form of communication and I need to ask more questions. I have learned to wonder more. I wonder what happened? I wonder what that behaviour is telling me? Solihull has given me more patience, made me think and ask more questions. It has helped me to understand that our young firesetters or children classed as having antisocial behaviour are telling me something and my role is to try and find out what that is.

Solihull has also taught me that I also need to be contained as well as my colleagues. We cannot be effective in our role if we are 'filled up'. We need to deal with our own needs emotionally before we can support our clients. In my role it is so easy to become over whelmed by the daily problems we face. Seeing children desperate for attention and parents struggling to get through each day never mind trying to cope with what they feel or been told is a demanding or bad child.

Solihull has also taught me that I can't solve all the problems and that I don't have the capacity to do that, but if I can provide that family with some head space and relieve the pressure to help them think more clearly, then it's a starting point.

So often we come away from a training day and think that was interesting, but how do I take this forward? How do I use it in my day to day life? Solihull was different; I could see where it fitted in on a daily basis, not just at work, but in my home life. It was an approach I could use and the more I saw it working the more confident I became. It did make me think and question my own parenting skills, but I always remember the phrase 'good enough is good enough.' I don't believe anyone sets out to be a bad parent. We do the best with what we know; if I can enhance that love with more knowledge and supporting words then I can make a difference.

Solihull is for everyone no matter their role, it gives you the tools to support both yourself, your family and colleagues and this helps you to support your clients.

Lynn Sweeney, Seconded Solihull Approach Trainer.

This quotation from Lynn shows the significant impact that the Solihull approach has had on her practice: She is now sharing this experience on a national level across the SFRS in Scotland.

This is very exciting and innovative work; national delivery has been spread across the three service delivery areas, providing up to seventy training places. The SFRS are offering places on the training to key partners e.g. the Police. This is further supporting interagency understanding and partnership working.

As previously mentioned, Scotland is currently experiencing a 'movement' initiated by Dr Suzanne Zeedyk and the organisation 'Reattachment' to increase awareness of ACEs and the impact of early trauma on the developing brain. The film 'Resilience: the biology of stress and the science of hope' has been shown across localities and services to share an understanding of the impact of ACEs. Due to the success and positive reaction to the film, Lynn recognised that this could be a valuable introduction to the SFRS training programme, as it links to the concepts of the Solihull Approach. It is now being shown to SFRS personnel across Scotland prior to Solihull Approach training. Evaluations from these sessions show that the film is being well received and this will hopefully create a thirst for the Solihull Approach training! Some of the comments from SFRS personnel who have attended the film session include:

'Very useful should be rolled out to operational crews.'

'It was a good addition to the Solihull Approach.'

'Thank you very much for your awareness training session this morning; it really was excellent, thank you very much for inviting me along.'

'This is an area I am quite passionate about because, as an adopter, I see the consequences of ACEs every day in life.'

This initiative would not have been a success without the support of Gordon McGuire, station manager in Cumbernauld, and Alistair Macintosh, youth engagement officer. Their forward thinking vision and drive led us to this point. More recently, the passion and enthusiasm of Lynn Sweeney will ensure that the Solihull Approach is firmly embedded in the practice of the SFRS.

So, in answer to the initial question...'What can Solihull Approach training offer to the Scottish Fire and Rescue Service?'

In short...lots! Here is a summary of what Solihull can offer and why it is relevant to the SFRS:

- Gives a theoretical framework to think about and respond to trauma experienced by the public and firefighters
- Helps SFRS personnel understand the WHY... and gives help to know HOW to respond
- Helps SFRS personnel be less judgemental towards people in the community, thinking less about their circumstances as being a choice and more about them as a result of experiences
- It supports the changing role of the SFRS with a greater emphasis on prevention and support
- It helps to change attitudes and values, hearts and minds of SFRS personnel
- Enhances multi agency working by creating a common language and shared understanding
- The benefits of Solihull Approach evolve with practice and reflection.

Conclusion

For me, working with the SFRS has been a privilege and I have enjoyed every part of this incredible journey. It has been challenging and enlightening but also fun! I have learned much about the challenges and demands faced by SFRS staff. They are a crucial service and do lots more than fight fires! As a facilitator, I have learned to adapt delivery style and content to suit the specific requirements of the SFRS and reinforce that, although a firefighter or community safety advocate's intervention may be short, it can have a significant impact on the person they are working with. As a result of the project's success, we submitted an application to the Scottish Government for a Quality Improvement award for this work under the category of 'MOST INSPIRING OR INNOVATIVE PROJECT AWARD' and were delighted to be short listed as a runner up for Scotland. The SFRS are now fully committed to continue this work and have the capacity with their own Solihull Approach trainers to sustain and extend the approach in the future.

The poster below was created to share this work.

INVESTING IN NURTURING LIVES AND COMMUNITIES

Across North Lanarkshire using the Solihull Approach

+ AIM

Provide Solihull Approach training for Fire Fighters to increase their knowledge and understanding of a relational approach to support early intervention for families and promote engagement with the Fire Service.

+ WHAT WE DID:

July/August 2015 - **tested the Solihull Approach with Fire Fighters in Cumbernauld Fire station**
August/September 2016 - **adapted the 2 day foundation course to suit the needs of Fire Fighters**
January 2017 - **use learning to test with Police Scotland**

Total number of Fire fighters trained at 3 November 2016 : 51.

"The training was very well delivered, good pace and good mix of listening and exercises. I think this training should be mandatory and delivered early to CFF's/CSA new in post. Thank you!"

"Excellent course with good input from trainer and good input from students. Good to see that I'm doing the correct techniques when engaging with people."

RESULTS: Rating on relevance to their role

- 94% HIGHLY RELEVANT
- 6% QUITE USEFUL
- 0% LIMITED VALUE
- 0% LIMITED VALUE

"It has made me look back at situations good and bad and now I can improve for the future"

IMPACT: Key learning that will be used in practice following training

- 38% Use in all aspects of role
- 50% Understanding with fire setters, an HFSV, working with vulnerable groups
- 17% Be more reflective
- 5% To support colleagues
- 11% Shared language with other partners

KEY LEARNING GAINED ON THE TRAINING

 44% Child/brain development
 11% How to support change of behaviour
 27% Validates current practice
 50% Reciprocity/containment/behaviour management
 39% The importance of patience/listening/not judging

NEXT STEPS

2 FireFighters now trained as trainers; deliver the adapted Solihull Approach training to fire service staff involved with community engagement; supporting vulnerable members of the public, fire setter interventions etc.

References

1. The Health Foundation. *Quality improvement made simple.* https://www.health.org.uk/sites/health/files/QualityImprovementMadeSimple.pdf

2. Scottish Government (2017). *Getting it right for every child.* https://www.gov.scot/Topics/People/Young-People/gettingitright

3. Children and Young People (Scotland) Act 2014. http://www.legislation.gov.uk/asp/2014/8/contents/enacted

4. Felitti, V.J., Anda, R.F., Nordenberg, D., Williamson, D.F., Spitz, A.M., Koss, M.P. and Marks, J.S. (1998). Relationship of childhood abuse and household dysfunction to many of the leading causes of death in adults. *American Journal of Preventative Medicine,* 14(4): 245-258.

19 Social workers and the Solihull Approach

Sheina Rigg

Introduction

In my role in the social work learning and development department in Belfast Health and Social Care Trust, I became a Solihull Approach trainer in 2014, which was part of the implementation of an infant mental health strategy in the agency and in the region. I focused upon the Solihull Approach for my Masters dissertation (as the final module of the Queens University Belfast Applied Social Studies in strategy and leadership), examining it from a statutory family and childcare social work perspective to see if the initial positive evaluations received were enduring. In addition, I wanted to gauge if my own enthusiasm and learning had resonance with colleagues and management in my organisation. I could see where social work (being a 'magpie' profession) already used some of the theories underpinning the Approach. However, I embarked upon this study to analyse the enablers and barriers for social workers in their implementation of the Approach and to discover whether it was valued as part of an emerging infant mental health strategy in my agency.

Background

The Infant Mental Health Strategy for Northern Ireland (NI) states that it is essential that practitioners receive support to embed new learning in practice 'to ensure that investment has an impact on children and families'[1].

My study explored the enablers and barriers for social workers implementing the Solihull Approach into their practice, and what they required in order to maintain the implementation of the model in their work with families, which could also inform the Infant Mental Health Strategy within my agency.

The Solihull Approach is a practical integrated theoretical model. It brings together theories from psychoanalysis, child development and behaviourism to provide a framework in which to explore relationships between children and their parents/carers. It aims to practically support a range of professionals, for example, social workers, health visitors, psychologists, school nurses, midwives and education practitioners.

My objectives were to conduct a literature review and evaluate or audit the impact of the Solihull Approach on social workers trained in the Approach to gain their views. In addition I wanted to audit through a succinct survey[2] what social workers valued in the Solihull Approach, if they implemented it in their practice and, if so, what helped them to do so. I had found that the evaluations following the 2 Day Foundation training had been consistently positive and further evaluation after the four practice sessions delivered in NI equally, if not more, positive.

It is worth noting that in NI there has been a slightly different training strategy compared to elsewhere: following the 2 Day Foundation training, all practitioners were strongly encouraged to attend practice sessions which were of two hours duration once a month for four months. In these sessions Solihull Approach themes were revisited by the group members and case examples were used for discussion and to embed implementation.

Therefore, it was important to explore what social workers said they needed in order to maintain the implementation of this approach. To provide balance it was also necessary to explore barriers that they encountered, to explore if there was any element of the Solihull Approach that challenged their professional values, or that was not understood. Part of this objective was to discover if the structures of the hierarchical and procedural organisation made taking on new approaches difficult, (even if the individual is enthusiastic about it). Thus, barriers would be identified, whether organisational, professional or personal.

Context

Early intervention approaches have been discussed in social work research, Child Abuse Inquiries (CAI, UK) and Case Management Reviews (CMR, specific to NI)[3,4]. Northern Irish society is beginning to emerge from several decades of civil conflict (the 'Troubles') and there is an increasing amount of research highlighting the issues for children who have been traumatised, some perhaps through transgenerational experience of trauma, in those decades. This is linked to recognition of the child's first three years as being an exponential time of brain development, which, if supported by 'good enough' parenting[5] or caring, establishes the positive wellbeing of that child. This also has long-term implications for the whole of the child's society.

There is a growing body of neuroscience research concerning the brain development of the unborn and new born child and, it can be argued, 'we are the first generation to have this knowledge at our fingertips, we ignore it at our peril'[6]. The Solihull Approach introduces this neurological information to social workers, for some for the first time, and sets it beside familiar theory. It is, therefore, an approach at once familiar and brand new which has received very positive training evaluations from a profession that can be weary and wary. Exploring what is effective in interventions across the range of family and childcare services is a matter for ongoing debate and research.

Through the Solihull Approach, it is argued that a range of practitioners can develop a shared language, and the method of training offers an opportunity to reflect upon the new research emerging over the last 15 years in terms of infant development, and specifically brain development. Cognisant of the caseloads, pressures and frustrations of social work in a statutory agency bound by budget restraints and increasing pressures of austerity, the Solihull Approach may offer an opportunity to change mind sets and reclaim skills that have become submerged under heavy caseloads and paperwork, in particular observation and analysis skills of parent and child interactions.

The training method used was a cascade model and funding was provided by the Public Health Authority under the scope of the NI Infant Mental Health Strategy. Nursing and specifically health visiting was well established in their familiarity to, and use of, the Approach. Therefore the strategy targeted professions and agencies less familiar to the Solihull Approach training in Belfast Health and Social Care Trust and social work

144   Sheina Rigg

was a key discipline who had not availed of the training. The new aspect, for those of the group without psychology or health backgrounds, was the research on infant brain development which has been growing dramatically over the last 15 years, enhanced by the developments of MRI technology (magnetic resonance imaging). The familiar aspect of the Solihull Approach was the concept of containment, although the language was new to some. This concept reflects the skills that social workers use regularly and the values inherent to the profession of respect and empowerment. In addition, the second theoretical concept of reciprocity emanating from the field of child development[7,8] appeared to be encouraging the fundamental social work skills of observation (observing the reciprocity between carer and child). Skills that, at times, can be lost in the profession's bureaucracy and frantic statutory child protection role[9,10].

A range of complex issues are common to family and childcare social work so there was a need to explore how the Solihull Approach might support social workers in their interventions and see if it fitted well with their professional expertise. In addition, I wished to consider if it did inform and support practitioners and how the organisation maintained the knowledge gained, to improve practice and ultimately inform decisions and deliver positive outcomes for children.

Methodology

The methodology of the study was a systematic literature review followed by a survey. The survey consisted of ten questions sent to 60 social workers who had all completed training in the Solihull Approach since the beginning of the strategy three years ago. Therefore a 'census' approach[2] was used as opposed to any sampling, as the numbers were deemed manageable. The role, grade and team of the social workers varied and reflected the strategic selection by the infant mental health steering group in the agency. Therefore, not all services within the family and childcare programme were represented (e.g. family intervention teams and residential social workers had not availed of the training due to time pressures and particular constraining factors in these agency teams over the last three years). Those who had been trained were from Looked After Children's teams, Fostering and Adoption teams, Children with Disabilities teams, Child and Adolescent Mental Health Services and a few from Adult Services, who had been targeted due to their roles as 'champions' in the Think Family strategy. The response rate was 47% (n=28) and a thematic analysis was conducted. The number of years working as a qualified social worker varied by 39 years. Themes from more newly qualified social workers and those with many years of experience were analysed to see if there were significant differences in views of the Solihull Approach.

Literature review

Globally there is increasing awareness of the need for early intervention in mental health issues across the life span and recognition that children and adolescents with disrupted nurturing are one group who disproportionately experience mental health problems[11]. Infants and children throughout the world have a right to be protected and their development supported through the provision of appropriate services[12]. The ACE studies (Adverse Childhood Experiences)[13,14,15] originating in North America, highlight that the number of adverse issues a child experiences can be directly correlated to the mental and physical health of the adult into whom they develop. This emphasises that the moral imperative is to intervene early and effectively and that there is logic and cost saving factors in doing so. In addition, some economists argue that this is more viable than increasing welfare.

Understanding of resilience[16,17,18,19] informs the social work profession; how children can cope with war, terror and deprivation if supported and buffered by concerned and available caregivers[20]. The impact of trauma upon young children must be considered in a broader understanding of infant development, but needs setting in the relevant cultural context.

The vast range of literature on infant mental health, significantly developed and contributed to over the last 25 years through the developments of neuroscience and MRI technology, drew attention to some of the disconnect between the research and how social workers are using the evidence base to inform their interventions. The enquiries regarding children and young people who have died tend to dominate social work practice[3,21], creating reactive responses. Best practice with families where there is a toxic combination of issues, namely domestic violence, mental ill health and addiction, is always a debate between practitioners, families, academics, government and the public. The Munro Review[3,9] draws attention to the increasing bureaucracy with which social workers contend. She observes how this has deskilled the workforce, created organisational cultures that are not learning based but procedurally based.

Transgenerational issues are familiar to many social workers who have worked in any given area for a time. In a post conflict or post Friday Agreement[22] Northern Irish society, discussion ensues regarding children being impacted upon due to their parents' (or grandparents') experience of 'Troubles' related trauma[23] and their resulting mental ill health. Transgenerational trauma may undermine the key areas of healthy infant development namely, attachment, self-regulation and resilience[24,25].

There is evidence of correlation to violence-experienced children who may pass this on to their own children though adapted genes[25]. The study of epigenetics is used to explain why we are seeing traumatised children despite them having no direct experience of the trauma[24].

The ACE studies also acknowledge that emotional trauma, exposure to toxic stress, whether transposed to a NI 'Troubles' context or any other, impacts upon the mental and physical health of the growing child[15,26].

Leadership

When implementing new strategies there needs to be effective leadership and influence. Some new strategies are disseminated from government down to local level[27] and then incorporated into specific policy such as the NI Infant Mental Health Strategy. The implementation of any new approach (and arguably a change of mind set) requires leadership in the partnerships involved in order to achieve goals (e.g. the Infant Mental Health Group in Belfast) and achieve them together. Good leadership in social work is based upon understanding of theories of change and having the tools to facilitate the change and analyse its process.

146 Sheina Rigg

There are common traits in effective leaders e.g. enthusiasm[28] and authenticity[29] appear vital. In terms of establishing a 'movement', Douglas and her team appear to have modelled a transformational leadership[30] in the Solihull Approach. This leadership has needed to be developed in NI to engage a stressed and weary profession in a new approach such as the Solihull Approach. There are views that social work is becoming a more compliant profession[31,32,33] where there is little evidence of radicalisation[34], lobbying of government or resistance to issues such as austerity. In addition, some of the demoralisation of the profession has resulted in a lack of confidence and a rise in procedurally driven work, which is routine and dull[35]. Consequently, this can lead to 'loss of opportunities for the exercise of creativity, reflexivity and discretion in direct practice'[36]. There can be a view of social work as a 'technical exercise'. However, social workers need to 'engage with the complexity that is embedded in social work due to the complex nature of human beings'[37]. Social workers may feel disempowered and helpless when faced with chronic and challenging parenting issues, resulting in poorer outcomes for the children in such families.

Leadership of the implementation of an approach such as the Solihull Approach needs to be based upon a sound evidence base of quality research and then championed effectively with enthusiasm and energy. If it is about changing mindsets this needs to be carefully considered. An appreciative inquiry approach[38] has characteristics of validating practitioner experience and expertise and due to this there may be increased ease of implementation. A successful implementation of an approach will also be more effective if it is seen to work on a number of levels. This could range from the direct work with families and children with a range of needs and issues, but also apply to work in team and peer situations and in supervision and management approaches. However, it may also be important that the leadership of new strategies acknowledge the limitations of any given approach. Social work should be a reflective, critical and creative profession with opportunities for leadership in many positions, whether in strategic groups, teams, case management or in direct work with one family. Therefore an approach that supports these aspects of the profession is inevitably more easily implemented.

De-professionalisation of social workers/lack of confidence

An aspect of this study was whether the Solihull Approach influenced the organisation as well as the individual social worker. Social work operates in an increasingly bureaucratic system. Procedural compliance dominates[2] and a culture of learning[39] is seldom apparent. Each of the five Northern Irish Health and Social Care Trusts may be influenced by different approaches and devise different strategies in order to fulfil their function to support families and protect children, despite the small regional population (1.862 million, NISRA 2016) and their collective need to be accountable to the Department of Health. In terms of multi-disciplinary working, there is then a further hierarchy of the different professions involved, which is particularly apparent in child protection, especially in court, where there is a reported sense of the low status of social workers. As a result, there can be a lack of confidence and indeed at times a reluctance to accept the risk of decision making by family and childcare practitioners. Munro[40] states, 'following rules and being compliant can appear less risky than carrying the personal responsibility for exercising judgment'.

However, the exercise of containment, a key element of the Solihull Approach, can support the uncertainty and anxiety associated with decision making in a highly pressured and often anxiety-provoking child protection arena and court context[41].

The structure and dynamics of teams in social work are important and can be where learning, supporting and containing often happens, both in a collegiate manner and in the supervision relationship between team leader and social worker. Confidence and professional judgement can be facilitated by an organisation that supports reflective practice, where learning takes place. Resilient organisations with resilient staff is a parallel process to building resilience in children and using concepts such as containment and reciprocity very deliberately in the social work process and in social work supervision will be an effective way to become a more supportive and containing context for child protection social work'[41].

Containment of social workers working with child protection

Within the review of Child Abuse Inquiries there is reflected a need for containment and reciprocity in the supervisory relationship. Ferguson[42] describes the 'deep emotional impact of child protection work on workers and their capacities to protect children'. The neglected practitioner[43] can become unable to protect the children they are working with due to the lack of effective supervision. Effective supervision means a situation where there is some degree of emotional intelligence[44], containment and reciprocity, that is, attunement of a supervisor to a worker, in addition to case management procedures. The existence of containment and reciprocity in the supervisory relationship should result in workers that are more effective.

The emotional regulation that is required of social workers is sometimes called 'emotional labour'[45], reflecting the arduousness of their task. Howe[46] stresses that social work is 'emotional work of a high order' and thus social workers require sensitive and containing supervision which supports reflection. Horwath[43] describes the unhealthy relationship between a neglected practitioner and the neglectful parent who is not meeting their child's needs as a 'toxic duo'. This again draws parallels with the social worker mirroring the family chaos that can occur when they are working with long-term neglect. Supervision then is the place where social workers must acknowledge these issues, using whatever frameworks are useful (e.g. Graded Care Profile 2 (NSPCC 2016); UNOCINI; Child Assessment Framework) to bring to supervision where the analysis, reflection and the emotional 'labour' must happen. Northern Ireland continues to be one of the areas of the UK with the highest relative poverty and child poverty and these, combined with persistent issues of sectarianism, puts strain on resources and the mental health of the wider community, but most significantly, the children and young people[25]. The improved provision of 'early help'[3] can only serve to support the professional resilience of social workers in parallel with the resilience of the children they try to protect.

Findings from the survey

Responses to the ten question survey provided both quantitative and qualitative information. Significantly, the number of years of experience in social work of the respondents spanned 39 years. This lead me to consider if established social workers

148   *Sheina Rigg*

would be more cynical, sceptical or weary of change and if their approach to the Solihull Approach might be more negative compared to those who responded who had three or four years' experience. However, overwhelmingly, it was noted that most respondents had embraced the model, seeing it as both stimulating and valuable, but also validating their best practice. Some also stated it was effective in developing their confidence as practitioners and ensured their responses and interventions were more evidence based and child centred.

Responses indicated that brain development was the most informative and useful aspect of the training and next were the key approaches of containment and reciprocity. The response to brain development research mirrored the feedback in training days and practice sessions that this was the most exciting and engaging aspect, much of which was quite new to the respondents and it was commented upon as being directly relevant to their work and their practice.

Containment was referred to frequently and the managerial role was particularly highlighted by some, either in how they were supervised or in their supervision of teams if they were team leaders or in senior management. Some social workers talked about 'containing' both parents and children; another specifically referred to containment of foster carers, and another, as a manager, talked of 'containing' teams of workers through supervision and in other aspects of management. Many of the social workers thus portrayed the implementation of the approach in their practice and its effectiveness on a number of levels.

One question regarding any changes in practice as a result of training and implementation of the Solihull Approach, resulted in some responses which might have been slightly defensive (on reflection it was a weighted question). However, others said that self-observed changes were in terms of increased confidence; they felt validated in their practice and their skills by the Approach. A practical response was that they felt more confident in case discussions with colleagues.

A range of skills were noted as being developed or changed as a result of the Solihull Approach training and information. Many of these were directly connected to the themes of the Approach e.g. some noted that their ability to contain others had developed and that they were conscious of doing this deliberately and skilfully and this took place not only in relation to parents, foster carers, but also with colleagues and in supervision with staff. In addition, increased knowledge of the brain development of both infants and adolescents enabled them to support parents/carers to develop insight into the meaning of their child or foster child's behaviour. Some stated that their own practice with adolescents improved as they gained insight and understanding. This increased empathy for the young people they worked with and they were then able to support carers of adolescents to be more empathic and insightful.

In terms of direct application to their work, the social workers made a range of comments. One said:

> I am able to use the Solihull Approach to support practice development in residential childcare, containment in particular is applied in reflective practice sessions.

Another commented:

> I am currently working with parents to help enhance their parenting skills…the concept of containment has been critical in helping me support parents. Strengthening the parents' skills and sharing with them strategies and approaches that they can use to support their children has been significantly informed by the Solihull Approach.

Supervision was specifically asked about, relating to the literature regarding the emotional 'labour' of social workers. The responses indicated that the concepts of reciprocity and containment appeared directly relevant to the supervisory relationship. However, I questioned if the Solihull Approach also had a role in informing the case management and decision making of social workers in the supervision context to advise planning, interventions and analysis. The majority of the respondents cited it as applicable to supervision, some saying they would specifically use their newly developed understanding of brain development in supervision.

Reciprocity, the second underpinning theory of the Solihull Approach, was specifically referenced e.g. one worker talked specifically about parent and baby interaction. This would imply that the detailed description of reciprocity and in particular Brazelton's studies[47] would give social workers particular insight into what they were observing in the infant parent dyad and this would inform their assessment. Four indicated that the whole approach was very useful to all their work.

Questions regarding barriers and enablers to the implementation of the Solihull Approach provoked a range of responses with 'personal interest' dominating; where social workers were self-motivated to develop professionally in order to learn and understand more effectively the families they were working with. However, the specific language of the Approach was commented upon as effective in formal professional settings and writing i.e. in court and case conference reports and in professional discussion. Others found the Approach had greatly enhanced their understanding of the therapeutic consultation sessions they accessed from psychology and principal practitioners. The practice sessions, of themselves, were seen to be very effective and enabling (64% of responses) and this is of note as they only appear to be facilitated in NI. This method of embedding learning was appreciated by the majority, although acknowledged as quite difficult to attend. However, the time element (strictly of two hours duration) was effective and the discussion and presentation of cases was interesting and grounded, which for many facilitated deeper understanding of the model.

The main barriers identified to implementation of the Solihull Approach was, as always, the lack of time to read, reflect or discuss. Others said ongoing practice sessions would be effective as they felt their learning was at the beginning stage. A need for the Approach to be collegiate was noted:

> I need all of my teams to complete the training and have regular Solihull Approach support groups.

Another commented:

> I need it to become common coinage in social work language so as to be able to communicate with my colleagues in the field of family and childcare.

Discussion

The professionals who responded to the survey were predominantly well established in their profession. I reflected that this could have had different ramifications e.g. positively in terms of the social worker's level of confidence and their approach to their work, or negatively in their increased potential to be 'burned out', cynical or exhausted. However, none of the feedback to the surveys conveyed a negative attitude toward the Solihull Approach. Training for experienced social workers may be required to be particularly well considered, with evidence based research, and a 'sound causal theory'[48]. In addition and integral to the training structure, there were opportunities for the Approach to be related to their years of experience. Of course it needs to be said that years of experience does not always equate to better practice. The responses indicate that the Approach 'made sense' to the social workers in terms of the whole approach being effective. The Approach appeared to validate their existing practice[48], but there was also reported a significant development of either knowledge, skills or values of these social workers. The majority of responses were very positive about the Solihull Approach content, delivery and the materials provided and the 'personal interest' that most indicated, would be related to this. Indeed the format of the training with its use of videos and the discussion based practice sessions encouraged and insisted upon participation, which is consistently cited as a more engaging, exciting and inspiring method for most practitioners.

Social workers are professional and skilled practitioners and there was a response to the Approach which indicated that it developed their reflective practice, was challenging and yet fitted well with existing skills, knowledge and values. Personal interest was mentioned as an enabler by almost all of the social workers, by far the most dominating enabler. Considering the significant years of experience of the respondents, this may indicate that experienced practitioners may derive more from an approach that has elements of newness (i.e. the neuroscience of infant development) but does not undermine their established practice. In addition, experience may bring recognition that there is a need for change and the Solihull Approach brings change that is manageable; it is not about paperwork or requiring technical expertise, it is about an approach. The Appreciative Inquiry[49] theory of change may describe well what is occurring in the implementation of Solihull Approach and its apparent effectiveness.

With established practitioners, the leadership needs to be sensitively engaged. 'Managerial leaders must verify and persuasively communicate the need for change'[48] and the practice sessions require leadership from the trainers/facilitators. The sessions became a form of group supervision which was not managerial[10,43], but consisted of peer support and peer sharing. For example, in the practice sessions I was facilitating, one social worker, more newly qualified than others in the group, greatly appreciated the chance to talk to a social worker about her case study. Others had opportunities to vent some frustrations about workloads in the practice sessions; this had to be managed carefully by the facilitators but generally was managed by the group themselves as a way of containing and ensuring that the practice sessions kept their focus. Some used the peer support to deeply analyse casework and consult with others regarding a child's development.

By the reported high attendance at practice sessions, it was indicated that the format was effective and that practitioners found it manageable to integrate a two hour monthly

Social workers and the Solihull Approach   151

practice session into their work schedules, as lack of time was stated to be the biggest barrier to implementation and maintenance of the Solihull Approach in practice. Practice sessions also served to maintain the momentum[50] initiated by the 2 Day Foundation training that is generally required to fully establish a new approach. However many respondents clearly stated that something similar to practice sessions was needed, probably for the long term. Effective leadership was originally modelled by the Solihull Approach team (in Solihull, England), as they recognised the sensitivity of introducing new approaches and the need for a strategy that supports embedding of the approach in an organisation. Indeed it reflected the theories of effective change, where there is a clear plan of implementation facilitated by a leader who understands the process, but is also authentic and enthused about it[29].

The format of two hour practice sessions always adhered to was validated by the high attendance rate. They were 'contained' by the time and by the assurance it would not run over, a modelling of containment by the leaders of the sessions that the practitioners appeared to appreciate. The format of the practice session as a practical forum which provided an opportunity to link theory to practice and to specific cases, was appreciated, as the responses indicated. Moving theory into practice validated their skills, knowledge and experiences, but provided new terms and language. The responses indicated that there was further and extensive learning gleaned from the practice sessions in particular. For some, this was where more of the actual learning took place, as they may have found the full days of training long and challenging to absorb completely.

Conclusion

Despite the limitations of the study and some flaws in the survey questions, the responses of the social workers did reflect much of what has been discussed through the themes in the research: enablers can be found in the structure of how a new approach is delivered or facilitated to the workforce. In addition, the leadership role of facilitators needs to be carefully executed so that a range of practitioners can embrace the approach. The years of experience of those who responded to the survey was very significant and therefore a balance between new research, information and language, coupled with an approach that validated practice wisdom, appeared to be of most effect. The neuroscientific explanation for behaviour needs to be reflected upon and balanced with the expertise that emanates from social work. It does provide fascinating new discoveries, for example, a 'Brave New World'[51], the name of the video used in the Foundation Training is apt, as the research can intrigue, fascinate and inspire professionals who may have been in practice for many years.

For the Solihull Approach to be embedded in the modern organisational structure there needs to be a range of enablers as reflected in the research and in the social workers' responses to the survey. For the Approach to be integral to practice, the supervisory relationship should be supportive on two levels; both a conscious use of the theory between supervisor and supervisee to do the emotional labour required of the profession, but also in its use as a framework for planning and decision making regarding the families on a social work caseload. Collegiate support from peers is cited as important and there is a call for this approach to be widespread across the family and childcare programmes. Trainers

152 Sheina Rigg

need to lead in an effective and responsive manner and consider how they support and respond to the time constraints of a busy workforce. Senior management needs to enable implementation of new approaches with a clear strategic response.

There is a need for containment of social workers, who are often working under pressure and making difficult decisions which are required to be child centred and in the child's timescale. The Solihull Approach appears to enhance observation skills to assess the quality of infant and parent interaction. It also can contribute to effective supervision techniques, therefore operating on a number of levels. In addition, effective supervision needs to be a reciprocal relationship, two way, reasonably attuned and not simply managerial. This is a theme of the Solihull Approach model, as reciprocity is observed in all relationships, not just in the parent/infant dyad. However, the barriers that remain are identified as the constantly cited time restraints, both to attend the initial training and subsequent practice sessions and in having time to reflect on the learning if training has commenced. In addition, the social workers stated they wanted a clear direction from senior management to support their potential to improve their practice and the outcomes for families.

The content of any approach also needs to carry with it credibility and gravitas. The Solihull Approach appears to do this. The appeal and newness is not only in the combination of factors as social workers recognise the theories as part of their core skills, but also that the Approach supports them by providing a new language with which to explain their practice. However, an enabler for social workers is their interest in the growth in neuro scientific research and the advance of MRI technology, which gives insight (but does not explain everything) into issues such as attachment and brain development, giving agency to this information through the lens of a social work practitioner with their broad range of skills.

The study attempted to explore the how, what and why of the implementation of the Solihull Approach. Validation of existing skills has been a key theme, as has confidence, linked to confidence of the whole profession. Concerns regarding the marked decline in confidence of the profession reside in the research and in the reviews conducted, recognising that despite having a broad range of practice wisdom, social work is demoralised as a profession, afraid of making mistakes due to the punitive response observed and perceived in CAIs and CMRs. The Approach, it is indicated by the respondents, will go some way to boosting confidence through giving the language and updated knowledge that can inform and support social work assessments, enhance their understanding and support their decision making for conferences and court. In addition, it may also support broader global and cultural issues. The increase of refugees coming to NI who have experienced trauma, as well as the indigenous population who have experienced the decades of the Troubles, may contribute to the studies of epigenetics, but also be informed by research on transgenerational experience of trauma.

As a strategy in social work, the Solihull Approach is in its infancy in this organisation and there is clear call for it to be adopted across the whole family and childcare programme. This in itself would be seen as an enabler: a collegiate understanding of the model. Also, there is a need for the agency to strive to be a learning organisation, to build in reflective opportunities and time, to develop or revisit skills and for social workers to feel able to justify them, be they skills of observation or time taken to develop the relationship.

Large, complex and messy caseloads and the subsequent shortage of time are often cited as barriers to learning and were specifically mentioned by social workers in this study. Some responses specifically mentioned the 'practice sessions' format as being effective, but also requested for more of the same for maintenance of the Solihull Approach and their developed knowledge. The format of the practice sessions catered for a range of learning styles and the total involvement of all the social workers attending. They were not passive recipients, but were engaged in the process of learning and implementation. In addition, the format of the practice sessions provided a group supervision experience. This at times could be challenging, for example, when a practitioner could be questioned by their peers on points of practice and process. However, the role of facilitators was to manage this process using effective and facilitative leadership skills. My own experience at times was to ensure the social worker presenting a case study did not feel criticised by peers, but was able to be contained in the group and experience reciprocity. The surveys indicated this often was their experience.

The study has sought to evaluate the Solihull Approach and its application to family and children's social work in Belfast Health and Social Care Trust. Through the literature and policy review, it has explored the research regarding infant mental health and the themes of leadership and social work in modern organisations. The social workers who responded to the survey provided valuable views of the approach and how the implementation of it is best supported. It has also drawn attention to how the approach can support the learning and confidence of a profession that is at times beleaguered.

References

1. Public Health Authority (2016). Priority 2 Workforce development, 29.

2. Campbell, A., Taylor, B. and McGlade, A. (2016). *Research Design in Social Work, qualitative and quantitative methods.* London: Sage Learning Matters.

3. Munro, E. (2011a). *The Munro Review of Child protection final report: a child centred system.* London: TSO.

4. Larkin, H., Felitti, V. and Anda, R. (2014). Social Work and Adverse Childhood Experiences Research: Implications for Health and Policy. *Social Work in Public Health,* 29, 1-16.

5. Winnicott, D.W. (1973). *The Child, the Family and the Outside World.* London: Penguin.

6. APPG (All Party Parliamentary Group) (2015). *Building Great Britons. Conception to age two: The First 1001 days.* http://www.wavetrust.org/sites/default/files/reports/Building_Great_Britons_Report-APPG_Conception_to_Age_2-Wednesday_25th_February_2015.pdf. (Accessed: 17 July 2017)

7. Brazelton T.B. and Cramer, B. (1991). *The Earliest Relationship.* London: Karnac.

8. Perry, B. D. (2002). Childhood Experience and the Expression of Genetic Potential: what childhood neglect tells us about nature and nurture. *Brain and Mind,* 3(1), 79-100.

9. Munro, E. (2011b). *The Munro Review of child protection interim report: the child's journey.* London TSO.

10. Trevithick, P. (2012). *Social Work Skills and Knowledge: a practice handbook.* 3rd Edition. Maidenhead, Berks: Open University Press, McGraw-Hill.

11. World Health Organisation (2014). *Investing in Children: the European Child Maltreatment Prevention Action Plan* 2015-2020. World Health Organisation (2017) FGM factsheet http://www.who.int/mediacentre/factsheets/fs241/en/ (Accessed: 9 August 2017)

12. UNCRC (1989). United Nations Convention on the Rights of the Child. https://www.gov.uk/government/publications/united-nations-convention-on-the-rights-of-the-child-uncrc

13. Felitti, V.J, Anda, R.F., Nordenberg, D., Williamson, D.F., Spitz, A., Edwards, V., Koss, M.P. and Marks, J.S. (1998). Relationship of Childhood Abuse and Household Dysfunction to Many of the Leading Causes of Death in Adults -The Adverse Childhood Experiences (ACE) Study. *American Journal of Preventive Medicine*, 14(4), 245-258.

14. Larkin, H. Felitti, V. and Anda, R. (2014). Social Work and Adverse Childhood Experiences Research: Implications for Health and Policy. *Social Work in Public Health*, 29, 1-16.

15. Davidson, G., Devaney, J. and Spratt, T. (2010). The Impact of Adversity in Childhood on Outcomes in Adulthood, research lessons and limitations. *Journal of Social Work*, 10(4), 369-390.

16. Daniel, B. and Wassell, S. (2002). *Assessing and Promoting Resilience in Vulnerable Children.* London: Jessica Kingsley.

17. Daniel, B., Wassell, S. and Gilligan, R (1999). *Child Development Child Care and Protection Workers.* London: Jessica Kingsley.

18. Gee, D.G. and Casey, B.J. (2015). The Impact of Developmental Timing for Stress and Recovery. *Neurobiology of Stress*, 1, 184-194.

19. Blackwell, D. and Melzak, S. (2000). *Far From the Battle but Still at War.* London: The Child Psychotherapy Trust.

20. Masten, A.S. and Narayan, A.J. (2012) Child Development in the Context of Disaster, War and Terrorism: pathways of risk and resilience. *Annual Review of Psychology*, 63, 227-57.

21. Brandon, M., Sidebotham, P., Bailey, S., Belderson, P., Hawley, C., Ellis, C. and Megson, M. (2012). *New Learning from Serious Case Reviews.* DFE-RR226. Department for Education: London.

22. Campbell, J., Duffy, J., Traynor, C., Coulter, S., Reilly, I. and Pinkerton, J. (2013). Social Work Education and Political Conflict: preparing students to address the needs of victims and survivors of the Troubles in Northern Ireland. *European Journal of Social Work*, 16(4), 506-520.

Social workers and the Solihull Approach   155

23. Commission of Victims and Survivors (2012). *Young people's transgenerational Issues in Northern Ireland*. QUB.

24. Downes, C., Harrison, E., Curran, D. and Kavanagh, M. (2012). The Trauma Still Goes On…: the multigenerational legacy of Northern Ireland's conflict. *In Clinical Child Psychology and Psychiatry*, 18(4), 583-603.

25. Commission of Victims and Survivors (2015). *Towards a Better Future: The Transgenerational Impact of the Troubles on Mental Health*. University of Ulster.

26. Devaney, J., Bunting, L., Davidson, G., Hayes, D., Lazenbatt, A. and Spratt, T. (2012). *Still Vulnerable the Impact of Early Childhood Experiences on Adolescent Suicide and Accidental Death*. NICCY, QUB and NSPCC.

27. Allen, G. (2011). *Smart Investment: massive savings*. London: Cabinet Office.

28. Goleman, D. (2012). *Emotional Intelligence: why it can matter more than IQ*. New York: Random House Publishing Group.

29. Kouzes, J. and Posner, B. (2007). *The Leadership Challenge (4th edition)*. San Francisco: Wiley and Sons.

30. Bass, B.M. and Avolio, B.J. (1994). *Improving Organizational Effectiveness through Transformational leadership*. Thousand Oaks, CA: Sage Publications.

31. Dominelli, L. (1996). De-professionalising Social Work: Anti-Oppressive Practice, Competencies and Postmodernism. *British Journal of Social Work*, 26, 153-175.

32. Featherstone, B.; Morris, K. and White, S. (2014). A Marriage Made in hell: early intervention meets child protection. *British Journal of Social Work*, 44(7), 1735-1749.

33. Das, C., O'Neill, M. and Pinkerton, J. (2015). Re-engaging with community work as a method of practice in social work: a view from Northern Ireland. *Journal of Social Work*, 0(0), 1-20.

34. Ferguson, I. and Woodward, R. (2009). *Radical Social work in Practice: making a difference*. Social Work in Practice series. Bristol: The Policy Press.

35. Wilson, G. (2011) Evidencing Reflective Practice in Social Work Education: Theoretical Uncertainties and Practical Challenges in *British Journal of Social Work*, 43(1), 154-172.

36. Healy, K. and Meagher, G. (2004). The Reprofessionalisation of Social Work: collaborative approaches for achieving professional recognition. *British Journal of Social Work*, 34, 243-260.

37. Ruch, G., Winter, K., Cree, V., Hallett, S., Morrison, F. and Hadfield, M. (2017). Making meaningful connections: using insights from social pedagogy in statutory child and family social work practice in *Child and Family Social Work*, 22(2), 1015-1023.

38. Cooperrider, D. and Whitney, D. (2005). *Appreciative Inquiry: a positive revolution in change*. San Francisco: Berret-Koehler Publishers.

39. Trevithick, P. (2014). Humanising Managerialism: reclaiming emotional reasoning, intuition, the relationship, and knowledge and skills in social work. *Journal of Social Work Practice: Psychotherapeutic Approaches in Health, Welfare and the Community,* 28(3), 287-311.

40. Munro, E. (2010). *A System's Analysis.* London: TSO.

41. Lees, A., Meyer, E. and Rafferty, J. (2011). From Menzies Lyth to Munro: the problem of Managerialism. *British Journal of Social Work,* 43(3), 542-558.

42. Ferguson, H. (2007). Working with Violence, the Emotions and the Psychosocial Dynamics of Child Protection: reflections on the Victoria Climbié case. *Social Work Education: the International Journal,* 24(7), 781-795.

43. Horwath, J. (2015). The Toxic Duo: the neglected practitioner and a parent who fails to meet the needs of their child. *British Journal of Social Work,* 46(69), 1602-1616.

44. Goleman, D. (2012). *Emotional Intelligence: why it can matter more than IQ.* New York: Random House Publishing Group.

45. Horwath, J. (2015). The Toxic Duo: the neglected practitioner and a parent who fails to meet the needs of their child. *British Journal of Social Work,* 46(69), 1602-1616.

46. Howe, D. (2008). *The Emotionally Intelligent Social Worker.* Basingstoke, Palgrave.

47. Brazelton, T.B. (1984). *Neonatal Behaviour Assessment Scale 2nd edition.* London: Blackwell.

48. Fernandez, S. and Rainey, H. (2006). Managing Successful Organisational Change in the Public Sector. *Public Administration Review,* March/April, 168-176.

49. Miller, R., Freeman, T., Davidson, D. and Glasby, J. (2015). *An Adult Social Care Compendium of Approaches and Tools of Organisational Change.* SCIE. www.scie.co.uk

50. Kotter, J. (2012). *Leading Change.* Boston Massachusetts : Harvard Business Review Press.

51. Brave New World (2001). In *Body Story,* Channel 4. Available from www.solihullapproachparenting.com

20 Delivering the 'Understanding your child' parent programme in a prison setting

Denise Kelly, Sean McCracken, Catarina Smith and Cheryl Valentine

This chapter has been co-written by the key people involved in delivering the 'Understanding your child' course for parents in HMP Shotts. We hope to share with you our experience of this initiative, exploring both the highlights and challenges we have faced along the way.

Note: In this Chapter, the Solihull Approach is often referred to as 'Solihull' and the 'Understanding your child's behaviour' course as 'Understanding your child'.

Introduction

HMP Shotts is a maximum security, long term prison which houses approximately 537 men at any given time. It is responsible for the care and rehabilitation of some of the highest profile offenders in the prison system in Scotland. All of the men housed at the establishment have been sentenced to a minimum of four years with many serving tariffs of 20 years plus.

The impact of facing a long term sentence affects these men in various ways. Many men feel that they will no longer be able to provide their children and families with the support and care they previously did and that their children and families would be better off, in the long term, without them in their lives. This results in men withdrawing from the people who can support them throughout their sentence and becoming depressed, isolated and more likely to reoffend upon release.

> For a prisoner who receives visits from a family member, the odds of reoffending are 39% lower than those who do not.
>
> The Importance of Strengthening Prisoners' Family Ties to Prevent Reoffending and Reduce Intergenerational Crime, Lord Farmer, August 2017.

The imprisonment of a parent has been recognised as an 'Adverse Childhood Experience' (ACE)[1] which can have far reaching and long lasting implications for children. Many children experience this loss as a bereavement, which can have a negative impact on their mental health. It can increase the risk of depression, anxiety and behaviour difficulties as well as affecting learning and long term prospects. Children may become dissociated and experience bullying from their peers, as well as enduring the stigma of the crime committed by their parent from their community and society as a whole. In many cases, young children are not informed of their parent's imprisonment and are told that their mum or dad is working away from home and that they can visit them at their new place of work; this results in extended family members and older siblings having to lie to the young child. When the child then discovers the truth, they feel emotions such as anger, betrayal and have issues in relation to trust. Children who are aware of their parent's imprisonment also suffer many challenges and conflicting emotions.

> How can I love my dad when he is in jail? Only bad people go to jail and I don't think my dad is a bad person. He loves me, looks after me and I always have fun with him.
>
> Child as cited in Families Outside.

The remaining parent also has to endure the stigma from the community of the crime committed by their loved one, which can result in the family moving from their home to another area less likely to be aware of the history of the family. In effect, the remaining parent becomes a single parent, having to be responsible for all aspects of raising children and making ends meet. Financial issues are a major factor. The remaining parent has to make adjustments to the family's lifestyle and in some cases will have to stop working due to childcare issues.

Mental health conditions such as depression and anxiety are also prevalent in family members with a loved one in prison. Many relationships deteriorate, with other family members not accepting the situation and not understanding why the remaining parent would want to continue to support their loved one while being imprisoned. Relationships between the convicted and their partner/spouse can also deteriorate and often break down completely. Evidence shows that 50% of prisoners lose contact with their families through the period of their sentence.

'Getting Better Together' (GBT) is a third sector, community based organisation established to tackle health inequalities experienced by the community of Shotts, North Lanarkshire. The organisation offer a wide range of services to support all age ranges of the community, from early years and youth groups to befriending and support for the elderly and isolated in the community. They also deliver community transport, a community garden and café as well as a community radio station. HMP Shotts is a community within the community of Shotts.

In 2012/2013 the family strategy group within the establishment identified parenting skills as a priority on their agenda. GBT, in collaboration with NHS Lanarkshire, secured funding to develop, improve and maintain familial relationships between prisoners and their children. GBT developed the Family Time Project to be delivered during children's visits within the prison.

Children's visits

Children's visits are in complete contrast to general visits within the establishment. In a general visit a prisoner has to sit on a designated chair and is unable to move for the duration of the visit. Physical contact between the prisoner and his visitors is limited, a hug upon arrival and when leaving is permitted, but no other physical contact is allowed during the course of the visit. The visit room at HMP Shotts can hold over 30 visits at any given session and each prisoner is permitted a maximum of three visitors. This can mean that, at times, over 150 people can be present.

Children's visits are restricted to a maximum of eight prisoners, their children and partner/spouse. This allows the family to play and move freely around the room. Contact is encouraged between the prisoner and his family. Prison officers remain at the back of the visit room to maintain security but not to impinge on the family's interactions.

The Family Time Project offers a range of activities suited to the children's age and stage of development, designed to promote positive interactions and build a strong familial bond. Staff aim to provide families with fun, exciting, enjoyable experiences and to help build happy memories from a period in their lives they would ordinarily try to forget upon release.

Family Time staff are also aware of the anxiety visiting a prison causes in children and aim to alleviate this by providing the children and parents with a nurturing and welcome environment in which to share quality time and grow their relationships.

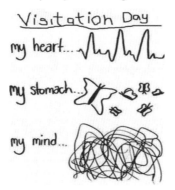

This diagram gives a visual representation of the feelings of a child on a visit day.

Working in collaboration with family contact officers in HMP Shotts, staff from GBT also deliver four family parties throughout the course of the year. These include Christmas, Easter, summer and Halloween. It is heart-warming to witness the 'hardest' men in society as daddies being turned into mummies during our Halloween parties or participating in a 'bunny race' at Easter!

160 Denise Kelly, Sean McCracken, Catarina Smith and Cheryl Valentine

> This is our first party here. It has been amazing and we really enjoyed it, thank you! You wouldn't know that we are in a jail!

Mother attending recent Easter party.

The catering department also help provide the families attending children's visits with normal family experiences, by providing pancakes for Shrove Tuesday and a traditional Burn's supper for Burn's Night.

One child played the part of Mary with her father being Joseph and her mother being Gabriel in a Christmas nativity play delivered by the Family Time Project and the chaplaincy department within the prison.

GBT staff are also available to offer a range of support to all visitors attending HMP Shotts in relation to a wide range of issues pertaining to the impact of the imprisonment of their loved one. This support is delivered via a purpose built visitor centre within the visit waiting area of the establishment. The visitor centre is comprised of a central office, a play room for children attending visits and a confidential meeting space. This service has been in operation since April 2017.

How did the partnership evolve?

Staff from GBT responsible for the delivery of the Family Time Project attended the Solihull Approach 2 Day Foundation training delivered by North Lanarkshire Partnership. This training helped to enhance interactions between staff members and the families who had engaged with the Family Time Project. It improved their understanding of the issues experienced by families attending visits and the behaviours exhibited by children in attendance. As a result, staff were better equipped to help parents identify new ways in which to interact with their children and understand what their children were trying to communicate through their behaviour.

GBT staff discussed the possibility of bringing the approach to HMP Shotts in the form of the 'Understanding your child' (UYC) course at a meeting of the family strategy group. They explained the positive impact the approach had on their practice and how it would be a valuable addition to the programme for children and families attending the establishment. It would also complement the Family Time Project and increase the quality of interactions between dads in prison and their children by providing fathers with the knowledge and understanding of their children's development, both emotional and physical.

The manager for the National Integration Centre (NIC) within the establishment recognised the value of piloting the course to the dads currently living in this area of the prison. Factors such as cost were raised. Staff assured him this would be delivered free of charge, which is always a selling point due to budget constraints! It also had the potential to 'transform life and unlock potential' of fathers who may feel that they can no longer be positive role models for their children.

First Line Manager (FLM), David Dalziel, is the forward thinking manager of the NIC within HMP Shotts who supported the initial pilot group.

> In my role as FLM I ensure that we have a full and varied regime for the prisoners within the NIC and when I first heard of the Solihull I agreed to take it to the NIC for

Delivering the 'Understanding your child' parent programme in a prison setting 161

a trial period as it was something new and it would fill some time for prisoners as well as it being provided for free, which due to budgets was very important.

I identified two Scottish Prison Service staff to support Cheryl and Denise who were going to facilitate the group. These two staff would organise the prisoners and ensure Cheryl and Denise were escorted to and from the NIC as well as providing supervision throughout the group to deal with any behaviour issues.

It quickly became clear that this group was so much more than just a space filler on my regime. After two or three sessions I could hear prisoners talking about it and praising the way they were treated in the group, as well as talking about their children and families with other prisoners which is really quite unusual in a prison setting. It led to better relationships between prisoners and the staff supporting the group and also better relationships between prisoners. Guys who, because of their crimes, were previously shunned by other prisoners were now being treated the same because they had a common interest - their children and the need to be a father. I also witnessed prisoners grow in confidence as they had support from staff and group facilitators and now felt ready to play a part in their children's lives where they had lost hope before.

Many prisoners when sentenced to eight years or over start to think they have no life left and in particular that they have no role as a parent, stating things like: they will be teenagers before I get out; I will be lucky to attend their 21st birthday party; my kids are better off without me!!

A particular example of this was a gentleman who arrived in the NIC on 1st May 2015. He hardly spoke to staff or prisoners and spent most of his time in his cell. He was sentenced to life and a tariff of 20 years and when he arrived in the NIC he was 39 years old and could see no future as he would be at least 59 before release. He thought his family would be better off without him and started to reduce contact with them both through visits and telephone. He was always polite and courteous to staff, but avoided communication if he could. He understood it was a requirement in the NIC to participate in the regime and attended a few discussion groups: Drug and Alcohol awareness; START (which deals with sentence management); and Respect Me anti-bullying group. He participated well in these groups, but was still withdrawn out in the flat and also from his family. When he started the Solihull programme it seemed to open the eyes to the fact he still had hope, not just for release but also to play a part in his children's lives and also grandchildren's lives. His whole attitude changed towards his time in custody and rather than participating in the regime because it was a requirement, he became a willing volunteer to participate in everything we had to offer.

David Dalziel, First Line Manager.

As previously mentioned, this work has been undertaken by three very different organisations; Scottish Prison Service, Getting Better Together and North Lanarkshire Council. As with all co-production initiatives there have been challenges! This is due to different working practices, procedures and of course, the fact that HMP Shotts is a maximum security prison.

What happened when we ran the first group?

Here is the experience of being involved from the prison officer perspective:

I've worked at Shotts prison now for 22 years. The past four years I've worked in the National Integration Centre based in HMP Shotts where we work with long term prisoners serving eight years or more. The NIC is set up to help prisoners settle into their sentence through staff working closely with their personal prisoners, identifying issues and needs. Courses are run in the NIC to help prisoners with stress, anxiety, anger management and alcohol and drug dependency. We hoped that we could use and run a Solihull Approach course for the dads within the NIC.

I jumped at the chance when my First Line Manager, David Dalziel, asked if I was interested in doing a course about parenting for two days. My wife had recently given birth to our first child and I wasn't given the manual before leaving the hospital. I was hoping that this course would help me to be a better dad. The course was being delivered to the fire service in a station in Cumbernauld. After driving around a couple of housing estates I eventually found a fire station, said the code word 'Solihull' and got in. I enjoyed the course and learnt a lot about containment, brain development and that the fire service provide a crackin lunch!

I then spoke with staff and dad's at the prison, to try to gauge who would be interested in the Solihull group, a few dads were sceptical and said, 'I am a good dad'. We arranged a drop in session for the dad's in the NIC to engage and inform as many of the dad's as we could. Cheryl Valentine, Melissa Keyes (GBT) and myself spoke with the dads explaining about the principles of Solihull, the group and a bit about ourselves. The drop in worked well; we had a list of dads interested in attending.

Our aim was to run the 'Understanding your child' course exactly as it would in the community, but as we ran the group we realised we would have to tailor it more for the dads inside. Each week the dads would get their homework for the following week, observations of their children. For most of the dads this was difficult as they weren't going home after the class and seeing their children. Some of the dads were only having a visit once or twice a month with their kids, other dads were relying on speaking with their children on the telephone with the odd visit here or there. We changed some of the language we were using in the Solihull course so it suited the prison environment and was sensitive to the dad's situation. The ice breaker and making a cup of coffee or tea helped the dads relax and feel welcome within the group. We encouraged the dads to say what went well and what didn't on the weekly feedback sheet. For us, this was important to know as this was the first time we had attempted running a Solihull course within a Scottish prison.

The course was held on a Tuesday morning in one of the group rooms within the NIC and it took time to break down some of the barriers and engage some of the dads. The pass cards were used a lot by some. As the course progressed, the dads relaxed and were more confident to speak about their kids, how they parent and how they were parented. Week five was a tough week for our first group as some of the

Delivering the 'Understanding your child' parent programme in a prison setting 163

dads felt that because they were in prison that they couldn't really be a dad for their children and that the children would be better off without them in their lives; some of the dads were serving sentences of 18 to 30 years. I was shocked at how open the dads had been with us. Fair to say that we all needed a bit of containment in the prison carpark for the facilitators at the end of that day.

As we neared the last few remaining weeks of the group, the dads said that they were gutted that the course was almost finished and didn't want it to end. Speaking with the dads about what they would like, we developed and planned a Dads Plus group and I organised Story Book Dads within Shotts prison. This is a programme where dads can read story books for their children and it's recorded. The audio is sent to HMP Channings Wood in Devon where they edit it and send back the finished CD. The dads and their children love this scheme and with books kindly given by the Scottish Book Trust, it means that the dads can hand out the recording with the book.

We used the all the information gathered from the weekly feedback sheets to give a review of the course to Jim Kerr, Governor of HMP Shotts. One of the dads agreed to come along and give his feedback and speak with the management team about how Solihull had helped him.

Sean McCracken, Prison Officer.

The experience of delivering the first group was a huge learning curve for the facilitators involved, especially those who did not work in a prison environment.

I was delivering a Solihull Approach 2 Day Foundation course to a very motivated group of multi agency practitioners, one of them being Melissa Keyes who at the time worked for GBT. She explained her role in HMP Shotts and we discussed the possibility of running the 'Understanding your child' parent group for dads. I was really interested in testing this out. However, this was very new territory for me. I appeared for the first day of delivery with my handbag over my shoulder, containing my mobile phone and a glass jar of coffee in hand for the dads. I was quickly informed of the security risks and that none of them could be taken into the prison! When I look back, I realise I have learned a lot about prison life and the emotive impact this has on all the family.

Cheryl Valentine, North Lanarkshire Council.

Over the 10 weeks of the first group, we improved the processes used to deliver the programme and made changes to the course content as a result of both facilitator's observations and feedback from the dads on the first group. We used the Quality Improvement[2] model to measure impact and identify changes we wanted to make to the subsequent groups. The facilitators from the onset of the group were keen that the participants were thought about and treated as 'dads' not prisoners. This helped to create a positive ethos from the start of the group, based on trust and respect.

Our first main learning point as we delivered the 10 week programme was in relation to the circumstances of the dads who were attending the group. One did not have regular contact with his children. As the group progressed he shared how difficult it was to hear other dads talking about their children. We offered him the opportunity to step down from the group, but he wanted to continue. In fact, during the course of the 10 weeks, he represented himself at court and gained the right for 'letterbox' contact (ability to send/receive letters and cards to/from his children). He also insisted on completing the group as he felt it may help his case to finally gain access to see his children again.

> I was a bit apprehensive at first about the group, because of the situation that my children are in. I felt as if I was a useless dad and I had let my children down because I had landed myself in prison. I fought for my kids through the courts even though I am not involved in their lives at the moment. I love my kids and am doing my best to be there for them, I miss them and love seeing them.
>
> Dad from Group 1.

We have used this learning in subsequent groups by asking the interested dads if they see or are in regular contact with their children before starting the group. If they have no contact, we discuss the content of the sessions to ensure they are aware that it could be sensitive and difficult for them to be involved. Several dads who are not in regular contact with their children have now completed the group and feel they have benefited from the experience, giving them a greater understanding of their children. However, two dads chose to start the group, but, as predicted, found it too difficult and stopped attending.

We quickly realised through observations and some comments from the dads, that some of them were not feeling very positive about joining the group, although the responses collated weekly (see graph below) shows a predominantly relaxed feeling. The facilitators felt some of the dads were reluctant to record accurate response, hence the evaluation forms gave a different impression. Later in the group, once relationships had become more established, the dads shared their thoughts of joining the group.

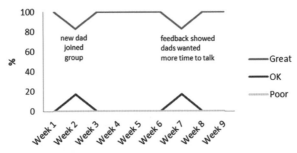

'I thought this would be another waste of time but let's just get on with it.'

'I felt some genuine reservations, but most of all I felt guilt 'cos I knew that I had real inadequacies as a father and having to admit them in front of other people was going to be hard.'

Delivering the 'Understanding your child' parent programme in a prison setting

> 'My first feelings about the group was that this was going to be another typical how to be an ideal father power point class.'

> 'I didn't really know what to think and what to expect. I didn't really want to talk about my family and personal things at the group as I felt uncomfy at first.'

This shows that we as facilitators were right in our feelings that the evaluation of how relaxed they felt did not represent the dad's actual feelings and it was only as the weeks progressed and trust and relationships developed that this changed.

As the group progressed, and the facilitators responded to the needs of the group, the dads later expressed how their feelings changed:

> 'I came to realise that my kids still needed me, even if I couldn't be with them and I also felt relaxed enough to join in with the classes.'

> 'I was looking forward to the next visit so I could try things I had learned in the class.'

> 'I felt totally different, Solihull showed me that it's not about how much time you spend but it's about how you spend that time....I used to spend my time chasing a smile and a cuddle off my son but I soon learned that using the Solihull Approach, using the techniques and watching his development, the smiles and the hugs come naturally and that's when you know that I am a dad, when you get a kiss without asking and a hug without asking, that really does make you feel like a dad.'

> 'As the group progressed I felt very comfortable talking about my children and family. We were made to feel like real dads. I knew I could be a good dad as the course went on.'

The graph below shows how they began to understand their children more. They later shared how the group helped them with their children.

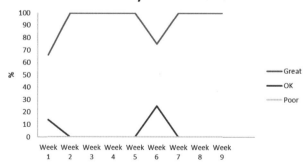

How helpful was the group to help you understand your child better?

> 'It helped with T directly as I was watching T develop and hearing stories about him developing,.....your partner comes up and tells you he did this.... he did that, Solihull taught me how to understand what he is developing and what he is looking for...... you then begin to develop with him, you don't watch him develop, you do it with him and it just brings the communication so much better.'

'Solihull helped me understand my children more and lets me know how they were and how they are feeling growing up.....helped me understand I can be a good dad to my children while in prison.'

At the end of the course the graph shows an increase in the dad's ability to make changes and they gave us some examples of the changes they had made.

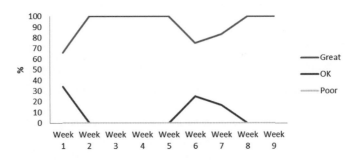

'I started father and child visits. I call every day and ask how they are and call every night to say goodnight, these are the things I hope they'll remember...even though I am not there every day and if some days they go...'oh no its dad again'.'

'It was wee things you noticed more, you were conscious of things you were doing in the past and no doing them any more.'

'I stopped trying to be a dad...........concentrated more on his development, me and my partner spoke more and in turn it lead us to being able to understand his development more which in turn made the visits a whole lot easier and everything else just fitted in.'

'I listen more to them and let them tell me what they have been doing in their own time so they don't think I am bossing them about, that is just one change I have made out of a lot of changes and I would say that all the changes have been for the best, Solihull has made a great difference to my life and my family's. Thanks for everything.'

'The Solihull Approach, it isn't about teaching you how to be a good dad, it simply reminds you that you are one.'

'I went from hardly speaking to my kids to now they are sick of me phoning.'

During the course of the 10 week programme, we made several adaptations to the delivery of the course. The weekly evaluations from the dads and our own evaluations supported us in identifying the changes we wanted to make.

The programme, as outlined in the facilitator's manual, has a strong focus on asking parents to observe and reflect on what we cover in the weekly classes and involves a weekly home task. As mentioned previously this was obviously not appropriate for the dads in our group as they did not see their children on a daily basis. We adapted the language of the tasks to ask them to observe their children on their next visit or, if they were not due to see their children, to reflect on this during their telephone conversations with their children or think back to a time in the past when they were with their child. It became apparent that the dads liked to talk about their children and share any achievements, special events etc. that their children had been involved in with the group. The facilitators recognised this and created space at the beginning of each session to informally ask how the families had been and ask the dads to share any news from home. This had the advantage of not only helping to build relationships in the group, but also allowed facilitators to contain any worries or concerns that the dads had about home circumstances and then allow them to move on and focus on the content of the session.

Another key learning point for the facilitators was to introduce visual aids and small activities to engage the dads. A short weekly 'icebreaker' was used at the start of each session; this helped to create a relaxed start to each session. It was however apparent that the icebreakers needed to be fun and not demanding.

We also recognised the need to respond to the dads by being very flexible and responsive. On occasions, dads could be feeling low and missing their families, this was especially apparent at holiday times e.g. Christmas and also if there was an issue or concern at home. On one occasion, one of the dads was concerned about his teenage son being involved in drugs. The other dads were very supportive and responded by containing him. We responded by giving time for this discussion. The dads admitted that they would not previously have had these types of discussions with the group, as they did not normally talk about their personal worries with each other. This shows that the relationships and trust built up within the group had the additional benefit of encouraging the dads to share concerns about their home life. The dads then informed us that this experience in the group caused a change and they began to contain each other outside the group e.g. when out walking for exercise in the yard.

The pass cards were well used, especially by one dad; we doubted that he would have continued to attend had the pass card not been available. (Pass cards are used in all Solihull Approach courses for parents. A parent can hold one up at any time to indicate that they don't want to participate in a particular exercise, no questions asked.)

All dads grew in confidence over the 10 weeks and showed great insight into their situation and the impact that this could have on their child/ren. We noticed that the dads' self-esteem and confidence in themselves and as fathers improved. They appeared more relaxed, had more eye contact and contributed more as the weeks progressed. We had increasing issues with time as the weeks continued and the dads wanted to discuss more. We were always short of time towards the second half of the course!

The prison staff noticed that some of the dads started to rely on each other for support outside the group and had formed friendships as a result of spending time together in the group.

The evaluation forms were distributed at the end of each group. The results collated showed that the dads scored the three questions very highly. We did however wonder if the dads were scoring 'great' to try to please us, as they were enjoying the group. It was different to other groups delivered in prison. In an attempt to gain more meaningful feedback, we decided to test a five point scale rather than the three point and changed the evaluation forms for the second group. This worked and made a difference to the scores received for the second group, allowing the dads greater variance in their responses. It also showed the differing moods and feelings of the dads more, as the ratings showed greater variation each week. The overall trend however is similar to the first group, in that the dads rated an increased understanding of their children and were increasingly able to identify changes they wanted to make.

It was obvious that the programme is very relevant for dads in a prison setting and has had significant impact on the dads and their families. Several of the family members have spoken to GBT staff at the visits, commenting on the positive impact the group has had and noticing a change in how the dads interact with their children. As facilitators, the impact was far greater than we could have hoped for.

In general, we were amazed by the response from not only the first but subsequent groups. It appeared that the group was filling a gap that none of the other groups offered in the prison could fill. The dads enjoyed the group and although they found talking about their children difficult on some occasions, they enjoyed the focus on their family and they could quickly relate to their child's age/stage of development and identify changes in how they would like to respond.

When we asked the dads on week 10 as part of our final evaluation.....'What do you do now as a result of the course?' they gave us some examples:

'Encourage children to do things more.'

'Encourage children more.'

'Look through child's eyes, tune into their thoughts more.'

'Explain more to them, previously I would have told little lies e.g. its broken rather than it needs more batteries.'

'Book more visits; I now realise the importance of the visits for the kids. Before I didn't book visits as I found it too difficult and questioned how I can be a dad while in prison.'

'Be more patient with children e.g. when doing up their jackets to go home.'

'I will treat them individually.'

We have been well supported by the prison staff who were required to be present with us when we delivered the group, for security reasons. Initially we thought that we could support the prison officers to become 'Understanding your child' facilitators and that they would then deliver the groups. This however was not welcomed by the dads. Although they understand the need for an officer to be present in the room and feel that their relationships with the officers developed during the group, they did not feel that they would open up as readily to the prison officers, as their relationship with them is very different to the one that we had forged. There has, however, been an improvement in the relationships between the prison officers who have participated in the groups and the dads.

Delivering the 'Understanding your child' parent programme in a prison setting **169**

It was also clear that other prison staff not involved were showing an interest in the group and wanting to know more about the approach; some also had some miscomprehensions about what the group was about. We delivered a 2 Day Foundation training for some key staff, to create awareness of the Solihull Approach and the results we found from delivering the 'Understanding your child' programme. The evaluations showed that the 2 Day Foundation course was highly relevant and the participants commented on how they felt after attending:

'Very good course, all prison officers and parents should do the course. Highly recommended.'

'It will help me to support my staff with their personal issues (family) but also understand what prisoners are discussing during the course and how difficult it is to maintain family relationships.'

'I will use this with my personal prisoners, being more involved with and discussing their relationships with their children.'

'Overall a fantastic and very resourceful course. It would be great to roll this out to more prison staff.'

'I will understand prisoners' behaviour, in relation to their upbringing, passing on new information to help them with their children.'

This shows that the 2 Day Foundation training is also beneficial to prison staff. The facilitators used their knowledge of the prison environment to adapt the training to make it more relevant for the prison officers. It is clear that there is a demand for more training.

A key driver for our early work was the support of Jim Kerr, Governor. When he was presented with the outcomes of the first group, he was keen to continue. We realised how important it is to have management support, especially in the environment in which we are delivering the group. Jim has since moved from his post in HMP Shotts and is now the Director of Operations in the Scottish Prison Service. We arranged a meeting with the new Governor to share this work and look forward to sharing our ongoing progress with her.

Impact on relationships

One of the authors, prison officer Catarina Smith, decided to carry out a short evaluation of the impact that programme has had on relationships.

Since getting involved with the Solihull I found my job as a prison officer easier and more rewarding, as a result of the relationship that developed with the dads in the group. As the dads opened up more and discussed their children with everyone in the group, the communication outside the group improved and I felt there was a greater element of trust overall.

In order to gain an insight into the thoughts of some prisoners who attended the course I distributed a questionnaire.

Survey Question 1:

'How do you feel about staff being in the group and interacting within the group setting?'

The dads reported thinking that this was a positive thing and provided some good insight from both parties. One comment was made that 'it broke down the barriers between staff and cons'.

Survey Question 2:

'How has the course improved your relationship between your family and your children?'

In general, the responses showed that the dads felt the group encouraged them to analyse not only their own emotions, but also their children's as they develop. It helped them to understand their children more.

Survey Question 3:

'How has your relationship with other prisoners in the group improved?'

The feedback from dads was that 'it lets you and others know that you're not the only one going through the same situation' and also 'the course has taught me patience not only with my children, but with fellow inmates inside prison'.

This shows that there have been clear examples of dads becoming more confident in being a dad while serving a prison sentence. Dads who participate in children's visits not only benefit themselves, but the family as a whole. There was great excitement recently when the dads took part in a very successful Gruffalo Play much to the delight of the children! More importantly it made the participants realise that you can be a parent in prison.

Cat Smith, Residential Officer.

How did we scale up?

Due to the success of the first group, we continued to offer the 10 week programme for other dads in the NIC. Our experience and skill as facilitators evolved and we realised that every group is very different! We offered a 'drop in' coffee morning for interested dads. Some of the dads who completed the first group attended and were instrumental in encouraging new dads to participate. They shared the impact it had on them and their relationships with their children. This has now been adopted as a key part of the process when recruiting new dads.

We have now delivered a total of seven groups in HMP Shotts impacting on 44 dads and 154 children...and still going! The prison now considers the programme as a core part of the ongoing support for families, underpinning the Scottish Prison Service vision statement and including it in the children and family strategy. We are delighted that the establishment have recognised the benefits and acknowledged the importance of this for families.

Delivering the 'Understanding your child' parent programme in a prison setting 171

One of the groups was delivered in another section of the prison, Lamont Hall. We were unsure how this would go, as this hall has a different regime from the NIC where we had previously delivered the group. The prisoners are more engaged in a prison regime and go to 'work' in the prison. We were, however, delighted that the group worked well and we had the highest number of dads yet complete the group! This shows that the group is beneficial to all dads in the prison and not just those in the NIC.

Unexpected outcomes

As men were approaching the end of the 'Understanding your child' course in the NIC they were eager to continue their learning and develop their knowledge on a range of topics which concerned them in relation to their children's interests and developmental stage.

This led to facilitators developing a follow-on group called 'Dads Plus'. This is a short group designed for dads, with the content being based on suggestions from the dads with their children in mind. The course runs for approximately six weeks and has covered topics such as Bookbug (an initiative developed by The Scottish Book Trust to develop a love of reading and positive attachment in children from birth), the importance of play, internet safety and drug and alcohol use in teenagers.

Dads who attended the Dads Plus programme shared with facilitators that they miss the opportunity to attend pantomimes or the theatre with their children and would welcome the chance to perform for their children. Facilitators suggested 'The Gruffalo' as a project for the men to work on for their children.

The script was written using the book 'The Gruffalo' by Julia Donaldson and each father identified a character from the book they would like to play. As the performance was scheduled during the Easter holidays, the dads decided the narrator should take the form of the Easter Bunny, who would also gift Easter eggs to all children in attendance at the end of the performance. There was much discussion between the dads about the different character roles in the book!

I'm not being the little brown mouse! He ain't gangster enough for me mate!

Dad from Dads Plus group.

This father changed his mind when he discovered that the little brown mouse was the cleverest character in the book, as he convinced the other animals wanting to eat him that he was the scariest creature in the wood which resulted in the Gruffalo being afraid of him in the end.

The Gruffalo character was undertaken by a father who had blossomed during the 10 week 'Understanding your child' group. He initially had stopped all contact with his children as he believed he could not have any influence on their lives and thought they would be better off without him. He used his pass card on many occasions and was reluctant to contribute to the sessions for the first few weeks of the group. He became a driving force for the production of 'The Gruffalo'!

The cast met each week to rehearse and plan their performance. It was amazing to witness! These men, who had reputations to uphold and who were perceived by society to be extremely dangerous, turned into scared, nervous and self- conscious men-children and had very little confidence in what they were trying to achieve. A mother of one of the cast members described how committed her son was to the play, during Family Time Project.

> My son phoned last night, almost in tears about doing this play! He has written his lines on sticky notes and posted them all over his walls so he can read them all the time.

When the men had learned their lines, facilitators noticed a massive increase in their confidence. The men began to act! They met outside the designated Dads Plus times to rehearse and it was apparent they had been learning their lines when they were locked in their cells every evening.

The dads took ownership of the play by designing invitations for their families and invited guests, including the Scottish Government, North Lanarkshire Partnership, NHS and GBT, in addition to various agencies within the establishment, such as psychology, social work and staff members from the NIC. The Governor, Deputy Governor and other members of senior management in the prison also attended.

The dad who played 'The Gruffalo' contacted the work sheds in the prison to arrange to have scenery made to depict the deep dark wood and the various homes inhabited by the characters. Upon completion of the scenery, it was taken to the NIC where it was painted by the Little Brown Mouse, the Fox, the Owl, the Snake and the Gruffalo…a real team effort!

All cast members purchased their own costumes from money in their PPC account to ensure that their families did not incur any financial difficulty as a result of the play.

The Scottish Book Trust kindly donated a copy of 'The Gruffalo' for every child who would be attending. Facilitators arranged various Gruffalo themed activities for the families to complete after the performance as well as arranging a Gruffalo themed snack for the families from the catering department.

The family who attended loved it! Here are some of their comments:

> 'Fantastic, brilliant, super excited' (adult).

> 'Good fun' (teenager).

> 'Good!' (Child).

> 'Great as we can't share this type of experience normally, it feels something special as we wouldn't normally get to do it with them' (adult).

> 'Didn't realise it was down to the guys, this is a great memory that T (child) will never forget' (adult).

> 'T (child) was so excited when she woke up today as she knew this was happening' (adult).

> 'He (dad) was very funny' (child)..

> 'It was great as our kids don't get to do what other children get to do with their dads' (adult)

Delivering the 'Understanding your child' parent programme in a prison setting

'I wish I could live with my dad' (child).

'This has been a great day for dads, kids and visitors' (adult).

'It feels more natural' (adult).

'It was brilliant, especially the Gruffalo, it feels very family orientated' (adult).

The dads were amazing in their performance...and felt very proud as a result! Here are some of the comments made by the dads after the performance:

'Communication has got better.'

'Depressed it's over, I'm deflated.'

'I feel more confident now.'

'There is now a common bond between the dads who took part.'

'We need more of this type of thing.'

'They should re-think the system to have more of this.'

'I feel good now, I want more!'

'Proud.'

'It has given good memories for the family.'

'Looking forward to the next one!'

'It helps the guys mix and mingle with each other that wouldn't usually.'

'Great for the kids and the family.'

'It gave me something to look forward to.'

'It was good to mix the Easter theme and the buffet was good.'

'It has boosted morale.'

Celebrating successes

We are very proud of the success of the programme, delivered in a prison setting and have had many occasions to celebrate its success. It has proved to be challenging on many levels, especially working as three different organisations and delivering it in a maximum security prison. However, the results have shown to be very worthwhile. The 'Understanding your child' team submitted an application for an award to the Scottish Government as part of the Quality Improvement awards and we were delighted to win for the category of 'Co-production'. This award has raised awareness of the benefits of the 'Understanding your child' programme and as a result we were asked to present our experience to the national learning collaborative at the Scottish Exhibition and Conference Centre to an audience of 700 to 800 delegates.

Denise Kelly, GBT, describes her experience of this:

> Presenting our Solihull journey to approximately 800 people at the Children and Young People Improvement Collaborative in the SECC was one of the most nerve racking experiences of my working life to date!

> Standing on the stage, wired for sound, I was convinced the audience would hear my heart beating over anything I was trying to say. Delivering my section of the presentation I was aware of the shaking tone of my voice and how my knees were softer than normal! I couldn't identify any audience members nodding or smiling at what I was saying due to the bright lights in my eyes and I was more than aware of the television cameras recording every move and word spoken!

> This experience helped me understand how some of the dads who engaged in the Solihull Approach at HMP Shotts may feel when talking in a group about their children and family lives, as this is completely out of their comfort zone. I discovered during this presentation that I have a tendency to become hyper aroused when under great stress and require masses of containment!

> Being short listed for and winning the Quality Improvement Award by the Scottish Government was another 'pinch myself' moment.

> The recognition of the work we deliver in the prison has been astounding to me. Having the recognition of 'real grown ups' such as Don Berwick requesting to visit the prison to speak with us and the dads involved in the Solihull Approach and him speaking about our work to the First Minister over dinner, highlights the importance of our work and the potential it has to change lives.

> I am delighted that HMP Shotts have decided to continue the spread of the Solihull Approach throughout the establishment to encompass all dads and look forward to improving outcomes for the children and families involved.

> Denise Kelly, GBT.

Delivering the 'Understanding your child' parent programme in a prison setting   175

The programme has also been showcased in the internal magazine produced by prisoners… for prisoners. The article below featured in 'Snapshotts' magazine.

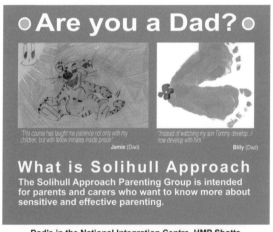

We were delighted to be asked to host a visit from Dr Don Berwick, MD, MPP, (President Emeritus and Senior Fellow, Institute for Healthcare Improvement) in February 2017. He visited the prison to hear how the Quality Improvement model has been used to develop the dads groups. It was an honour to host the visit and even more rewarding when he expressed how impressed he was that we could evidence the improvements and the impact on the dads and their families.

What's next?

The word is out about the group and we are delighted that other dads in HMP Shotts are now showing an interest and want to attend. HMP Shotts are committed to continue to offer the programme to dads across the whole prison and have now included the Solihull Approach 'Understanding your child' programme in their core family strategy. We have identified that the partners/mums of the children could also benefit from attending the 'Understanding your child' group and are keen to pursue a joint mum and dad 'Couples' group. This is still a 'work in progress' due to the security issues and sourcing a suitable location for the group to run.

As a result of the Quality Improvement award we achieved, we were asked to attend a Quality Improvement Practicum with Scottish Government. This is a year long programme to help teams use the Quality Improvement model in a work context. We would like to use the Couples group as a project to focus on for this work.

Other prisons are also interested in offering the programme and work has already started in HMP Addiewell. The first group recently completed the 10 week programme with similar results to HMP Shotts.

In summary the whole experience has been challenging and rewarding. Here are some thoughts from some of the core team members:

> I have been involved in the delivery of The Family Time Project at HMP Shotts since 2014 and I have found working with families and children affected by imprisonment to be both challenging and rewarding. The implementation of the Solihull Approach throughout the services we offer has been of tremendous benefit in our aim of improving outcomes for these families that statistics paint a very bleak future for.

> The delivery of the UYC course has enhanced my practice and more importantly it has enhanced the relationships of the families I work with. Fathers who have completed the course are more confident in their role as fathers and have told us on occasion that they have found Solihull to be beneficial in their interactions with Prison Officers and other prisoners.

> I have been surprised on many occasions with the information dads on the course are willing to share about their own childhood and the fears that they have for their children. Over the period of the course I have witnessed dads being tearful, frightened and lacking in confidence in their role as dad. Watching them grow in confidence and understanding has been the highlight of my work at HMP Shotts.

Denise Kelly, GBT.

Delivering the 'Understanding your child' parent programme in a prison setting 177

The Solihull Approach has changed both my personal and professional life. I am a better mum and much better practitioner. I consider it a privilege to be involved in delivering training for practitioners and also the UYC programme for parents. Delivery in the prison setting has been particularly rewarding and fascinating. I have enjoyed building relationships with the dads and getting to know them as dads and not prisoners. They have taught me lots about adverse childhood experiences and I am both amazed and grateful for their openness, honesty and trust in us. However, the proudest achievement has been the impact that the group has had on their children. The knowledge that the groups have enhanced the interactions and relationships that the dads have with their children and knowing that this will make a difference to their children's future, is the greatest reward of all.

Cheryl Valentine, Solihull Co-ordinator, NLC.

References

1. Felitti, V.J., Anda, R.F., Nordenberg, D., Williamson, D.F., Spitz, A.M., Koss, M.P. and Marks, J.S. (1998). Relationship of childhood abuse and household dysfunction to many of the leading causes of death in adults. *American Journal of Preventative Medicine,* 14(4), 245-258.

2. The Health Foundation. *Quality improvement made simple.* https://www.health. org.uk/sites/health/files/QualityImprovementMadeSimple.pdf

21 Solihull Approach for adults: Keeping Trauma in Mind

Clea Thompson and Andrew Summers

The beginnings of an idea

When Clea Thompson joined the Fife Clinical Psychology department ten years ago, the Child Psychology Head of Service had a strong interest in attachment informed and systemic practice. The Child Psychology specialty quickly embraced the Solihull Approach as a methodology for disseminating useful concepts of child development and attachment informed practice to multi agency colleagues through a cascade process, and developed a large pool of Solihull Approach trainers from a range of services. Trainers were able to deliver two Solihull Approach trainings a year, including follow up workshops and theory/practice sessions. This cascade, which has continued in Fife for over ten years, was supported by recurrent funding from a Changing Children's Services funding stream that paid for several sessions of clinician time per week and money for resource packs. Many of the original trainers are no longer in post, but several trainings a year are still offered.

More recently, Fife moved to a model in which services would become self-sustaining and no longer reliant on trainers from the Child Psychology specialty. This involved providing more training sessions for facilitators (train the trainer), enabling other services to sustain the approach and deliver their own in-house training. The Solihull Approach has now been adopted within children's services in Fife as a universal approach to understanding children in the context of family relationships and training has expanded into education and third sector agencies. As has been reflected in the rest of the UK, the training is well regarded and positively received. The follow up theory practice sessions, although difficult to implement, have been highly valued as mechanisms for enabling the embedding of the Solihull Approach.

The Child Psychology specialty in Fife is hosted in an area wide Psychology Service. This enables strong links with adult psychology colleagues and allows the possibility of close collaborations between practitioners who work across the age range. Several years ago a colleague, who worked with adults who have experienced complex trauma in childhood, invited Clea to deliver a talk to adult services about developmental trauma in childhood and make the case for adopting a lifespan, trauma informed, services approach.

The case for trauma informed care

A trauma informed approach changes the question from 'what is wrong with you?' to 'what has happened to you?' This paradigm shift has huge implications for the delivery of services and organisation of delivery of care to the most vulnerable populations. The rationale for trauma informed services developed from an understanding that most clients seeking mental health services have experienced some kind of trauma[1]. Adults with a history of complex trauma often present repeatedly in primary care, with diffuse and chronic health problems, a lack of confidence and self-esteem and frequent self-harming and addictive behaviours.

Research findings have demonstrated that childhood stressful life events can impact adult health. The Adverse Childhood Experiences study[2] (ACEs), a longitudinal US study, has highlighted that adverse childhood experiences (such as child abuse, neglect, and repeated exposure to domestic abuse) are associated with whole range of negative health outcomes, including heart disease, stroke, lung and liver disease, alcoholism, drug abuse, depression and other mental health issues.

In fact, many studies have shown the link between trauma, abuse, witnessing violence, repeated abandonments and sudden or traumatic loss on adult mental health[3]. Further, statistics repeatedly show that the traumatic experiences of persons with the most serious mental health problems are:

- interpersonal in nature
- prolonged and repeated
- occur in childhood and adolescence
- extend over years of a person's life.

This is received wisdom from the clinician perspective. However, this is now supported by the scientific evidence, requiring a seismic shift both in attitude and in response to dealing with the impact of childhood trauma.

Why choose the Solihull Approach?

The Solihull Approach was first developed in 1996 and is now used by a wide range of professionals from different agencies to work with families. It is particularly suited to multi-professional work and has a solid evidence base (e.g. included in NICE guidelines). Once practitioners are trained, information booklets or resource packs are available to support the approach. The combination of a universal approach for agencies, with adaptable resources, makes it very accessible to a wide range of practitioners.

Although the case for trauma informed care is compelling, the roadmap for this paradigm shift is somewhat unclear. Following Clea's initial talk on this topic and some months of reading and research, she learned that the most effective trauma informed services training taking place in the US had certain similarities with the Solihull Approach, which were already being delivered in children's services in Fife. Brown[4] examined the impact of curriculum-based Risking Connection (RC) trauma training on the knowledge, beliefs, and behaviours of 261 staff trainees. Risking Connection training teaches a trauma framework that asserts that childhood trauma experiences interrupts the trajectory of development in three critical areas: attachment[5,6]; brain and nervous system[7,8]; and self-capacities or self-regulation skills[6]. The results showed positive outcomes and suggested a 'Train the trainer' model of dissemination is an essential means of bringing change.

180   Clea Thompson and Andrew Summers

Clea was struck by the resonances with the Solihull Approach training, including the adoption of a cascade training approach and wondered if it would be possible to adapt the Solihull Approach training for adult practitioners and include a focus on complex developmental trauma. This would serve two aims: to enable practitioners in adult services to have a greater understanding of the impact of past traumatic experiences that lead people to present to services with diffuse or troubling 'symptoms' of distress, and to promote the early intervention agenda for new parents who present to adult services in the perinatal period with difficulties around attachment and bonding. She became aware that, coincidentally, Hazel Douglas, Director of the Solihull Approach, was working on a one day trauma training manual for practitioners working in children's services, which could be delivered by cascade.

How did the idea become reality?

Following a launch event at a department research conference, to lay the groundwork for discussions with the adult service about the importance of early intervention, Clea worked with Andy Summers, who has a lead role within the Fife Adult Psychology specialty for complex trauma, and with Hazel Douglas to set up a series of crucial meetings to discuss the feasibility of developing a new Solihull Approach training manual for adult practitioners.

These discussions focused on the need for a more joined up and integrated approach to addressing the needs of families referred to child services, where the parents had an extensive trauma history and required input from adult services, or the reverse situation, where parents with complex trauma were referred to adult services. The frequent difficulty coordinating input between child and adult services in these types of situations was recognised. Some of this appeared to stem from difficulty at the more fundamental level of case conceptualisation, partly due to the lack of a shared language between child and adult services. It was hypothesised that adopting the Solihull Approach as a basis for training and extending this into adult services could ameliorate some of these difficulties in the collaboration and delivery of services. This led to consideration about what would be required from a training programme and the following requirements were identified:

1. A developmental trauma focus. This was considered essential to creating connections between and a shared language for services across the lifespan.

2. The training needed to lead to sustained change in the knowledge, skills and behaviour of practitioners. It is well recognised that training often does not 'stick' when practitioners return to their workplaces and that although this is often due to organisational or systems reasons, the training needed to support this as much as possible. This led to looking for a way of training that promoted sustained practice and reflection on practice.

3. Following on from the point above, it was thought that there was a particular risk that just training practitioners in facts, for example, about trauma prevalence and consequences, might leave them feeling overwhelmed and lead to reactions such as avoiding working with those affected, or going on a 'quest' for skills that might never give them the confidence they were seeking. Therefore, training

should help practitioners develop confidence in applying the skills they already possess, by giving them a framework for understanding trauma and helping them think about how to apply their skills within this framework.

4. The model needed to emphasise the importance of supervision in maintaining the wellbeing of practitioners and also in supporting them to continue to practice in a reflective fashion. It was recognised that the Psychology Service lacked the resources to provide supervision directly. Therefore, there was an intention to create a network of trained practitioners who could support each other to address some of these needs.

5. Recognising the very large number of practitioners who might need to be trained, the programme needed to be capable of delivery at scale, for example through a cascade training model.

Andy secured support from colleagues within Adult Psychology and the Head of Psychology Service for this development. Through links with colleagues in other services interested in trauma, he began to assess the demand for this training outside the Psychology Service. The Child Psychology Head of Specialty suggested the name 'Keeping trauma in mind' (KTIM). Clea, Andy and colleagues met Hazel Douglas in January 2016 to review existing Solihull Approach materials and identify what was required to modify these for practitioners working with adults.

The Solihull Approach team developed the training programme and the manuals with further input from Clea, Andy and colleagues. In the meantime, Andy worked with colleagues in Psychology and other services to identify the first cohort of KTIM trainees, who would play a crucial role in piloting the materials, becoming ambassadors for KTIM, and, for many, to go on to become trained trainers and be involved in the subsequent cascade of KTIM. This involved securing the agreement of line mangers to release their staff to be trained and to train others in future. This was accomplished by targeting services that had at least some awareness of the significance of trauma for their service users. Established working relationships were also important in this process.

The first KTIM training began in June 2016, with 15 trainees, delivered by Clea and the Head of Child Psychology, both experienced Solihull Approach trainers. Theory into practice sessions continued through to September 2016 and a 'Train the trainer' day ran in November 2016. By this time Andy, supported by the Fife Psychology Head of Service, had secured funding from the Scottish Government's Mental Health Innovation Fund to support the cascade training process.

The KTIM Programme

The 'Keeping trauma in mind' Solihull Approach training programme is designed for staff working with adults who may have experienced adverse childhood experiences (ACEs), also known as complex or childhood trauma. The training provides staff with a framework for understanding the effects of ACEs and helps them to understand current difficulties/ symptoms as the consequence of underlying trauma. The training focuses on increasing confidence in the importance of the therapeutic relationship, builds on existing skills and enables a shift away from primarily behavioural or symptom focused approach.

Beyond the initial two day training, four theory into practice sessions enable practitioners to discuss ways in which they are using the knowledge and implementing the approach. These sessions have been developed in a multi-professional way to develop a shared understanding of roles and responsibilities and a way of thinking about the challenges that clients can face.

Topics covered by the training include:

- Solihull Approach model: containment, reciprocity, behaviour management
- Brain development
- Stress response to trauma
- Neurology and trauma
- Recognising trauma
- Trauma and attachment
- Recovery from trauma
- Levels of intervention: scope for practice
- Community and organisational trauma

Implementation of KTIM and the cascade process

NHS Fife are currently evaluating the training by collecting pre, post and follow-up quantitative data from participants, measuring confidence, skills and knowledge. Qualitative anonymous feedback is also requested at the end of Day Two. 84 participants have completed the training so far. All participants rated the training as relevant to their work and 80% rated it as highly relevant. All participants rated the training as good or better, with 61% rating it as excellent.

The findings, so far, have shown that the training is highly valued and there are plans for further cascades. As the funding from the Mental Health Innovation Fund comes to an end, KTIM is currently being embedded in the general Health Improvement training programme for Fife. This ensures that the administration will be mainstreamed and that KTIM becomes part of the core training provision within Fife.

Delegates' experience of the training

'I value my skills of listening and reflecting more now. Having a language and a model for what I was doing already has increased my confidence as a practitioner.'

'It gives me permission not to give advice and gives me confidence to go at the person's own pace'

'Interesting, refreshing, informative, new and exciting, helpful and useful'

'I am using the model pretty much daily, changing relationships with clients for the better'

'Overwhelmingly positive. Really resonated with my current job and client group'

The Solihull Approach in Action

The following case example is from an Adult Community Psychiatric Nurse (CPN) and demonstrates the value of a universal approach between services and the value of an attachment informed approach for adult services.

> In my capacity as a CPN I received a referral to work with a young woman who was struggling with low mood and anxiety postnatally. She had a five week old baby and had not been able to bond with him, reporting to the health visitor that she felt as though he was not her baby. Prior to my visit I contacted the health visitor. This was to get some history and context to the presenting situation. I am involved in the development of the perinatal mental health pathway and as a result of my Solihull Approach training, was aware of the importance of attachment and the importance of intervening to prevent problems for both the mother and child in the future. I was able to have a valuable conversation with my health visiting colleague about attachment issues and reciprocity. She shared her delight that as a worker in adult services, I was aware of the Solihull Approach and what it entailed, which enabled a consistent approach and way of working with the family. It allowed us to have a common language to discuss the needs of both child and mother. The client informed us it was helpful in allowing her to make connections between her behaviour and the impact it has on others, especially her baby son. It has also allowed her to reduce some of her anxiety, as she has a framework of reference rather than feeling she was/is failing. She no longer requires further appointments and was pleased with the support she received.

Reflections (Clea):

> It has been a great source of satisfaction to be part of this work and part of the movement taking place across Scotland to develop trauma awareness at the general population level. It has become possible to imagine a society where the prevention and healing from childhood and adult traumatic events are given the priority they require, so that all can benefit from a healthier and more resilient population. There is now a cross party working group in Scotland for the prevention and healing of childhood trauma, which is quite something, considering that shining a spotlight on the almost unbearable presence of child abuse in our world, takes bravery and courage for all involved.

Reflections (Andy):

> My experience of delivering Solihull Approach (KTIM) is that adult practitioners find the neurodevelopmentally informed approach helpful. Typically, they are quickly able to relate to the concept of containment and apply this to their work. It often seems to give practitioners a shared language for talking about the importance of their relationships with their clients and to 'legitimise' focusing on the relationship.
>
> The containment exercise, of discussing times when they have personally felt contained versus not contained, seems very helpful in making this concept come alive. Reciprocity has seemed a less intuitive concept, but developing the materials

to have more focus on adults e.g. adult case studies, appears to have helped here, leading to ideas such as engaging clients at their own pace. Most services for adults do not have an overt focus on behaviour management, but ideas around boundary setting and the importance of working on the relationship through containment and reciprocity to improve the chances of behavioural change appear to resonate with adult practitioners. The observation of adult and child interactions between the first two days of the Solihull Approach KTIM, and the reflection on this in Day Two, appear to be key parts of this training. It is clear that KTIM can lead to participants feeling powerful emotions, including delegates who are parents in the group reflecting on their own interactions with their children. However, these emotions have always felt contained within the training group and participants appear to finish KTIM feeling motivated and empowered to work with adults who have experienced developmental trauma, rather than overwhelmed or hopeless.

References

1. Elliot, D.E., Bejelac, P., Fallot, R.D., Markoff, L.S. and Reed, B.G. (2005). Trauma-informed or trauma-denied: Principles and implementation of trauma-informed services for women. *Journal of Community Psychology*, 33(4), 461-477.

2. Felitti, V.J., Anda, R.F., Nordenberg, D., Williamson, D.F., Spitz, A.M., V.Koss, M.P. and Marks, J.S., (1998) Relationship of childhood abuse and household dysfunction to many of the leading causes of death in adults. *American Journal of Preventative Medicine*, 14(4), 245-258.

3. Clarke, D. and Layard, R. (2014) *Thrive: The power of evidence based therapies*. London: Penguin.

4. Brown, S. M., Baker, C. N. and Wilcox, P. (2012). Risking connection trauma training: A pathway toward trauma-informed care in child congregate care settings. *Psychological Trauma: Theory, Research, Practice, and Policy*, 4(5), 507-515.

5. Bowlby, J. (1998). *Loss: Sadness and depression (Vol. 3)*. London: Random House.

6. Schore, J. R. and Schore, A. N. (2008). Modern attachment theory: The central role of affect regulation in development and treatment. *Clinical Social Work Journal*, 36(1), 9-20.

7. Perry, B. D. (2009). Examining child maltreatment through a neurodevelopmental lens: Clinical applications of the neurosequential model of therapeutics. *Journal of Loss and Trauma*, 14(4), 240-255.

8. Saxe, G. N., Ellis, B. H. and Kaplow, J. B. (2012). *Collaborative treatment of traumatized children and teens: The trauma systems therapy approach*. New York: Guilford Press.

22 The evidence

Rebecca Johnson

Introduction

My task in this chapter is to summarise a couple of decade's worth of research related to the Solihull Approach. The discerning reader can download up to date summaries of all the research projects and/or a full reference list from the Solihull Approach website[1]. There is also a list, available to download, of government documents which cite the Solihull Approach, for example, as a model of good practice, so I will not replicate that here. Instead I will try to summarise the themes in the research, give a sense of the narrative arc to date and give the reader an insight into the process of going from idea to publication.

Thanks to the contributions of university students and trainees, (honorary) research assistants, independent practitioners, researchers across the UK and of course, willing participants who have committed their time and energy to filling in questionnaires and being interviewed, there is now a strong research base. This includes various designs, from case studies to a randomised controlled trial, using both qualitative and quantitative methodologies.

Everything that has been studied has been, or is in the process of being, published. This is significant because it means there are no non-significant studies. The studies have also tried to capture real world samples, rather than investigating the impact of Solihull Approach activity on highly specific groups because, whilst this would be interesting, it is not so relevant to service providers who tend to offer services to parents in a range of circumstances, with a range of challenges.

What does the research say?

Unlike other programmes, the Solihull Approach is principally a theoretical framework or model. As this book illustrates, the applications of this theory based 'way of thinking' are wide and varied. Resources and trainings have been developed over years to reflect these, including a structured, manualised group for parents. However this does not mean the Solihull Approach *is* any one element of the whole package. And as its scope is broader than, for example, a parenting programme, and so must its research output be.

The initial focus was on how the model impacts upon professional practice. Trainee clinical psychologists were valued partners as they had to complete doctoral standard research and were looking for innovative applications of psychological theories as topics for their projects.

186   Rebecca Johnson

As a result there is a strong research base of evidence relating to using the Solihull Approach as a practitioner on a 1:1 basis, i.e. with individual families on a caseload. This shows that:

- It doesn't take any more time than practitioner would normally give to a family[2].
- Usually parents require fewer sessions to elicit behaviour changes[2].
- Practitioners have a better understanding of the problem or issue and are more aware of parents views[2,3,4].
- Practitioners are more confident[2,3,5] and effective[4] in working with families.
- Using the Solihull Approach decreases anxiety in parents[5].
- The referral of cases is more appropriate and consistent within professionals[6].
- Following training 88% health visitors changed their practice and consistently used the Solihull Approach[2,3,6,7].
- There was enhanced practitioner reflection, and a greater focus on parents' and children's feelings after Solihull Approach training[6,8].
- Other professionals, such as family support workers, also find the Solihull Approach training beneficial[3,7,8].
- Using the Solihull Approach has been shown to increase practitioners' job satisfaction[2,6].
- Parents and young people value the support they have received from Solihull Approach trained practitioners, in particular the trust, understanding and reliability within the relationship between them and the practitioner[8,9,10].

As the Solihull Approach spread both geographically and in scope and areas started to take a strategic approach to rolling out training, independent practitioners, some of whom had links to academic institutions in their professional roles, became interested in undertaking research. An example is some of the research relating to schools:

- Solihull Approach Whole School training resulted in an increase in teachers' satisfaction with their helping role, self-esteem, and a decrease in feeling burnt out/stressed, compared to teachers who did not receive the training[10,11].

Some publications are about the use of the Solihull Approach in managerial settings and about the benefits of the training across disciplines and agencies:

- Supervision, consultation and managerial support are important for implementing the approach in practice and the Solihull Approach model itself can be used as a model for delivering consultation and supervision[7,8,12,13,14,15].
- The Solihull Approach facilitates multi-agency working[6,9,10].

Individuals began to write up their experiences of using the Approach. There are case studies showing:

- The Solihull Approach can be used effectively with children with complex neurodevelopmental difficulties[16,17].

The evidence   187

- Attendance at a Solihull Approach group for parents is enjoyable, beneficial and recommendable for all[18].
- The group for parents can be successfully delivered in Urdu in Pakistan, resulting in an 89% completion rate, and self-reported improvements in communication, parental confidence and parent-child relationships[19].

Publications have also emerged out of the necessity to pilot new 'interventions' thoroughly, using in-house expertise. Members of the core Solihull Approach team and the Child and Adolescent Mental Health Service in which it grew, have research skills through their professional trainings and these have been supported by the enthusiasm and sheer graft of honorary research assistants.

There are various research papers relating to the face to face groups and online courses for parents:

- 'Understanding your child's behaviour' (UYCB) results in improvements in: parental anxiety and child behaviour problems[20]; parental sense of competence and locus of control[21]; a more empathic parenting style and self-reported improvements in behaviour management[22].
- Parents attending the group report increases in closeness and decreases in conflict in the relationship with their child, improvements in prosocial behaviour in the child and decreases in conduct problems[21,22], compared to a control group[23].
- Gains were maintained at follow-up (3 months)[24].
- Parents rate UYCB highly[21,25,26].
- UYCB can be used successfully as a 'fathers only' group[27].
- The online version of the course, 'Understanding your child – online', resulted in increased closeness in the parent-child relationship, and decreased conflict[28]. The online version of the antenatal course, 'Understanding your pregnancy, labour, birth and your baby – online', resulted in feeling closer to the baby, less anxious and increased intention to breasfeed[29].

Outcomes for foster carers have been explored:

- The Solihull Approach Foster Carer group results in carers' rating of child hyperactivity and attentional disorders reducing[30].
- The group helps carers: understand the effects of trauma; 'step back' and reflect on the meaning of a child's behaviour; improve their relationship with the child, and be able to look after themselves[31].

There are also publications about the antenatal offer[32,33]:

- The Solihull Approach antenatal groups (both face-to-face and online versions) result in an increase in feelings of attachment in mothers and fathers, a decrease in maternal anxiety about pregnancy, labour and birth, and an increase in mothers' intention to breastfeed[29,34].

188   Rebecca Johnson

- The Solihull Approach can be used as a model to underpin peer breastfeeding supporters[35,36].

What's in the pipeline?

The Solihull Approach is constantly evolving so inevitably research lags behind development. Gaps at the time of writing include measuring the impact of the Advanced training seminar series on professional practice, the impact of Foundation training on the emergency services, prison staff, housing officers, perinatal mental health teams, international practitioners and so on. Long term outcomes are also hard to measure, particularly when the drivers (trainees and students) are transient, or on short term timelines to suit academic work streams. None of this is insurmountable of course, but it hopefully gives a flavour of the day to day challenges facing institutions based in service delivery sectors, rather than in academic institutions, when it comes to generating research output.

At the time of writing there are also some promising collaborations in the pipeline. More is needed to investigate and corroborate the evidence around the groups for parents, using control groups and long-term follow-ups. There is promise in working with specialists in the research field; those who revel in running towards projects with complex challenges when everyone else is throwing their hands in the air and walking away defeated. Fingers crossed and watch this space!

Challenges

Research and evaluation are essential pieces of the jigsaw when it comes to operationalising good practice on a large scale. No commissioner worth their salt is going to back something based on the intuition of front-line practitioners, no matter how passionate they are. Those practitioners may be gathering evaluations as they go, they may produce reports for service managers, providers, and commissioners. Sometimes they share them with the Solihull Approach team. However, ask them to embark on a research project with a view to achieve dissemination nationally, or further afield, and paralysis kicks in. Where does one get the time in a busy working day to sit down at a blank screen and write an ethics proposal or a research protocol, let alone an abstract, introduction, method, results and conclusion according to a specific set of guidelines for a specific journal? Which, incidentally, needs to be selected from a wide range of options. This work is anxiety provoking and overwhelming!

Over the years there have been several collaborations with academic institutions, some resulting in successful co-publications, some in bid writing for research grants and some relationship brokering. The journey is always long, slow and detailed and when unsuccessful, as has been the case for a couple of bids for large grants to run full scale randomised controlled trials (RCTS) over the years, can be disheartening.

These are just some of the practical challenges. Then there are methodological ones. Recruiting enough participants into a control group is one challenge, solved by including parents on a waiting list for a group in the first RCT about the Solihull Approach. However this requires a long time period (five years in that case) which tends to be incompatible with academic studies or transient personnel timescales.

At the time of writing the hierarchy used to weigh up the strength of evidence, valued by organisations such as the Early Intervention Foundation, has the randomised controlled trial at the apex and testimonials way down at the bottom. Whilst some have challenged the value of this perspective, particularly for real world programmes, the RCT is still seen as definitive. In our experience local testimonials and stories are also highly valued, rightly or wrongly, on the ground by commissioners. Perhaps this is because they bring to life the impact of their hard-won decision making. Clearly a range of research methods are valuable.

Other methodological challenges are more perplexing. There are two types of online courses, those that are paid for, such as the Solihull Approach online courses, and those that are free, known as Massive Open Online Courses (MOOCs). Evaluators of both must grapple with working out a whole new research paradigm. For example, if you want to know if online courses are effective and you start designing a beautiful research protocol with inclusion and exclusion criteria and a recruitment process, you have already veered away from the naturalistic sample of anonymous, unrestricted learners who want to access the course. If you take that sample and start interrogating them for their age, number of children, ethnicity, relationship status, dress size, eye colour, etc., you risk putting them off : who wants to enter such personal data into the internet in this age of cyberattack and 'big data' intrusion? So you may lose the very people who seek out an online version of a programme precisely because it is anonymous and private with no hurdles. This is a challenge being discussed within the academic research community[29].

The Solihull Approach team are keen to bring together: people who have expertise in research methods, people who have the energy and drive to undertake research, practitioners delivering services to parents (who therefore have contact with potential participants, whose views and experiences are the subject of interest).

We are always happy to support practitioners to turn their service need for data into a published article. We can make suggestions about measures, design, and journals. We can support you with choosing a journal and help with writing up. We may also be able to put you in touch with others with similar interests or experiences.

Round up

In summary there are over 50 published research papers, evaluation reports and articles, all of which support the mantra heard uttered on many occasions by both practitioners and parents: 'The Solihull Approach just works!'

However, the testimonials and feedback from parents and practitioners that regularly come into the Solihull Approach office, giving encouragement to keep growing this project, are a heart-warming reminder that all the evidence in the world is meaningless unless practitioners and, most importantly, parents like and value the model.

References

1. www.solihullapproachparenting.com/research
2. Douglas, H. and Ginty, M. (2001) The Solihull Approach: changes in health visiting practice. *Community Practitioner*, 74(6), 222-224.

3. Lowenhoff, C. (2004) Practice development: training professionals in primary care to manage emotional and behavioural problems in children. *Work Based Learning in Primary Care*, 2, 97-101.

4. Milford, R., Kleve, L., Lea, J. and Greenwood, R. (2006) A pilot evaluation study of the Solihull Approach. *Community Practitioner*, 79(11), 358-362.

5. Douglas, H. and Brennan, A. (2004) Containment, reciprocity and behaviour management: Preliminary evaluation of a brief early intervention (the Solihull Approach) for families with infants and young children. *The International Journal of Infant Observation*, 7(1), 89 –107.

6. Whitehead R. and Douglas H. (2005) A qualitative evaluation of health visitors using the Solihull Approach. *Community Practitioner*, 78(1), 20-23.

7. Vasilopoulou, E., Afzal, A., Murphy, K and Thompson, C. (2017) The Solihull Approach pros and cons. *Community Practitioner*, 90(5), 40-42.

8. Maunders, H. Giles, D. and Douglas, H. (2007) Mothers' perception of community health professional support. *Community Practitioner*, 80(4), 24-29.

9. Moore, T., Adams, M., Pratt, R. (2013) A service evaluation on the Solihull Approach training and practice. *Community Practitioner*, 86(5), 26-27.

10. Hassett, A. (2015) Evaluation of the Solihull Approach in Kent: drawing conclusions from the data. Project Report. *Canterbury Christchurch University CReaTE website*, http://create.canterbury.ac.uk/15229/

11. Hassett, A. and Appleton, R. (2016) Understanding your pupil's behaviour: A pilot study from two schools in Kent. *Canterbury Christchurch University CReaTE website*. http://create.canterbury.ac.uk/15228/

12. Lumsden, V and Sarankin, M. (2014) The Process of consultation to a Health Visiting team based on the Solihull Approach: a critical reflection. *Community Practitioner*, 87(10), p34-36.

13. Brigham, Lindsay and Smith, Ann (2014). *Implementing the Solihull Approach: A study of how the Solihull Approach is embedded in the day to day practice of health practitioners.* The Open University in the North, Gateshead.

14. Stephanopoulo, E., Coker, S., Greenshields, M. and Pratt, R. (2011) Health Visitor views on consultation using the Solihull Approach: a grounded theory study. *Community Practitioner*, 84(7), 26-30.

15. Drea C., Lumsden V. and Bourne J. (2014) Using practitioners' feedback to contribute to organisational development in health visiting. *Community Practitioner*, 87(12), 30–33.

16. Williams, L. and Newell, R. (2012) The use of the Solihull Approach with children with complex neurodevelopmental difficulties and sleep problems: a case study. *British Journal of Learning Disabilities*, 41(2), 159-166.

17. Bains, S. (2015) A carer's journey. *Community Practitioner*, 88(12), 10-11.

18. Rogers, E. (2014) Lessons in parenting. *Children and Young People Now*, July, 2014.

19. Norman, L. (2013) Delivering Solihull Approach training in Pakistan. *Community Practitioner,* 86(8), 42-43.

20. Bateson, K., Delaney, J. and Pybus, R. (2008) Meeting expectations: the pilot evaluation of the Solihull Approach Parenting Group. *Community Practitioner,* 81, 28-31.

21. Cabral, J. (2013) The value of evaluating parenting groups: a new researcher's perspective on methods and results. *Community Practitioner,* 86(6), 30-33.

22. Vella, L., Butterworth, R., Johnson, R. and Urquhart Law, G. (2015) Parents' experiences of being in the Solihull Approach parenting group, 'Understanding Your Child's Behaviour': an interpretative phenomenological analysis. *Child: Care, Health and Development,* 41(6) 882–894.

23. Douglas, H. and Johnson, R. (*submitted, 2018*) 'A randomised controlled trial of the Solihull Approach ten week group for parents'.

24. Baladi, R., Johnson, R. and Urquart-Law, G. (2018) Understanding Your Child's Behaviour (UYCB): Evaluating a Solihull Approach face to face 10 week group for parents. *Community Practitioner,* November Issue, 45-47.

25. Johnson, R. and Wilson, H. (2012) Parents' Evaluation of 'Understanding Your Child's Behaviour', a parenting group based on the Solihull Approach. *Community Practitioner,* 85(5), 29-33.

26. Appleton, R., Douglas, H. and Rheeston, M. (2016) Taking part in 'Understanding Your Child's Behaviour' and positive changes for parents. *Community Practitioner,* 89(2), 42-48.

27. Dolan, Alan (2013) 'I've Learnt What a Dad Should Do': The Interaction of Masculine and Fathering Identities among Men Who Attended a 'Dads Only' Parenting Programme. *Sociology,* 48(4) 812-828.

28. Johnson, R. (2018) 'Improvements in parenting achieved with innovative online programme: Preliminary evaluation of 'Understanding Your Child – Online' (UYC-OL) – A Solihull Approach course for parents and carers'. *Educational and Child Psychology,* 35(1), 40-50.

29. Shahid A., Johnson R. (2018) Evaluation of an online antenatal course 'Understanding pregnancy, labour, birth and your baby' by the Solihull Approach. *Evidence Based Midwifery,* 16(3), 101-106.

30. Brown, Suzanne (2014) Clinical Update: A Small Service Evaluation of a Solihull Approach Foster Carer Training Group Pilot Study Practice. *Social Work in Action,* 26(1), 37-52.

31. Madigan, S., Paton, K and Mackett, Naomi. (2017) The Springfield Project service: evaluation of a Solihull Approach course for foster carers. *Adoption and Fostering,* 41(3), 254-267.

32. Fagan, E., Land, S., Meadows, Z., Raza, M., Gavin, J. and Douglas, H. (2016) Midwives' experience of delivering the Solihull Approach Antenatal Group. *International Journal of Birth and Parent Education,* 4, 31.

33. Douglas, H. (2016) The Solihull Approach Antenatal Parenting Group: Understanding pregnancy, labour, birth and your baby. *International Journal of Birth and Parent Education,* 4, 29-31.

34. Douglas, H and Bateson, K. (2017) A service evaluation of the Solihull Approach Antenatal Parenting Group: integrating childbirth information with support for the fetal-parent relationship. *Evidence Based Midwifery.* 15(1), 15-19.

35. Thelwell, E., Rheeston, M and Douglas, H. (2017) Exploring breastfeeding peer supporters' experiences of using the Solihull Approach model. *British Journal of Midwifery,* 25(10), 639-646.

36. Monique, Tan., Rheeston, M and Douglas, H. (2017) Using the Solihull Approach in breastfeeding support groups: Maternal perceptions. *British Journal of Midwifery,* 25(12), 765-773.